Women and Child Development

Women and Child Development

Kalpana Roy

Commonwealth

Women and Child Development

ISBN : 81-7169-614-7

Edition - 2027

Published by :
COMMONWEALTH PUBLISHERS (P) LTD.
4831/24, Govind Lane,
Ansari Road, Darya Ganj,
New Delhi - 110002
Ph. : 23272541, 23242541
e-mail : commonwealthpublishers2016@gmail.com

Distributed by :
ARJUN PUBLISHING HOUSE
4831/24, Govind Lane,
Ansari Road, Darya Ganj,
New Delhi - 110002
Ph. : 23272541, 23242541
e-mail : arjunbooks2001@gmail.com

Laser Typesetting by :
Dimple Computers
Delhi

Printed at :
Divine Digital Press
Delhi

Preface

The department of women and child was, for most of the year under the minister for human resource development. The Department has 3 autonomous organisations. These organisations are fully funded by the Government of India and assist the Department in its functions including implementation of some programmes/schemes.

Programmes for women and children implemented by the Department, though not exclusively for SC/ST, are primarily directed towards the most disadvantaged groups of population like scheduled castes and scheduled tribes and other economically backward classes living in backward rural, tribal and urban slum areas.

The World Bank assisted ICDS projects are being implemented exclusively in the predominantly backward/tribal areas of the 4 States of Andhra Pradesh, Orissa, Madhya Pradesh and Bihar. In these projects certain additional services, like functional literacy for women, skill development training for empowerment of women, interventions for adolescent girls, rehabilitation of the severely malnourished, strengthened inputs in the spheres of communication, monitoring, and so on are provided. With a view to provide a sharp focus, the ICDS monitoring formats have been revised to include caste-specific information on beneficiaries. Similarly, under the scheme of condensed courses of education for Adult Women, the institutions are required to make efforts to enroll Scheduled Caste and Scheduled Tribe women for the courses.

Efforts are made to encourage more voluntary organisations to come forthwith proposals to start welfare programmes in tribal and backward rural areas by extending special concessions and relaxation under grant-in-aid rules.

Editor

Contents

1

Introduction

The department of women and child was, for most of the year under the minister for human resource development. The Department has 3 autonomous organisations viz. National Institute of Public Cooperation and Child Development (NIPCCD), Rashtriya Mahila Kosh(RMK) and the Central Social Welfare Board (CSWB) working under its aegis. NIPCCD and RMK are registered under the Societies Registration Act, 1860, whereas CSWB is a charitable company registered under Section 25 of the Indian Companies Act, 1956.

These organisations are fully funded by the Government of India and assist the Department in its functions including implementation of some programmes /schemes. The National Commission for Women was constituted as a national apex statutory body in 1992 for protecting and safeguarding the rights of women.

A meeting of the Parliamentary Standing Committee on Human Resource Development was held under the Chairpersonship of Shri S.B. Chavan on 19 June 1998 to examine the Demands for Grants of the Department of Women and Child Development for the year 1998-99. The Action Taken Report (ATR) on the 66th Report of the Standing Committee was submitted to the Rajya Sabha Secretariat on 28th January 1999.

The Lok Sabha constituted a Committee on

Empower-ment of Women during March 1997 to consider the report of NCW and to report on the measures required by the Union Government for Empowerment of Women. Two sittings of the Committee were held on 6th January 1999 and on 15th January 1999 at New Delhi, to take oral evidence of Secretary (WCD) on the subject of "Developmental schemes for Rural Women"

The Plan and Non-Plan outlays for the year 1998-99 were fixed at Rs.1225.95 crore and Rs.48.28 crore respectively. The outlays have been revised to Rs. 1134.48 crore under Plan and Rs.45.45 crore under Non-Plan during the year 1997-98.

The Planning Commission, with a view to converge the benefits in the social and economic development sectors for women in the 9th Plan had requested all the Secretaries of the various Departments of the Government to draw up a women's component plan to identify allocation in all the sectors at the Centre by aggregating them in an integrated manner in this context, the Minister for Human Resource Development had requested all the Ministers for their personal intervention in the matter of inclusion of an identifiable women component plan in the programmes of the respective Ministries/Departments right from the planning process and thereafter to monitor allocations and implementation of programmes to ensure the reach of benefits to women. The Cabinet approved one of the recommendations of the National Perspective Plan for Women (19982000), which says that the Planning Commission and all the Ministries/Departments should have a women cell and the Annual Reports of the Ministries/Departments at the Central and State levels should document and review the work done concerning women. The Department, accordingly, requested all the Ministries/Departments to set up advisory committees for women in each sector to help in the preparation, monitoring, and implementation of the women component plan, to set up a women's cell, and to include a chapter on women component plan in their annual reports.

Special Component Plan (SCP) for Scheduled Castes and Tribal SubPlan (TSP) for Scheduled Tribes

Programmes for women and children implemented by the Department, though not exclusively for SC/ST, are primarily directed towards the most disadvantaged groups of population like Scheduled Castes and Scheduled Tribes and other economically backward classes living in backward rural, tribal and urban slum areas.

About 80% of the Department's Annual Plan outlay is earmarked for ICDS. Selection of these projects are made in areas inhabited predominantly by SCs/STs and other disadvantaged/vulnerable groups in both rural and urban areas. Of the A200 ICDS Projects operational in the country, 750 are tribal projects, located in areas predominantly inhabited by tribes.

In addition, the World Bank assisted ICDS projects are being implemented exclusively in the predominantly backward/ tribal areas of the 4 States of Andhra Pradesh, Orissa, Madhya Pradesh and Bihar. In these projects certain additional services, like functional literacy for women, skill development training for empowerment of women, interventions for adolescent girls, rehabilitation of the severely malnourished, strengthened inputs in the spheres of communication, monitoring, and so on are provided. A With a view to provide a sharp focus, the ICDS monitoring formats have been revised to include caste-specific information on beneficiaries. All the States/ Union Territories have been requested to ensure transmission of the said information on prescribed formats to facilitate the review of coverage of SC/ST population under the ICDS Scheme.

The Central Social Welfare Board made the following stipulations under its grant-in-aid rules to encourage voluntary action in tribal areas:

Normally, only suck institutions are eligible for grant-in-aid from the Board which are engaged in social welfare activities for a minimum period of three years; this condition is relaxed in the case of institutions located in tribal areas.

Institutions are normally given assistance under the grant-in-aid programme on an equal matching basis (50% grant from the Board and the other 50% raised by the institutions). In regard to the institutions in tribal areas, the Board allows grants upto 75% of the approved expenditure and in certain deserving cases, grants even upto 95%.

Further, the Central Social Welfare Board has been implementing the scheme of Socio-economic programme providing work and wages to women belonging to the weaker sections of the society. The beneficiaries under the programmes include, mostly, the members belonging to SC and ST communities. Specific instructions have also been issued to maintain separate records of the number of beneficiaries belonging to SCs and STs.

Similarly, under the scheme of Condensed Courses of Education for Adult Women, the institutions are required to make efforts to enroll Scheduled Caste and Scheduled Tribe women for the courses. In the case of SC and ST candidates, conditions regarding educational qualifications for admission to the courses are relaxed wherever necessary. Records are kept of the SC and ST candidates admitted to these courses.

Under the Scheme of Hostels for Working Women implemented by the Department, there are stipulations that 15% of the seats in hostels will be reserved for SCs and 7.5% for STs. The schemes of the Food and Nutrition Board (FNB) are aimed at improving the nutritional status of people, in general, and of the vulnerable sections of the population including SCs and STs, in particular. The major thrust of the programmes of the Board is on the rural and tribal areas and urban slums.

Efforts are made to encourage more voluntary organisations to come forth with proposals to start welfare programmes in tribal and backward rural areas by extending special concessions and relaxation under grant-in-aid rules.

Annual action plan

The Department, at the instance of the Cabinet Secretariat, prepared the Annual Action Plan (AAP) for the schemes and activities of the Department, setting out the targets, both financial and physical, for the four quarters of the year. This AAP was monitored on a quarterly basis in the Department to review the financial and physical achievements as per the targets fixed at the beginning of the year.

Implementation of programmes the north-east

At the instance of the Prime Minister, the Ministry of Home Affairs vide their Order No. 9/19/97-T, dated 9th October, 1997 constituted a Committee of Secretaries under the Chairpersonship of the Home Secretary to look into the development programmes of the Central Government in the North-East (in which Secretary, Ministry of Human Resource Development is a member). The Department under the scheme of Integrated Child Development Services (ICDS), National Creche Fund (NCF), Assistance to Voluntary Organisations for Creches for the Children of Working and Ailing Mothers, Hostels for Working Women, Support to Training-cum- Employment Programme (STEP), Socio-Economic Programme (SEP), Condensed Courses of Education and Vocational

Training for Women, Awareness Generation Projects for Rural and Poor Women, Food and Nutrition Board, National Institute of Public Cooperation and Child Development and other schemes of the Department allocated 10% of the budget available during the year for implementation of programmes in the North-East.

Reservation for SCs and STs

The reservation Policy of the Government of India is being followed by this Department. Out of the 30 Group "A" officers, 5 belong to the Scheduled Caste and 2 belong to the Scheduled Tribe category. Similarly, out of 95 Group 'B' officers, 17 officers belong to the SC community and A belong to the ST community. In respect of 69 Group 'C' posts, 12 officers belong to SC community and 4 belong to ST community. Out of 54 Group 'D' posts 25 officials belong to SC community and 3 belong to ST community.

Use of Hindi in official work

During the period under report, efforts were made to achieve the targets for the use of Hindi fixed by the Department of Official Language in their Annual Programme for 1998-99. Article 3(3) of the Official

Language Act, 1963 is being complied with in the Department. Letters received in Hindi were replied to in Hindi. Check points were strengthened to ensure better compliance of the provisions of the Official Language Act and Rules framed thereunder.

Quarterly Progress Reports received from the offices under the administrative control of this Department were reviewed. A representative of the Department has regularly been attending the meetings of the Official Language Implementation Committee of Central Social Welfare Board and National Institute of Public Cooperation and Child Development. Hindi Fortnight was celebrated from 1-15 September, 1998. During this period, debate, essay and noting and drafting competitions were held. In all, 40 officials appeared in these competitions, out of which 10 officials have been awarded prizes.

In addition to the routine work, the important material translated into Hindi relates to the Annual Report of the Department for the year 1997-98; Performance Budget, 1997-98; Parliament Questions; Cabinet Note on Rural Women's Development and Empowerment Project; Cabinet Note on Short Stay Homes; Cabinet Note on ICDS Training; Papers for the Conference of State Ministers and Secretaries-in-charge of WCD; Parliamentary Consultative Committee; Parliamentary Standing Committee; and National Nutrition Week, National Children's Award for Exceptional Achievements, 1997; World Breast Feeding Week

2

Women's Development

The Government of India has continuously been formulating strategies and initiating processes, to bring women into the mainstream. Women constitute half of the country's population (accounting for 407.1 million in absolute numbers as per the 1991 census), and it is abundantly clear that there can be no development unless their needs and interests are fully taken into account. In addition, the Government of India has brought about specific legislation to protect and safeguard the rights of women. Although there have been various shifts in policy approaches in the last fifty years from the concept of 'welfare' till the '70's to 'development' in the '80's and now to 'empowerment' in the '90's, the Department of Women and Child Development, since its inception has been implementing special programmes designed to improve the socioeconomic status of women. The Bureau of Women's Development, and Micro Credit Development, in the Department play a major role in this national endeavour for the advancement and empowerment of women. In its nodal capacity, the Department also formulates policies and programmes, enacts/amends legislations affecting women and coordinates the efforts of both Governmental and Non-Governmental Organisations working to improve the lot of women in the country. Employment, credit facilities, training, awareness generation, income-generating activities have been major interventions for improving the position of women. In addition, provision is made for support services of various kinds, including help to the women of vulnerable groups. Capacity building through training, awareness generation and gender sensitisation also constitute a thrust area of the Department.

These programmes play the role of being both supplementary and complementary to the other general development programmes in the sectors of health, education, labour and employment, rural and urban development, etc. In line with this integrated approach to the empowerment of women and enhancement of the status of the girl child, the, Department has sought to change attitudes in the family, the community and society towards women and the girl child and to mobilise these social units to play their rightful role in creating a conducive environment for women and girls. The interventions undertaken by the Department are directed to empower women and girl children legally, socially, economically and politically.

Social and economic empowerment

The Rural Women's Development and Empowerment Project has been sanctioned on 16 October 1998 as a Centrally-sponsored project for a period of 5 years in states of Uttar Pradesh, Madhya Pradesh, Bihar, Haryana, Karnataka and Gujarat with an estimated outlay of Rs. 186.21 crore. In addition, an amount of Rs. 5 crore will be provided over the project period, but outside the project outlay, for facilitating setting up, in the project states, of Revolving Funds for giving interest-bearing loans to beneficiary groups primarily during their initial formative stage. The overall objective of the project is to strengthen the processes, and create an environment for empowerment of women. Its specific objectives are:

— Establishment of between 7400 and 12000 self-reliant women's Self-Help-Groups (SHGs) having 15-20 members each, which will improve the quality of their lives, through greater access to, and control over, resources.

— Sensitising and strengthening the institutional capacity of support agencies to pro-actively address women's needs.

— Developing linkages between SHGs and lending institutions to ensure women's continued access to credit facilities for income generation activities.

— Enhancing women's access to resources for better quality of life, including those for drudgery reduction and time-saving devices.

— Increased control of women, particularly poor women, over income and spending, through their involvement in income generation activities which will indirectly help in poverty alleviation.

The implementing agencies will be the Women's Development Corporations of the concerned states in Bihar, Haryana and Karnataka, Gujarat Women's Economic Development Corporation in Gujarat, M.P. Mahila Arthik Vikas Nigam in Madhya Pradesh and Mahila Kalyan Nigam in Uttar Pradesh, who will actively associate NGOs in the implementation tasks. Funds needed by the implementing agencies will be provided by the Government of India in the form of grants-in-aid.

A substantial part of the outlay for the project will become available as soft-term loan/credit to the Government of India from the International Fund for Agricultural Development (IFAD) and International Development Association (IDA or World Bank). Almost the entire credit needs of the beneficiaries will be met from institutional sources.

Funds needed for setting up of the Revolving Funds in project states will be provided by the Government of India itself. The project, at the end of 5 years, is expected to bring about the following qualitative and quantitative benefits:

— Organisation of nearly 7,400 to 12,000 .Self -Help-Groups (SHGs) involving 2.14 lakh rural women and strengthening their ability to control their own affairs and to further their own development;

— Increased self-esteem, confidence and self-reliance of women to address the constraints which the society has imposed and is imposing on them;

— Improved management and technical skills for women;

— Improvement in the women's social status in both the family and the community;

— Increased mobilisation of various public and private sector services for women's benefit;

— Capacity building and strengthening of the support agencies, such as NGOs and Women Development Corporations, to enable them to be more effective in addressing women's needs.

— Orientation of financial institutions and line departments, to facilitate their sensitisation to gender issues and better services to women, especially rural women;

— Development of training modules and material which can be replicated and extensively used elsewhere, with such adaptations as may be warranted by local situations;

— Enhanced involvement of women in economic activities, additional income and control over it, thereby leading to upgradation of standards;

— Integration of women into the social mainstream, especially in the areas of control over and/or access to finance, including credit from institutional and other sources; and

— Improvement in women's well-being through improved conditions of living, including drudgery-removal and time-saving devices.

During next 5 years, under the project Rs. 191.21 crore will be required out of which Rs. 5.00 crore will be required as revolving fund. For 1998-99, an amount of Rs. 8.00 crore will be required as the project was sanctioned on 16 October, 1998 by the Planning Commission.

Indira mahila yojana

The Indira Mahila Yojana (IMY) is a programme launched by the Government of India in August 1995 as a central sector project for the holistic empowerment of women. The vision of IMY is to develop empowered women who will:

— Demand their rights from family, community and the government;

— Have increased access to and control over material, social and political resources;

— Have enhanced awareness and improved skills; and

— Be able to raise issues of common concern through mobilisation and networking.

It is premised on recognition of the fact that empowerment is a multifaceted process. It seeks to achieve this by the following objectives:

— To generate awareness among women by disseminating information and knowledge, so as to bring about an attitudinal change;

— To help women achieve economic strength through micro-level income generating activities; and

— To establish convergence of various services such as literacy, health, non-formal education, rural development, water supply, entrepreneurship, etc.

The IMY is based on the idea of the strength of the Self-Help Groups. The development of Indira Mahila Kendras (IMKs) at the Anganwadi level and also recognising other women's groups under the adult literacy programmes, health programmes, etc. and integrating, or associating them with the IMKs at the Anganwadi level would provide a grass-root level organisation for women to interact,

Achievements during the year

More than 37,000 small homogenous women's groups have been formed under the Scheme till December 1998, out of which 9000 women's groups have been formed during the period under reference.

For the purpose of sensitising implementors of IMY at the state/district level, a series of state/district level workshops are being conducted throughout the country with the assistance of National Institute of Public Cooperation & Child Development (NIPCCD). This process continued during the current year also. A total number of 2.4 state level workshops have been conducted so far, out of which 4 have been conducted this year.

Two training programmes of five days duration were organised at the Lal Bahadur Shastri National Academy of Administration (LBSNAA), Mussoorie for Chief Executive Officers, District Magistrates and District

Officers of the concerned districts where Indira Mahila Yojana is implemented, to sensitise them towards IMY.

The third training programme for the child development project officers (CDPOs) and Non-Governmental Organisations (NGOs) under the collaboration of Department for International Development (DFID) and Department of Women and Child Development was organised this year. 26 persons took part in the Indian module held between November 2 and 14, 1998 at Bankers Institute of Rural Development, Lucknow. This Indian module was funded by Rashtriya Mahila Kosh (RMK). 15 participants will be given intensive training at UK for 8 weeks and the other group will be taken on a study tour of 10 days duration to Bangladesh.

A teleconference inaugurated by Minister for HRD on IMY and group formation was organised from October 14-16-1998 covering six Hindi speaking states namely, Bihar, Gujarat, Haryana, Himachal Pradesh, Jammu and Kashmir, Madhya Pradesh and NCT of Delhi in collaboration with Indira Gandhi National Open University and Indian Space Research Organisation. Prior to this, a Master Trainers workshop was organised at NIPCCD by IGNOU between 6 - 7 October, 1998.

Resource material development

The main book on IMY has been translated into regional languages by some states. A Hindi version has also been brought out.

— Detailed guidelines for creation of a revolving corpus with Indira Mahila Block Society (IMBS) have been issued.

— A booklet on the Role of State Level Steering Committee (SLSC) and District Level Coordination Committee (DLCC) under Indira Mahila Yojana (IMY), has been compiled.

— A Handbook on IMY has been prepared with assistance of NIPCCD and with funding from the British Council and RMK.

— A project book on Micro-enterprise credit & Development Training (CREME) has been prepared by the IMY Desk and published by the British Council.

— All the important circulars of IMY and other related information has been compiled. A booklet containing this information will be published soon.

A new collaborative project "Training for Women Empowerment" has been launched in September 1998 in 21 IMY blocks of Maharashtra. A project launch workshop was held in Pune on 10-11 September, 1998 and the concerned Chief Executive Officers and Deputy Chief Executive Officers were sensitised.

An Aus-Aid assisted training-cum-workshop on micro-financing women's groups under India-Australia and capacity building project has been approved. Under this project, a training programme for senior/ middle level officials was conducted at BIRD, Lucknow from 14-18 December , 1998. Secretaries / Commissioners / Directors in charge of Women & Child Development of 8 states, 4 institutional faculty members and one official from this Department have been sent to Bangladesh, Indonesia, and Australia on a study tour from 8 - 31, January 1999, under this programme.

The DWCD and the Planning Commission conducted a rapid joint evaluation of the Scheme during 1997-98 and its report has been finalised this year. The evaluation study highlighted that although IMY had a potential to bring a major change in women's lives, the training requirements, resource material, personnel, etc. provided under the Scheme and its monitoring system should be strengthened. Based on the report and after further discussions with the Planning Commission, it has been decided to recast the Scheme incorporating provisions for removing the shortcomings. The recast Scheme is under finalisation. It is expected that the recast Scheme will be implemented in the next year.

Mahilla samriddhi yojana

Mahila Samriddhi Yojana, started in 1993 for the economic empowerment of women and to inculcate the habit of saving among rural women, is being recast and merged with Indira Mahila Yojana.

Women and structural adjustment

The department has taken up, in collaboration with International Labour Organisation, a project on 'National Network on Structural Adjustment, Women's Employment and Equality'. The project's objective is to ensure that women's needs in relation to employment and working conditions are fully incorporated and taken into account in Structural Adjustment Programmes and Policies.

A Tripartite Advisory Group headed by Secretary of the Department and comprising representatives of line Ministries, selected trade unions, National Commission for Women, employers organisations and leading NGOs and researchers has been set up to network with organisations interested in the subject focusing on labour market changes, etc. The project which started in January, 1997 has been successfully concluded in June, 1998. Under the prcject the following 4 studies have been conducted through reputed voluntary organisations:

i) Impact of Structural Adjustment Programme on Women's Employment in Unorganised Sector.

ii) Structural Adjustment Programme—Impact of Women's Work Participation.

iii) Structural Adjustment Programme—Impact on Women's Work.

iv) Impact of Structural Adjustment Programme on Women's Productive Work and Employment.

Haryana Integrated Women's Empowerment and Development Project

Haryana Integrated Women's Empowerment and Development Project with assistance from United Nations Fund for Population Activities (UNFPA) was under implementation from July 1994 to July 1998. The project areas were Mahendergarh district and 70 villages of Rewari district. The total cost of the project was Rs. 1382.00 lakh out of which UNFPA contribution was Rs. 812 lakh. The project comprised of components on (i) Empowerment, (ii) Health, (iii) Education, (iv) Adolescent Girl and (v) Economic Endowment.

Recently an independent evaluation was done for the Project. In view of the positive findings of the evaluation, 2nd phase of the Project in the same project area with assistance from UNFPA is about to begin.

Training employment and education

Self-Help Groups have emerged as one of the major strategies in group formation and various schemes of the Government of India have shown that strong women's, groups could contribute substantially to the development and convergence of services and activities. Experiences with various programmes and projects has highlighted the benefits of formation of women's groups for building confidence and focusing on developmental tasks. Different groups in various states all over the country have focused on skill development and awareness generation, promoting economic development through income generation activities, inculcating thrift, credit management activities among poor women.

The experience of running these schemes had shown that the sustainability of the majority of these groups was a major problem and one of the prime reasons for that was lack of a proper training strategy. Because of incomplete or ineffective training, full potential of women's groups formed in different states could not be realised. Many of the women's groups are neither homogenous nor sustainable. The vast geographical canvas also impedes transmission of messages in time and without distortion. The project called "Distance Education for Women's Development & Empowerment" aims to address some of these critical areas of concern. It is the first such programme of its kind in the country.

The scheme proposes to launch a certificate course by IGNOU to train a large mass of trainers from amongst village level implementors of the projects, their supervisors and district level functionaries. Such trainers after their successful participation in the project would be able to guide sustainable group formation work in their areas. Such an approach will also speed up the whole training process since a large number of centres could be activated simultaneously and the grass-root level trainers could be directly accessed. Considering about 7 lakh Government supported women's groups in the country at present, there will be a need of about 2.30 lakhs facilitators and 11,600 supervisory level functionaries who will require training on a best case scenario,

The implementation of the project is being jointly undertaken by the Department of Women & Child Development, Indira Gandhi National Open University (IGNOU) and Indian Satellite Research Organisation (ISRO). The Department of Women & Child Development would provide support of policy direction, sharing of available material and funds for the programme. The scheme would use IGNOU's experience in development and accreditation of software so that a standardised package consisting of self-instructional print, audio and video material with tutorial support through tele-conferencing could be developed. ISRO will provide the satellite linkage for at least 80 hours per year for the programme and will arrange some of the hardware related support. There would be 7 training cycles in English and 5 cycles in Hindi during the next 5 years.

The total cost of the project is about Rs. 3.90 crore consisting of Rs.105 lakh towards hardware, Rs. 166 lakh for software preparation and rest for printing, distribution and support services. The project also covers the installation of 150 units of receiving terminals with T.V. facilities and 250 new telephone connections at the identified centres.

The Programme will be open to employees of various Government bodies, NGOs and students.

Support to training and employment programme for women (STEP)

This programme launched in 1987, seek to provide updated skills and knowledge to poor and assetless women in the traditional sectors, such as agriculture, animal husbandry, dairying, fisheries, handlooms, handicrafts, khadi and village industries, sericulture, social forestry and wasteland development for enhancing their productivity and income generation. This would enhance and broaden their employment opportunities, including self employment and development of entrepreneurial skills. Women beneficiaries are organised into viable and cohesive groups or cooperatives. A comprehensive package of services such as, extension inputs, market linkages, etc. are provided besides linkage with credit.

Since the inception of the programme, about 4,16,000 women have been covered under 72 projects launched in the states of Andhra Pradesh, Bihar, Gujarat, Haryana, Himachal Pradesh, Kerala, Karnataka, Maharashtra, Manipur, Madhya Pradesh, Orissa, Tamil Nadu, Tripura, Uttar Pradesh and West Bengal. So far, women in the dairying sector have been receiving the maximum support. This is followed by handlooms, handicrafts, sericulture and poultry.

In the year 1997-98, 6 projects to benefit 53,325 women were sanctioned and an amount of Rs. 15 crore was released. During the year 1998-99, 5 projects have been sanctioned to benefit 31,320 women and an amount of Rs. 4.83 crore was released.

A sensitisation programme for the managers of new projects approved under the scheme of STEP during 1997-98 was organised in July, 1998 at the National Institute of Public Cooperation and Child Development (NIPCCD), New Delhi. This programme was attended by representatives from all new projects. Programme modules for legal literacy and health and nutrition education prepared earlier were finalised by the participants for use in the projects.

Trade-wise position of STEP projects sanctioned during 1997-98 and 1998-99 is given at Annexure V and trade-wise beneficiaries under STEP programme are as follows:

Setting up of employment-cum income generation-cum production units (NORAD)

The NORAD (Norwegian Agency for Development Cooperation) assisted programme launched in 1982-83 aims to improve the lives of poor women. Under this programme financial assistance is provided to Women's Development Corporations, Public Sector Corporations, Autonomous Bodies and Voluntary Organisations to train women, especially school drop-outs and semi-literates, in mostly non-traditional trades and to ensure their employment in these areas. Some of the trades are electronics, watch assembling, computer programming, garment making, secretarial practice, community health work, embroidery, weaving, etc. Financial assistance is also given to the grantee organisation for hiring of training-cum-production sheds, training costs, stipend to trainees and for training machinery and equipment.

The assistance under this Scheme is normally confined to Rs. 8000/- per beneficiary.

Since 1982-83 when the NORAD assisted programme was started, 1365 projects benefiting 1.99 lakh women have been approved. Since 1996-97 the assistance by NORAD has been supplemented with domestic resources. In 1997-98, out of an outlay of Rs. 17 crore, Rs. 12 crore was from domestic resources. During the year 1998-99, the Department has sanctioned 81 projects to benefit 6805 women and an amount of Rs. 3.01 crore has been released.

Since the inception of the Scheme the outlay has increased manifold, and the number of projects sanctioned so far has become large. Feeling a need for better monitoring of these projects, special emphasis has been given to monitoring during the current year. Desk (Monitoring) is looking after the monitoring work of the Projects sanctioned under the Scheme at Central Level. The projects functioning in the states of Andhra Pradesh and Uttar Pradesh have been inspected. On the basis of the inspection reports, appropriate action is being taken in each case.

An agreement was signed between the Government of India and Government of Norway on 13 November, 1997 for the extension of the assistance provided by the Norwegian Government for the next 5 years. As per the agreement, an amount of NOK 38 million (equivalent to about Rs. 20 crore) is to be provided by the Norwegian Government under the Scheme for the years 1997-2002. The contribution for the year 1997 and 1998 has been received from NORAD.

Attitudinal change towards the girl child

Balika samriddhi yojana

The scheme of Balika Samriddhi Yojana is under implementation since 199798. The main objective of the scheme is to raise the overall status of the girl child while changing family and community attitudes towards her and her mother. The lower status of the girl child is borne out by declining sex ratio, incidence of female foeticide and infanticide, lower nutritional intake, neglect of health as per hospital statistics, lower rates of literacy, enrolment and retention in schools, etc.

Under the scheme, an amount of Rs. 500/- is paid to the mothers of girl children born on or after 15 August 1997, in families below the poverty line. An amount of Rs. 60.00 crore has been released to the district level implementing agencies as identified by the State Governments/Union Territory administrations during 1997-98.

National Plan of Action for SAARC Decade of the Girl Child, 1991-2000 AD

National Plan of Action for the Girl-Child is under implementation since November, 1992.

Implementation of the Plan of Action is an inter-ministerial effort. The concerned Ministries/ Departments of Government are responsible for implementing the points of the Plan of Action through their girl-child specific or girl-child related programmes. In other words, targets/goals laid down in the NPA are to be achieved by different Ministries/Departments like Health, Education, Labour, etc. In view of this an

Inter-Ministerial Coordination Committee of Secretaries was constituted in 1993 to review the progress of implementation of the National Plan of Action. The Committee meets at regular intervals for the purpose.

Support services

Working women's hostels

Many women—single, divorced, married, widowed—migrate to towns and cities, where employment opportunities are available. A large number of young women also migrate for purposes of technical training, or in pursuit of professional courses of various kinds.

One of the vital support services enabling enrolment of women in employment and work and in technical training is the provision of safe and inexpensive hostel accommodation. Besides promoting gender equity, these services are crucial to enhancing productivity and efficiency at work.

Catering predominantly to working women, the Scheme is implemented through voluntary organisations, registered societies, public trusts, women's development corporations, universities, schools/colleges of social work and local bodies, etc. State Governments and UTs are also eligible for assistance. Financial assistance is extended to the extent of 75% of the cost of construction of the hostel building and 50% of the cost of land. The income-ceiling for eligibility of hostel accommodation has been raised from Rs. 5,0001- and Rs. 4,5001- per month to Rs. 16,000/- and Rs. 15,000- p.m. in metropolitan cities and other cities and towns respectively w.e.f 14 July 1998. A resident is allowed to stay in the hostel for a maximum period of five years.

Tata Institute of Social Sciences, Mumbai was entrusted with a National level Research Study on the working of women's hostels. The Institute has since submitted its report entitled 'Working Women's Hostels in India'. The study covered the states of Maharashtra, Gujarat, Tamil Nadu, Delhi, Orissa, Rajasthan and Kerala. The study revealed that the majority of the boarders were satisfied with the safety, security, cleanliness and sanitary conditions afforded by the working women's hostels. In most of the hostels, Hostel Management Committees were functioning. There is an emergent demand for expansion of the hostel facilities for working women. The State Governments and Voluntary Organisations have been advised to take follow up action. The Master Plan of Operations (MPO) prepared by the Department in 1991-92 indicated a need to provide hostel accommodation to an estimated 1.35 lakhs working women all over the country. During the year 1998-99, 5 hostels have been sanctioned to provide accommodation to 614 working women. In four of these hostels, day care facilities for 110 children of working women have also been provided. Since the inception of the Scheme, 815 hostels have been sanctioned to provide accommodation to 57,683 working women. Day care facilities have been provided to 7528 children in 288 hostels. The State-wise/ UT-wise position of the hostels sanctioned and number of beneficiaries of the Scheme is at Annexure VII.

Short stay homes for women and girls

The Government of India launched a programme in 1969 in the Central Sector called the Short Stay Homes for Women and Girls to protect and rehabilitate those women and girls who are facing social and moral danger due to family problems, mental strains, social ostracism, exploitation or other causes. The services extended in these homes include medical care; psychiatric treatment; casework services; occupational therapy; education-cum-vocational training and recreational facilities.

The need for providing Short Stay Homes for

women and girls has been due to the changing pattern of life, rapid urbanisation and industrialisation and the resulting migration from rural to urban areas. The break-up of social institutions like the Pint family, contributes considerably in creating problems of adjustment for women and young girls. Cases of marital conflict and emotional disturbance occur. This effort is made to help the women to rehabilitate themselves within a short period of time. These Short Stay Homes have been established by voluntary organisations.

At present, 272 Short Stay Homes receive grants from the Department, covering approximately 8160 beneficiaries. Under the scheme, the grant is being released at the existing financial norms on the recommendation of the State Governments, to the extent of Rs. 2,12,300 (Recurring and Non-recurring) when approved by the Government of India and subsequently, recurring grant of Rs.1,87,300 is given to the Home every year on the basis of 'C' Class city.

The Cabinet Committee on Economic Affairs has recently approved a proposal for revision of the norms and financial patterns of the scheme. The recurring cost as per the changed norms will now be Rs. 4,01,350 per Home per annum in 'C' class city and non-recurring cost would be Rs. 4,15,350. There is also a provision for some increase in subsequent years on the component of rent and the maintenance cost for residents. Provisions have also been made for upgrading skills and capacities of staff and residents as well as education of the children of residents. The implementation of the scheme will now be transferred to the Central Social Welfare Board.

During the year under report, a provision of Rs. 5.15 crore (Rs.4.00 crore under Plan and Rs. 1.15 crore under Non-Plan) (RE) has been made.

The Government of India sponsored Rashtriya Mahila Kosh (RMK) which was constituted as a registered Society on 30th March, 1993. RMK was also given, on its inception, a one time corpus fund of Rs. 31 crore by the Government. The policy directives of RMK come from the Governing Board of RMK, which comprises 16 members.

The main objective of RMK is to facilitate credit support or micro finance to poor women for income-generating activities. RMK mainly uses NGOs running on sound lines as its channelising agencies for identification of borrowers, delivery of credit support and recovery. RMK has completed more than five years of its existence. Since its inception, upto 31 January 99, RMK has so far been able to sanction credit limits of Rs. 57.09 crore through 367 NGOs to benefit 2,77,662 women. In addition, RMK has also supported the formation of women's thrift and credit societies popularly known as SHGs through its partner NGOs.

Eligibility for RMK's loan Assistance under the main scheme

i) NGOs/Women Development Corporations and Cooperative Societies (that have at least 33% women members) and are running on sound lines, and working inter-alia for the socio-economic upliftment of the poor women, who have experience in thrift and credit administration of at least 3 years.

ii) Recovery performance of such organisations should be around 90% during the last 3 years.

Lending Terms

— Loans are given to the poor women for their income generation activities.

— Amount of loan: Short-term (ST) loan upto Rs. 50001- and Medium-term (MT) upto Rs. 75001- per borrower.

— Repayment: Short-term loans are repayable in 15 months. Medium-term loans are repayable in 3-5 years. Repayments will be made quarterly/half yearly after providing for the requisite gestation period of A to 6 months.

— Lending rate of RMK both for ST and MT loans is 8% per annum to the NGO. The ultimate borrowers or their SHGs will be charged interest @ not exceeding 12%.

— In case the lending is done to the SHGs, they are free to fix a rate for their members, not exceeding 17.85% for this year.

— Interest is repayable at the end of each quarter. In addition to the 4% margin available to the NGOs/ SHGs, the following further incentives have been provided:

i) Incentive equal to 1% of the loan amount to NGOs for timely disbursement of loan.

ii) Interest relief of 1/2 % for timely repayments.

iii) I % grant is available to NGOs for skill upgradation or for training of women borrowers in credit management/ administration and for training in-group dynamics.

Promotional and other innovative scheme

Micro-credit or micro-finance is gaining world wide acceptance as a means of poverty alleviation. RMK has therefore evolved some promotional schemes to encourage the inexperienced NGOs to start off with a small amount of loan from RMK. Further, financial assistance is also made available for forming SHGs which are valuable and effective mechanisms for collecting and revolving savings of group members. This process lays a firm foundation for the future good repayment behaviour of the members. Details of RMK's SHG support scheme are as follows:

SHG Development Scheme

NGOs eligible to get assistance under this scheme should have been registered for 3 years and having a positive potential for becoming a collaborator of RMK in the course of another one or two years. Financial assistance by way of interest free loan convertible into grant of upto Rs. 1 lakh is given to the NGOs for formation, promotion and development of 25 Self-Help Groups. The homogenous groups will be of 15 to 20 women each. Upto 31 January 1999, an amount of Rs. 127.980 lakhs has been sanctioned under this scheme, out of which Rs. 89.430 lakhs has been disbursed. 113 new NGOs who have potential and interest in undertaking micro-credit activities have been covered.

Loan Promotion Scheme

The objective of this scheme is to encourage smaller NGOs so as to make them eligible for full finance from RMK in due course. The eligibility criteria for this scheme are the some as for the main scheme (noted above) except that the criterion relating to previous experience of credit and recovery is reduced to one year and the maximum amount kept at Rs. 2 lakh.

NODAL Agency Scheme

During the last 4 years of its existence, RMK has been making efforts to reach credit to as many poor women in the unorganised sector as possible. However, beginners still need detailed practical guidance on their proposed partnership with RMK. It is also natural that this guidance, if given in their own language, is even more effective. In this context, as a substitute to having regional offices, RMK has launched its "Nodal Agency" scheme to enlist the support of some major organisations not necessarily involved in savings and credit programmes, but who have suitable infrastructure for logistics and faculty support. These Agencies will identify the potential NGOs and will help them in group formation, in canvassing their credit limit applications to RMK and prior to that, in the preliminary scrutiny of the proposals, submission of credit limit papers and also later in drawal of applications, utilisation certificate, and so on. The nodal organisation will also attend to the queries raised by the small organisations. So far, 28 NGOs have been appointed Nodal Agencies of Rashtriya Mahila Kosh.

Tutoring of the new NGOs by old NGOs and dissemination of information on best practices in the field of Micro Credit

At least 30 new organisations were given the opportunity of visiting those NGOs at work, who are adept at micro-finance and SHG formation. Notable tutor NGOs were MYRADA, ASSEFA, Grama Siri and VJNNS, Annapurna Mahila Mandal, PEDO (Rajasthan), RIDO (Tamil Nadu) and Mass Education (Calcutta).

Resource NGO Scheme

The NGOs designated as Resource NGO (RN) amongst RMK's partners are those NGOs who have the capacity to educate and train the beginners in this field. The Resource NGOs are to play a role in guiding them in formulation of credit and savings programmes, giving training and exposure to the staff of smaller NGOs. RMK is to cover the expenses of these trainings. Resource NGOs have to be RMK's strong partners.

Revolving Fund Scheme

Rashtriya Mahila Kosh has introduced its "'Revolving Fund"' scheme to provide lumpsum funds to partner NGOs having more than 5 years experience in thrift and credit to provide them more elbow room in preparing new areas for credit, and to recycle loans to the poor women in need of credit. The other objective is to sharpen the experience of its large partner agencies in their fund management, and to provide them incentive in expanding their activities in the states which so far have a poor coverage of RMK. Under this scheme, upto 31 January 1999, an amount of Rs. 7.88 crore has been sanctioned to 41 NGOs. Out of this, an amount of Rs. 6.99 crore has already been disbursed.

Indira Mahila Yojana

Indira Mahila Yojana (IMY) has so far been adopted in 200 blocks of the country. Under IMY, a very strong emphasis is laid on the formation of women's Self-Help Groups at grass-root level under the Indira Mahila Kendras (IMKs).

The Self-Help Groups are a good conduit for RMK's credit support. Thus, credit facility available under RMK could be passed on to the IMBSs for on-lending to poor women provided they have formed Self-Help Groups and have also started savings on a regular basis and some members are keen to expand their income generation activities with credit support. In this context, RMK has funded the training of trainers at BIRD, Lucknow. These trainers have also had exposure in U.K. and Bangladesh. RMK is also involved in implementation of IMY, as it is expected to play a crucial role in giving exposition on the role and nature of SHGs. All RMK's officers have had the benefit of attending 3 days course on SHG at MYRADA, Karnataka.

Death Relief Rehabilitation Fund

The Death Relief and Rehabilitation Fund Scheme was launched on 15th August, 1995, to make provisions for writing off of loans outstanding against a woman borrower in case of her death or loss/damage of assets due to natural calamities, fire, riots, and so on. The Scheme is operational and, at present, 24 NGOs have become its members. It is a contributory scheme and matching contribution is provided by the kosh. A Coordination Committee consisting of the members of the Strategic Planning Group was set up to finalise/discuss the long-term planning of the scheme. The same Committee was also vested with the powers of settling claims of more than Rs. 15000/- *i.e.*, beyond the power of Executive Director to finalise the claims. Coordination Committee in its meeting held on 3 June 1998 has finalised claims to the tune of Rs. 1,20,654.45 received from 51 borrowers of 3 NGOs *i.e.*, Gramasiri, Prajashakti Vidya Sangham and Jinns.

Marketing Finance Scheme

Under the Scheme, an amount of upto 40% of the value of the goods produced by RMK's women borrowers expected to be sold is made admissible on the same parameters as applicable for loans to RMK's partner NGOs under the main Scheme. Upto 31 January 1999, an amount of Rs. 37.25 lakh has been sanctioned under this Scheme out of which Rs. 17.25 lakh has been disbursed.

Centrally Sponsored Rural Sanitation Programme (CRSP)

Rashtriya Mahila Kosh is also assisting in the Rural Sanitation Programme of the Ministry of Rural Areas & Employment, Department of Rural Development. The Ministry of Rural Areas and Employment has placed an amount of Rs. 2.25 crore as grants-in-aid at the disposal of Rashtriya Mahila Kosh for the implementation of Rural Sanitation Programme through its collaborating NGOs. Upto 31 January 1999, RMK has approved proposals for construction of 11765 sanitary toilets involving sanction of Rs. 255.72 lakh. RMK has already disbursed Rs. 205.19 lakh to the NGOs for implementing the programme.

In order to give a thrust to the health, environment improvement at sanitation programme in the country, RN has advised its partner NGOs, making incumbent upon them to motivate at least 25 to 30% of the families whose women members are provided loans out of RM assistance, to construct their own sanitary toilets from the savings or the surplus generated from the income generating activities and teach them the importance a health and hygiene.

Programmes in connection with 50 years of India's Independence

Workshops/Awareness Camps

As a part of celebrations of 50 years of India's independence, Rashtriya Mahila Kosh organised 11 workshops and 100 Awareness Camps in various parts of the country to generate awareness about RMK schemes and also highlight the socioeconomic empowerment of women since independence. These workshops/awareness camps were organised in those areas of the country where no NGOs have come forward so for or no Self-Help Groups have been formed. Emphasis was to be laid on dissemination of information in uncovered and backward areas of the country. Reports on 37 Awareness Camps and 5 Workshops have since been received.

Organisation of a Photo Contest

A photo-contest open to NGOs on RMK assisted women beneficiaries was organised. The first three prize winning photographs were awarded prizes of Rs. 5000/-, Rs. 3000/- and Rs. 2000/respectively.

Short Films

RMK has produced three short films to spread awareness about its schemes through the medium of television. The films have been completed and a dialogue is on with Doordarshan (Prasar Bharati Broadcasting Corporation of India) for the telecast of these films on national network.

Publicity Material Developed

RMK has been striving to develop publicity and informative material to help NGOs in the better performance of their tasks. During the year 1998-99, RMK has brought out the following publications:

i) A compendium of suggestions on micro-credit

A publication has been brought out which contains experiences of 6 leading NGO partners of RMK in micro-credit topics such as financial sustainability in Self-Help Groups, Management of credit support to poor women, Organisation of Training Complexes for Women Entrepreneur Development, Management of Accounts at SHG level. Many new NGO's will pick up useful ideas from the experiences highlighted in the Compendium to advance the cause of women's development. The Compendium was released by Secretary (WCD) at a function on 2nd November, 1998.

ii) 42 Questions on RMK

A number of queries are raised on various schemes/ programmes of RMK during workshops and training programmes. A need to bring out a publication giving clarification on the points often raised has been felt. To fulfil this need, a booklet on.42 questions often raised at various fora of RMK along with their clarifications has been compiled. This booklet was also released by Secretary (WCD) on 2nd November, 1998.

Workshops

RMK has been holding workshops in various parts of the country to spread awareness about RMK programmes and building up of capabilities among the concerned functionaries to monitor micro-credit programmes. RMK has organised 53 workshops up to 31 January 1999 which were attended by 3315 participants representing 1965 NGOs.

During the year 1998 RMK had taken new initiative calling through newspaper advertisements particulars of NGOs interested in micro-finance and then inviting them to business workshops. The applications of such NGOs are screened on the spot. Three business workshops were conducted at Bhopal, Patna and Bhubaneswar upto 31st March, 1998. One more business workshop has been conducted during the year at Lucknow. Apart from this, four workshops were held during the current year upto 31 January 1999. Through these workshops/business workshops, RMK hopes to involve a number of new NGOs as its partners in the task of micro-finance.

Achievement

Year-wise details of amount sanctioned, released and disbursed by the RMK upto 31 January 1999 since inception is given in the Annexure XVIII.

Smt. Heerama, a 53 year old woman from Doddabathi village, Davangere Taluk and District, Karnataka lives with her husband Sri Thotanagoudar. Her husband is very old and unable to work in the agriculture field. She did not have the means for a regular income to support her family consisting of six children and husband. She opened a mini snack shop in front of her house in the beginning she could not bring raw material for preparing the snacks due to shortage of finance. She contacted Sri Shakthi Mahila Mandali (R) for availing of loan. She availed a loan of Rs. 3,000/under the RMK scheme. Then she could bring raw material and built a reputation in that area for her snacks. Now she is remitting the loan instalments regularly and leading a happy life.

"The RMK is a very good scheme. It has helped me in proper time to overcome poverty. I am grateful to RMK and Sri Shakthi Mahila Mandali (R)".

Rathnamma, a 35 year old woman from Karnataka, lives with her husband in a small house, is unemployed and she did not have any income to support her family. Her house was located near an industrial area. She decided to open a Mess for industrial employees in her house and contacted Sri shakthi Mahila Mandali (R) for availing of loan. She availed a loan of Rs. 5,000/- under the Rashtriya Mahila Kosh. Her Mess has become very popular in that area. She returned the loan amount and took another loan for the expansion of the Mess, which she is repaying regularly. She has a good and regular income now. In her words "The Rashtriya Mahila Kosh is the best scheme. It has helped me at the right time to overcome my problems. Now, I can manage my family affairs without difficulty". She is now well prepared to face the challenges of life.

3

Child Development

The Constitution of India emphasises the importance of improving the well-being of children. Article 39 deals with the Directive Principles of State Policy, which stipulates that the State shall, in particular, direct its policy to ensure: that health and strength of workers, men and women, and the tender age of children are not abused, and that citizens are not forced by economic necessity to enter into avocations unsuited to their age or strength; that children are given opportunities and facilities to develop in a healthy manner and in conditions of freedom and dignity and that childhood and youth are protected against exploitation and against moral and material abandonment.

Article 24 stipulates that no child below the age of 14 years shall be employed to work in any factory or mine or be engaged in any other hazardous employment. According to Article 45, the State shall endeavour to provide free and compulsory education for all children until they complete 14 years of age.

As per 1991 Census, India has around 1500 lakh children below the age of 6 years, constituting 17.5% of its population. A large number of these children live in economic and social environments which impede their physical and mental development. These conditions include poverty, poor environmental sanitation, disease, infection, inadequate access to primary health care, inappropriate child caring and feeding practices.

While each crucial indicator including Infant Mortality Rate, Child Mortality Rate and levels of malnutrition have shown significant improvement, all of these are still considered abnormally high when viewed against the country's capabilities to protect and promote the development of children. Further, high population growth is also as much a cause for concern as infant and child mortality as we are still faced with human resource wastage of about 11% by the age of 5 years and most of it is avoidable. While significant success has been achieved in addressing vaccine preventable diseases and malnutrition, yet a large number of infants die each year. Inadequacy of care of women is also evident from prevailing high rates of low birth weight. Further, though the proportion of nutritional blindness has reduced drastically to 0.4% from 2% in 1973, sub-clinical deficiency of Vitamin 'A' is still prevalent.

Iron Deficiency Anaemia (IDA) is prevalent among women of child bearing age and preschool children. While over a period of time, use of iodised salt at the household level has significantly improved, yet no state in India is free from iodine deficiency.

To combat these problems, the Government of India in 1974 formulated a National Policy for Children which describes children as a supremely important asset. To look after the welfare and development of children, the Department of Women & Child Development is implementing various programmes, which are as follows:

The Integrated Child Development Services ICDS) Scheme aims to improve the nutritional and health status of vulnerable groups including pre-school children, pregnant women and nursing mothers through providing a package of services including Supplementary Nutrition, Pre-school Education, Immunisation, Health Check-UP, Referral Services, and Nutrition and Health Education. In addition, the Scheme envisages effective convergence of inter-sectoral services in the Anganwadi Centres.

The ICDS Scheme has now come to be regarded as the most viable vehicle for achieving the goals set in the National Plan of Action for Children, to be achieved by the year 2000 A.D. These, inter-alia, include reduction of Infant Mortality Rate (IMR) to less than 60 per thousand; reduction in Child Mortality Rate (CMR) to less than 10 per thousand; reduction in Maternal Mortality Rate (MMR) by at least 50 per cent; reduction in severe and moderate malnutrition among children under 5 years by at least 50 percent and universal enrolment and retention in primary schools.

Objectives

— Improve the nutritional and health status of children below the age of six years.

— Lay the foundation for the proper psychological, physical and social development of the child.

— Reduce the incidence of mortality, morbidity, malnutrition and school dropouts.

— Achieve effective coordination of policy and implementation among various departments to promote child development.

— Enhance the capability of the mother to look after the normal health and nutritional needs of the child, through proper health and nutrition education.

In addition to children below six years of age, ICIDS also takes care of the essential needs of pregnant women and nursing mothers residing in socially and economically backward villages and urban slums. The large network of ICIDS provides vital services in the disadvantaged areas to the most vulnerable groups.-

Services and beneficiaries

The programmes provide an integrated approach for converging basic services for improved child-care, early stimulation and learning, health and nutrition, water and environmental sanitation targeting young children, expectant and nursing mothers and women's/ adolescent girls groups. They are reached through well trained community-based Anganwadi Workers, an equal number of helpers and through the supportive community structure and women's groups. ICIDS provides increased opportunities for promoting early development, associated with improved enrolment and retention in the early primary stage and by releasing girls from the burden of sibling care, to enable them to participate in primary education. ICIDS today reaches out to 39 lakh expectant and nursing mothers and 203 lakh children (under six years of age), of disadvantaged groups. Of these, 114 lakh children (three to six years of age) participate in centre-based preschool education activities.

The following section deals with various aspects of the ICDS Programmes

- Nutrition
- Health
- Early Childhood Care and Pre-school Education

Nutrition

— Growth monitoring and promotion

- Supplementary feeding

— Nutrition and health education (NHED).

— Growth monitoring and promotion

Growth monitoring and nutrition surveillance are two important activities that are in operation at the field level in ICIDS. Both are important for assessing the impact of the health and nutrition related services.

Children below the age of three years are weighed once a month and children from three to six years are weighed quarterly. Fixed-day immunisation sessions on days when mothers come to take home rations for younger children (below two years of age) are used as opportunities for growth monitoring and promotion of younger children. In ICIDS, weight-for-age growth cards are maintained for all children below six years. Their growth is charted both to detect growth faltering and also to assess their nutritional status.

Growth monitoring and promotion helps the mother/family and AWW/ANM in taking timely, cost effective preventive action, to arrest any stagnancy or slipping down in weight, through early detection of growth faltering. Through discussion and counselling, growth monitoring also increases the participation and capabilities of mothers in understanding and improving child-care and feeding practices, for promoting child growth. It helps families understand better, the linkages between dietary intake, health-care, safe drinking water, environmental sanitation and child growth. Growth monitoring and promotion can thus also be an effective entry point for primary health-care.

Recently, the concept of community-based nutrition surveillance has been introduced in ICDS. A community chart for nutrition status monitoring is maintained at each Anganwadi. This chart reflects the nutritional status of all children registered with the Anganwadi, at any given point of time, helping the community in understanding what the nutrition status of its children is, why it is so and what can be done to improve it. This mobilises community support in promoting and enabling better child-care practices, contributing local resources and in improving service delivery and utilisation.

Supplementary feeding

All families in the community are surveyed, to identify low income families and deprived children below the age of six years, pregnant and nursing mothers and adolescent girls. They avail of supplementary feeding support for 300 days in a year. By providing supplementary feeding., the Anganwadi attempts to bridge the caloric gap between the national recommended and average intake of children and women in low income and disadvantaged communities. This pattern of feeding aims only at supplementing and not substituting for family food. It also provides an important contact opportunity with pregnant women and mothers of infants and young children, to promote improved behavioural actions for the care of pregnant women and young children. Specifically, it serves to reinforce the key message to promote appropriate and timely complementary feeding at home, starting among infants who are four to six months of age, with a full diet for young children by one year, and continued breast feeding up to two years.

The type of food varies from State to State, but usually consists of a hot meal cooked at the Anganwadi, containing a varied combination of pulses, cereals, oil, vegetables and sugar. Some States provide ready-to eat meals containing the same basic ingredients. There is flexibility in the selection of food items, to respond to local needs. The expenditure towards supplementary feeding is met by the State under the Plan budget available for Minimum Needs Programme. Special care is also taken to reach children below the age of two years, and to encourage parents and siblings to either take home ration for them or to bring them to the Anganwadi for supplementary feeding. The take-home ration is a contact opportunity for growth monitoring and promotion of children under two years of age and nutrition counselling of mothers, for improved childcare and feeding practices.

The national prophylaxis programme for prevention of blindness caused by vitamin A deficiency, and control of nutritional anaemia among mothers and children, are two direct interventions integrated in ICDS. Dietary promotion is an important part of nutrition health education and targetted supplementation is also provided. At nine months of age, 100,000 International Units (IU) of vitamin A solution is administered to infants, along with immunisation against measles, Children in the age group of one to five years receive 200,000 IU of vitamin A solution every six months, with priority to children under three years of age.

Tablets of iron and folic acid are administered to expectant mothers for prophylaxis and treatment and to children with anaemia. These supplements are distributed in Anganwadi Centres, and their utilisation is monitored by them. The usage of iodised salt is promoted, especially in the food supplement provided.

Nutrition and Health Education

Nutrition, Health and Education (NHED) is a key element in the work of the Anganwadi Worker. This has the long term goal of capacity building of women -especially in the age group of 15-45 years -so that they can look after their own health and nutrition needs as well as that of their children and families. All women in this age-group are expected to be covered by this component.

Anganwadi Workers use fixed-day immunization

sessions, mother-child days, growth monitoring days, small group meetings of mothers/Mahila Mandals, community and home visits, village contact drives and other women's groups meetings (DWCRA, Mahila Samakhaya, etc.), local festivals and gatherings, for nutrition and health education. Presently there are nearly 1,00,000 Mahila Mandals which are actively involved in extending nutrition and health education activities.

All efforts are made to reach out to women, including pregnant women and nursing mothers. Sustained support and guidance has to be provided in the period spanning pregnancy and early childhood, to mothers of young children, building upon local knowledge, attitudes and practices. This helps promote antenatal care, maternal nutrition, exclusive breast-feeding of infants upto four to six months of age, timely immunisation, introduction of timely and appropriate complementary feeding at home of infants at four to six months of age with a full diet by 12 months of age and continued breast-feeding up to two years. NHED also promotes appropriate prevention and management of diarrhoeal diseases (through ORT and continued feeding) and management of acute respiratory infections, to promote proper growth of the child.

Health

— Health Care

— Immunisation

— Referral Services

— Treatment of minor illness

Health Care

This includes

- Ante natal care of expectant mothers;

- Post natal care of nursing mothers and care of new born infants; and
- Care of children under 6 years of age.

The various health services provided for children by AWWs and PHC staff include regular health check-ups, recording of weight, immunisation, management of malnutrition, treatment of diarrhoea, deworming and distribution of simple medicines, etc.

At the Anganwadi, children, adolescent girls, pregnant women and nursing mothers are examined at regular intervals by the Lady Health Visitor (LHV) and Auxiliary Nurse Midwife (ANM) who also diagnose minor ailments and distribute simple medicines. They provide a link between the village and the Primary Health Care Subcentre. Maternal and child health facilities are geared towards providing adequate medical care during pregnancy, at the time of childbirth and subsequently. It is aimed at reducing complications during pregnancy and reducing perinatal mortality.

Immunisation

Immunisation of pregnant women against tetanus and immunisation of infants against six vaccine- preventable diseases -poliomyelitis, diphtheria, pertussis, tetanus, tuberculosis and measles - protects children from these diseases. These are major preventable causes of child, mortality, disability, morbidity and related malnutrition. Immunisation of pregnant women against tetanus also reduces maternal and neonatal mortality.

PHC and its subordinate health infrastructure carries out immunisation of infants and expectant mothers as per the national immunisation schedule. Children are also given booster doses. The AWW assists the health functionaries in coverage of the population for immunisation. She helps in the organisation of fixed-day immunisation sessions. She maintains immunisation records of ICDS beneficiaries and follows up to ensure full coverage.

Referral services

During health check-ups and growth monitoring, sick or malnourished children in need of prompt medical attention are provided referral services through ICDS. The AWW has also been oriented to detect disabilities in young children. She enlists all such cases in a special register and refers them to the medical officers. The effectiveness of this service depends on timely action, cooperation from health functionaries and the willingness of families to avail of these services. The Health Department in States/UTs identifies one hospital at the district level, which attends to the referral cases coming from the ICDS areas.

Early childhood care and pre-school education

— Early Childhood Care

— Early Childhood Education

Early Childhood Care and Pre-School Education under ICDS-non-formal pre-schooi education is a crucial component of the package of services envisaged under ICDS scheme, aims at universalisation and qualitative improvement of primary education in remote and socio-economically backward areas with primary attention being given to the girl child. The Early Childhood Care and Pre-school Education (ECCE) component of the ICDS may well be considered the backbone of the ICDS programme, since all its services essentially converge on the AW. This is also the most joyful play-way daily activity, visibly sustained for three hours a day. It brings and keeps young children at the Anganwadi Centre - an activity that motivates parents and communities. ECCE, as envisaged in the ICDS, focuses on the total development of the child, in the age range of up to six years, from the underprivileged groups. It includes promotion of early stimulation of the under-threes through intervention with mothers/ caregivers. Child-centred play-way activities which build on local culture and practices, using local support materials developed by Anganwadi workers, through enrichment training, are promoted. The early-childhood, pre-school education programme, conducted through the medium of play, aims at providing a learning environment for the promotion of social, emotional, cognitive, physical and aesthetic development of the child. Through ICDS, 11 A lakh children (3-6 years of age), from disadvantaged groups, are participating in centre-based, pre-school, play-way activities.

The ECCE component of the ICDS is a significant input for providing a sound foundation for development. It also contributes to the universalisation of primary education, by providing to the child the necessary preparation for primary schooling and offering substitute care to the younger siblings, thus freeing the older ones -especially girls - to attend school.

For this, improved coordination between the Anganwadi Centres and primary schools, in terms of timings, location and supportive linkages between the Anganwadi Worker and primary school teacher - are being promoted.

Convergence

ICDS scheme supports convergence with other supportive services, such as safe drinking water, environmental sanitation, women's empowerment programmes, nonformal education and adult literacy, and health and nutrition.

Targetted beneficiaries

The Scheme targets the most vulnerable groups of population including children upto 6 years of age, pregnant women and nursing mothers belonging to poorest of the poor families and living in disadvantaged areas including backward rural areas, tribal areas and urban slums. The identification of beneficiaries is done through surveying the community and identifying families living below the poverty line.

The ICDS team

The ICDS team comprises the Anganwadi helpers/ Anganwadi Workers (AWWs), the supervisors and the Child Development Project Officers (CDPOs). In larger rural and tribal projects, Additional Child Development Project Officers (ACDPOs) are also a part of the team. The medical officers, the lady health visitors and female health workers from nearby primary health centres and sub-centres form a team with social welfare/women and child development department functionaries to implement ICDS.

The AWW is a community-based voluntary frontline worker of the ICDS programme. Selected from the community, she assumes a pivotal role due to her close and continuous contact with the people, especially women she works with. As a crucial link between the village population and the Government administration, she becomes a central figure in helping the community identify and meet the needs of their children and women. The AWW is expected to monitor and promote the growth of children, with the active participation of community/ mothers. She enhances their capability for preventive and promotive action for child growth - through improved childcare and feeding practices. She also enables them to prevent disease infection. The AWW organises supplementary feeding, helps organise immunisation sessions, distributes vitamin A supplements and iron and folic acid tablets, treats minor injuries and ailments, and refers cases to medical services. The more visible aspects of her role is in making the Anganwadi literally a courtyard play centre - nurturing and joyful -with play-way activities attracting and sustaining the participation of children and families. Considering the valuable services provided by the Anganwadi Worker and Anganwadi Helper, their honoraria has been increased by 25% and 30% respectively.

The Supervisor (Mukhya Sevika) is responsible for 17-25 Anganwadis, depending upon the nature of the project. She supports and guides AWWs and assists in recording home visits, organising community meetings and visits of health personnel, and providing on-the-job orientation to AWWs. The CDPO provides the link between ICDS functionaries and the Government administration. This officer is also responsible for securing Anganwadi premises, identifying beneficiaries, ensuring supply of food to centres and flow of health services, and monitoring programmes and reporting to the State Government. At the community level, other frontline workers, including the Gram Sevika, primary school teachers, also link with the Anganwadi worker. Local women's groups, Mahila Mandals, youth clubs, local organisations, Panchayat Samitis and Bal Vikas Mahila Samiti members also support the Anganwadi Workers.

The ICDS team facilitates creation of partnerships between frontline workers and community/ women's groups, ensuring an integrated approach for improved childcare, health, nutritional well being and development at the Anganwadi Centre, literally a courtyard play centre, a childcare centre located within the village or the slum area itself. It is the focal point for the delivery of services at community level to children below six years of age, pregnant women, nursing mothers and adolescent girls. Besides this the AW is a meeting ground where women's groups can, come together, with other frontline workers, to promote awareness and joint action for child development and women's empowerment.

In addition to the job responsibilities of AWW originally envisaged, AWW is discharging additional activities in various sectors in different State and UT's. Throughout the country, the Anganwadi Worker and Helper have been utilized for schemes related to health and family welfare. Further her services are vital in implementation of the RCH (Reproductive Child Health) programme and National AIDS Control Programme during the Ninth Five Year Plan. Apart from this ' the Anganwadi Worker and Helper are significantly contributing in implementation of various other programmes and schemes of both Central Government and State Government.

Setting up of the National Committee for Reviewing benefits/facilities being provided to Anganwadi Workers and Helpers

During the conference of State Ministers and Secretaries of the Department of Women and Child Development held on 22nd and 23rd July, 1998, the Minister for HRD stated that a Committee will be constituted with definite terms of reference for going into the whole gamut of the issues affecting the service conditions of the Anganwadi Workers and Helpers and exploring the avenues for increasing the honoraria being paid to Anganwadi Workers and Helpers. It was, therefore, decided to set up a National Committee in the Department of Women and Child Development in order to take stock of the service conditions and duties of the

Anganwadi Workers and Helpers and to identify the Ministries/

Departments/States, etc. which can provide additional remuneration to the Anganwadi Workers and Helpers functioning under the centrally sponsored ICDS Scheme. Besides the representatives of the concerned central departments, representatives of some State Governments who have taken initiative to increase the honoraria of Anganwadi Workers have also been included in this Committee. The Committee set up under the chairpersonship of Joint Secretary, in the Department, is in the process of finalising its report.

Coverage and outreach

Started on an experimental basis during 1975-76 in just 33 blocks of the country, the Scheme has gradually expanded and till November 1998, 4200 projects are in operation with sanctioned strength of 5.92 lakh Anganwadi Centres. However, while approving the enhancement of honoraria to Anganwadi Workers and Helpers working under the Scheme in May 1997, Ministry of Finance imposed a freeze on further operationalisation of ICDS projects beyond 4200 and Anganwadi Centres beyond 5.92 lakhs (approx.).

An in-depth review with each State/LIT was undertaken in the month of July/August-to ascertain the macro-picture regarding ICDS. The review included reconciliation in the number of sanctioned ICDS blocks, operational blocks, number of sanctioned Anganwadi Centres and operational Anganwadi Centres besides financial review. The focus of the review was to firm up the number of operational blocks state-wise as also to identify these blocks. With the approval of HRM, reallocation of operational 4200 ICDS blocks was carried out during August 1998.

Financial resources and funding pattern under the ICDS Scheme

The ICDS Scheme is a centrally sponsored Scheme implying thereby a Central share and a State share in the total costs. While the Central Government bears the full cost of meeting the operational requirements, the States provide for funds for supplementary nutrition component.

In addition to mobilising domestic resources, significant contribution also comes from UN Agencies, bilateral donors and the World Bank. Swedish Industrial Development Agency (SIDA) was providing support to 47 ICDS projects in Tamil Nadu upto June 1997 which has been extended upto 31st December 1998. SIDA supported ICDS projects were evaluated by a joint evaluation team comprising of representatives of Government of India, Swedish Embassy and Government of Tamil Nadu who conducted various studies. The joint evaluation is now complete and report is awaited.

Expenditure on ICDS

Alongwith the gradual expansion of the Scheme, there has also been a significant increase in the Central Government's spending on implementation of the Scheme during the 8th Plan period. As against the expenditure of only Rs. 1190.21 crores during 17 years, i.e. 1975-76 to 767.1 98-99 (uptoFeb'99) 1991-92, the expenditure during the 8th Plan period was Rs. 2271.28 crore. During 1997-98 against the provision of Rs. 479. 40 crore in BE, the central expenditure was to the tune of Rs. 608.35 crore. During 1998-99, against a provision of Rs. 768.41 crore in RE, the expenditure incurred up to February 1999 has been to the tune of Rs. 767.1 A crore.

Monitoring and evaluation

Management Information System

The ICDS programme is characterised by a built-in

monitoring system for promoting assessment, analysis and action at different levels at which data is generated. A central cell established at the Department collects and analyses periodic work reports. Based on this, programme strategies are refined, and timely interventions made -ensuring effective programme planning, implementation and monitoring. A national ICDS Management Information System (MIS) working group facilitates this process. Each State Government also has a MIS coordination cell. Districts with more than five projects have a district level ICDS monitoring cell, to facilitate programme monitoring.

MIS ensures a regular flow of information and feedback between each Anganwadi and the project, between the ICDS project and the State Government, and between the State Government and the Government of India. The flow of information is not only upwards - it is a two-way process and constitutes the basis for discussion and improved action at the level at which it is generated. This is done through a Monthly Progress Report (MPR) and a Monthly Monitoring Report (MMR).

Under the National Plan to monitor ICDS, Anganwadi Workers compile standardised monthly and half-yearly reports based on their register data. These reports are forwarded through supervisors to Child Development Project Officers (CDPOs) who are responsible for forwarding the reports (MPRs) to the State and Central ICDS Cell at the Department of Women and Child Development. MPRs quantify the status of key input, process and output indicators pertaining to the major component of ICDS service delivery, which can be used to manage operations.

Through monthly review meetings of ICDS and health functionaries at various levels - block, district, division and state - both MMRs and MPRs are discussed, for Promoting joint action. Efforts are underway to strengthen this process further.

The Department compiles computerised quarterly monitoring reports from the CDPOs. A State level performance statement is prepared on 8 indicators, comparing the performance of each state with the national performance. Copies of these reports are also sent to the Planning Commission, Prime Minister's Secretariat, National Institute of Public Cooperation and Child Development (NIPCCD) and other Ministries/ Organisations involved in the ICDS Programme. Quarterly status reports and performance reports are sent to the State's nodal departments for faking necessary corrective action.

ICDS Scheme: Strengths and impact

The impact of ICDS, however, has been quite dramatic on the health of the participant families. As a service delivery programme, the ICDS has certain unique features which constitute its areas of strength as enumerated below:

— The programme is village based and conducted by workers (Anganwadi Workers & Helpers), who are normally residents of the same village;

— The Anganwadi Worker is supposed to maintain close contact with individual households of the village.

— The programme enlists the active help and participation of voluntary organisations, social activists, academic institutions and professionals;

— There is a built-in scope for convergence of Health, Nutrition and Childhood Education Services at the Anganwadi level;

— Two-third of the population covered by the ICDS programme comprise scheduled castes, scheduled tribes and other backward communities.

ICDS scheme has been subjected to intensive research since the beginning. The impact of the programme is evident from:

— Decrease in prevalence of malnutrition among pre-school children

— improvement in the nutritional status of the children

— Improved immunisation coverage

— Decrease in IMR

— Improvement in school enrolment and reduction in school dropout rate

The most important impact of the Scheme is clearly reflected in significant declines in the levels of severely malnourished and moderately malnourished children in the country as also in significant decline in Infant Mortality Rate. The percentage of children suffering from severe malnutrition have significantly declined from 15.3% during 1976-78 to 8.7% during 1988-90 (figures published by National Nutrition Monitoring Bureau). The Infant Mortality Rates have significantly declined from 80 per 1000 live births in 1991 to 73 during 1994 (Sample Registration System).

ICDS - Evaluation and Research -1975-88 conducted by Central Technical Committee highlighted that the impact of the ICDS on the decline in Infant Mortality Rate is extremely favourable.

Major initiatives

A number of new initiatives have been taken during recent years to strengthen the impact. These chiefly include the adolescent girls scheme for girls in the age group of 11-18 years, effective involvement of the NGOs, provision of income generating activities for women and monitoring. The scheme is viewed as a major national vehicle for achieving the goals of the health and family welfare sector, education and rural development. The provision of income generating activities for women under this scheme is a major step for mobilising women in the rural areas and ensuring their empowerment.

Improving nutrition levels

The monthly monitoring formats have been amended to include frequency aspect of delivery of supplementary nutrition and gender and age specific information. This has also helped in timely detection of interruptions in the nutrition component and in taking early corrective actions. The cost norms of nutrition have been revised upwards to provide minimum calories/proteins on each day and supervisors of the projects have been made directly responsible for monitoring the growth of severely malnourished children and mothers. Further, in order to enable the community to assess the nutritional status of their children on a regular basis, Community Growth Charts have been designed and supplied to all the States for use in the Anganwadi Centres. In addition, Food and Nutrition Board (F&NB) with its 43 Community Food and Nutrition Extension Units (CFNEU) located in 27 States/ UTs is being effectively used for dissemination of vital nutrition and health education to ICDS functionaries/ beneficiaries. Further, 43 CFNEUs are also being used in monitoring the quality and delivery of supplementary nutrition in Anganwadi Centres under the ICDS Scheme.

Pre-school education

Resource Centres have been located in the CDPO's Offices and the necessary tie up has been done with NCERT and SCERTs for development of pre-school material in the local languages for use in the Anganwadi Centres. In addition, instructions have been issued for coordinating the timings between the primary schools and Anganwadi Centres and for regular visits of primary school teachers to the Anganwadi Centres. This has been done to ensure enrichment of pre-school component and better enrolment and retention in the primary schools.

Community partnership

The 73rd and the 74th Constitutional Amendments have created vibrant new partnerships to reach the most disadvantaged and the most vulnerable young children. In some States, devolution of powers to Panchayati Raj institutions has also involved the transfer of some functions for managing and monitoring ICDS to district Zila Parishads, Block Panchayat Samitis and Gram Panchayats.

This constitutes a major opportunity for rooting development programmes more firmly in the community with the active participation of women. The Department has recently initiated steps for the constitution of Baal Vikas Mahila Samitis at village, block and district levels, with representations from women panchayat members, NGOs and ICDS functionaries. This is for integrated community-based monitoring of all programmes for women and children -especially ICDS.

Mobilising women for promoting their own health, nutritional well-being and self development as well as that of their children is an underlying principle of ICDS. This was furthered by the introduction of the ICDS adolescent girls' scheme in 507 blocks.

With the recently launched Indira Mahila Yojana (IMY), new possibilities are unfolding for ICDS to promote the process for women's empowerment. The Indira Mahila Yojana has three components: convergence of inter-sectoral services; awareness creation; and income generation activities. It has been initiated in 200 ICDS blocks during 1995-96.

Opening of Mini-Anganwadis to cover remote and low populated hamlets

Universalisation of the Integrated Child Development Service (ICDS) Scheme has been made in the country in 1995-96 by covering all the Community Development Blocks by the Scheme. There are, however, some small hamlets/villages in the country in Tribal Blocks having population of less than 300 and situated in far flung areas where the actual beneficiaries might be deprived of the benefits of the Scheme. To make full use of the ICDS Scheme and provide benefits of the Scheme to each and every child who is entitled to it, it has been decided by the Department to open Mini-Anganwadis in small hamlets/pockets in Tribal Blocks which are in far flung and remote areas. The guidelines to open Mini-Anganwadis in an ICDS project for such hamlets/ pockets are as follows:-

10 Mini Anganwadi Centres can be opened in lieu of a full fledged Anganwadi. There may be one main Anganwadi out of 10. A Mini Anganwadi can be opened with a population of 150 in a village/hamlet. It should be located within 1 km. from the main Anganwadi and there should be 15 to 20 beneficiaries therein. A woman/ adolescent girl is made responsible for distribution of nutrition diet to beneficiaries. An honorarium of Rs.50 is to be paid to the Mini Anganwadi Worker who provides cooked hot food to the Anganwadi beneficiaries. The maintenance of 10 Mini Anganwadis is managed within the cost of an Anganwadi norm of Rs. 11,200 per annnum. The provision of nutrition is to be ensured by the State Government from their own resources, being provided by them under ICDS Scheme as per norms. Uptil now, 1881 Mini-Anganwadi Centres have been sanctioned in tribal blocks of Maharashtra, 25 Mini-Anganwadi centres in Andhra Pradesh, 1708 in the tribal blocks of Orissa and 2878 Mini-Anganwadi Centres

were sanctioned in Madhya Pradesh with World Bank Assistance.

Integration of ayurveda and Indian system of medicines in ICDS scheme

The issue of inclusion of Ayurvedic medicines in Medicine Kits given to Anganwadis under ICDS Scheme was undertaken during this year. Instructions have been issued to State Directors of Ayurveda to further instruct ISM&H doctors to regularly visit AWCs in rural and remote areas. A list of simple home remedies for common ailments and a list of Ayurvedic medicines to be included in the Medicine Kits is being procured by this Department to be supplied to AWCs. A training module for AWWs in Ayurveda and Ayurvedic concept of life style is being developed which can be accommodated in the basic training course meant for AWWs. Department of ISM&H has been requested to forward a proposal with area-specific intensive intervention for meeting full integration of Ayurveda and ICDS Scheme.

Convergence strategy of intersectoral services in the anganwadi centres

Recognising the need for securing convergence of various services in the Anganwadi Centres so as to improve the efficiency of sectoral programmes and to ensure that the services are provided to the beneficiaries in a cost effective manner, the Department of Women and Child Development has identified specific thrust areas relating to various Departments including Ministry of Health & Family Welfare, Rural Development, Education, Urban Development. Welfare and this Department for convergence. These thrust areas were communicated to all concerned for taking necessary action towards integration and convergence of services of this Department.

World Bank assisted ICDS projects

The World Bank provided credit for the Centrally sponsored ICDS Projects, viz. ICDS-I Project in Andhra Pradesh and Orissa, and ICDS-11 Project in Bihar and Madhya Pradesh. Apart from providing normal ICDS services the Project also includes additional components like construction of AW buildings and CDPOs office cum godowns on a selective basis, strengthening training and communications components, improved health facilities, income generation activities for women and Women's Integrated Learning for Life.

ICDS-1 Project

The Project in Andhra Pradesh and Orissa became operational in January, 1991 initially for a period of 6 years i.e. upto 31st December, 1997.

The Project covered 191 blocks in Orissa and 110 blocks in Andhra Pradesh. The Project covered tribal areas, dominated by schedule castes and other backward classes.

The approved provision for the Project was Rs. 303.22 crore (Rs. 130.79 crore for Andhra Pradesh and Rs. 172.43 crore for Orissa) exclusive of the cost of the supplementary nutrition. This was subsequently revised to Rs. 343.69 crore (Rs. 1 59.40 crore for Andhra Pradesh and Rs. 184.29 crore for Orissa).

All the blocks covered under the Project in both the States have become operational. The available credit for the project was of the order of US $ 740 lakh which was fully disbursed.

ICDS-11 Project

The World Bank assisted ICDS-11 Project in Bihar and Madhya Pradesh became operational in September 1993 for a period of seven years, i.e., upto ' March 2000. The

Project covered 210 blocks in Bihar and 244 blocks in Madhya Pradesh in predominantly tribal and difficult areas, in a phased manner.

Additional inputs

In addition to the normal six ICDS services, the additional input being given in the project is as follows:

— Construction of Anganwadi buildings at village level and godown-cum-CDPO's office building at Block level in the most needy areas.

— Experimentation with Nutritional

— Rehabilitation Centres

— Schemes for Adolescent girls

— Skill upgradation / development for women

— Income Generation Schemes for Women

— Strengthening health and nutrition, awareness generation, community participation, communications, training, supervision, operations research, monitoring and evaluation components.

The Government of India has released an amount of Rs. 322.69 crore to the States of Bihar and Madhya Pradesh upto 31st March, 1998.

The approved provision for the Project is Rs. 596.23 crores out·of which Rs. 257.13 crore for Bihar, and Rs. 339.10 crore for Madhya Pradesh. So far Rs. 133.38 crores have been released for the Government of Bihar, and Rs. 223.41 crores have been released to the Government of Madhya Pradesh. State Government of Bihar has reported an expenditure of Rs. 92.85 crores and Government of Madhya Pradesh has incurred expenditure worth Rs. 184.80 crores.

The approved IDA credit for the project is US $ 1910

lakh out of which US $ 630 lakh (approx.) has been disbursed.

ICDS-111 Project

The third phase of the World Bank assisted ICDS (ICDS-111) Project has been approved by the World Bank. The project would cover the States of Kerala, Tamil Nadu, Maharashtra/Rajasthan and Uttar Pradesh including the training component of ICDS Programme being implemented in the country.

The total cost of the Project as approved by the Expenditure Finance Committee is around Rs. 1600 crore; Rs. 1000 crore for the Project in five states and Rs. 600 crore for the training component in the entire country for a period of five yea rs. The IDA has committed US $ 3000 lakh (including US $1000 lakh for the training component) for the project.

Andhra Pradesh Economic Restructuring Project (APER)

The Project proposal for World Bank assisted ICDS component of Andhra Pradesh Economic Restructuring (APER) Project in Andhra Pradesh, a Centrally Sponsored Project, is under process in this Department.

The Project proposes to cover 251 blocks at a total cost of about Rs. 392 crore for a period of five years. The project would form a part of the US $ 543.2 million assistance package committed by the World Bank for APER project.

World food programme (WEP) project 2206

World Food Programme (WFP), a United Nations agency, extends food aid under its Project 2206 for supplementary nutrition to children below 6 years of age and to expectant and nursing mothers under the Integrated Child Development Services (ICDS) programme. The WFP Project 2206 has completed 5 phases from March 1976 to June, 1995.

The Plan of Operations for Expansion Phase VI of WFP Project 2206 was signed between the Government of India and the WFP on 4 July, 1995 for a period of three years to cover 22 lakh beneficiaries (including 80,250 Anganwadi Workers / Helpers / adolescent girls) in the five states of Assam, Kerala, Madhya Pradesh, Rajasthan and Uttar Pradesh. There is a Country Programme (CP) for India for the five year period from Ist April, 1997 to 31st March, 2001. As resources are limited, the WFP has reduced its food assistance for India to 70,000 MTs out of which 40,000 MTs is earmarked for Project 2206 (ICDS) annually. As a consequence WFP was able to cater to 16.8 lakh beneficiaries under ICDS w.e.f. 1st September, 1997. Due to carry over stocks and outstanding deliveries, 50,667 MTs of food is available w.e.f. I April, 1998. In addition to this, 3500 MTs of food is also available from Canandian International Development Agency (CIDA) assistance through WFP for the state of Rajasthan which will cover an additional 2.30 lakh beneficiaries. WFP is providing a single micro-nutrient fortified blended food-either Corn Soya Blend (CSB) or locally produced 'Indiamix'. CSB is being imported through the Ports of Cochin, Calcutta and Jamnagar and can be cooked with jaggery and condiments to suit local tastes. The WFP Project 2206 is being reviewed by the Department of Women and Child Development, Government of India biannually in the meetings of the Food Aid Advisory Sub-Committee (FAASC).

WFP assistance for non-food programmes

The Better Health and Nutrition (BHN) Project (with a total cost of Rs. 175.67 lakhs) in Sirohi and Udaipur districts in the State of Rajasthan for a period of two years starting from March, 1997. The project is in collaboration with CARE India. The project's aim is to improve the nutritional status of women and children and reduce the rates of malnutrition and mortality.

Improving Child Survival through the ICDS (with a total cost of Rs. 81.65 lakhs) in Banswara district of Rajasthan for a period of two years w.e.f. December, 1996. The project mainly aims to reduce the extent of childhood malnutrition through a campaign on timely initiation of complementary feeding and increased convergence of on going women and child development programmes.

CARE - India assisted programmes

Government of India signed an agreement with CARE (Cooperative for Assistance and Relief Everywhere) on 6th March, 1950. The primary purpose of this agreement is to facilitate and maximize voluntary gifts of food and other urgently needed commodities by individuals and organisations outside India. The Department of Women ' and Child Development, Government of India is the nodal Department for implementation of CARE-India's programmes. CARE-India assisted programmes have been broadly classified in two parts (1) Food Programme, and (ii) Non-Food Programmes.

Food Programme

CARE-India extends food aid for supplementary nutrition to -children below 6 years of age and pregnant and nursing mothers in the ICDS programme. In accordance with the List of Provisions (LOP) approved for 1998-99, CARE-India has supplied food aid to 66.05 lakhs beneficiaries distributed in the States of Andhra Pradesh, Bihar, Madhya Pradesh, Orissa, Rajasthan, Uttar Pradesh and West Bengal. The food commodities include vegetable oil and a highly nutritious blend of corn and soya. These are cooked with other food items such as jaggery and condiments to make the food tasty and acceptable. CARE food is received in India at the ports of Calcutta, Vishakapatnam, Jamnagar and Paradeep.

Non-Food Programmes

The Integrated Nutrition and Health Programme (INHP) has been approved by this Department for a period of 5 years w.e.f. April 1996 to March 2001 A.D. with a total budget of Rs. 1,13,16,35,505. The INHP seeks to improve the health and nutritional status of women and children by directing resources and efforts to achieve those changes in health behaviour which lead to a reduction in mortality and malnutrition. The INHP is being implemented in the seven states where CARE is presently functioning in collaboration with the State Governments. State level advisory groups have also been set up in each of the seven states to facilitate implementation.

Improving Women's Reproductive Health & Family Spacing Project in the State of Uttar Pradesh for a period of five years with a total budget of Rs. 32,251,014 The project is in two districts of Uttar Pradesh namely, Sitapur and Shahjahanpur. The project aims to empower women to take informed decisions about their reproductive health including the number and spacing of children.

Improving Women's Health in Urban Slums Project in Allahabad, Uttar Pradesh for a period of six years with a total budget of Rs. 89,64,879. The project aims to significantly reduce mortality among 28,000 women (15-45 years) in 65 of the neediest authorised slums of Allahabad. Community based women's reproductive health care services are - created and extended, along with increased proficiency of Private Medical Practitioners (PMPs) and public sector personnel in providing reproductive health care,

Improved Health Care for Adolescent Girls in Urban Slums Project in Jabalpur, Madhya Pradesh for a period of six years with a total budget of Rs. 2,22,43,210. The project aims at a significant reduction in the morbidity and mortality associated with reproductive health among adolescent girls, both unmarried and married, in the slums of Jabalpur.

Girls Primary Education (GPE) Project for a period of five years with a total budget of Rs. 6,80,01,325/- in the States of Rajasthan and Uttar Pradesh. The project's aim is to increase girls' access to education in collaboration with local NGO's and community groups.

Credit Rotation for Empowerment and Development through Institution Building and Training (CREDIT) Project for a period of 5 years at a total cost of Rs. 11,22,05,790. The proposal is a joint venture of the WFP and CARE-India. The project proposes to expand the savings and credit portfolio of rural women in partnership with local NGOs in the States of Orissa and Bihar, Maternal and Infant Survival Project with Canadian International Development Agency (CIDA) assistance in the State of Madhya Pradesh. The total cost of the project is estimated at Rs.19,65,80,762/- for a period of two years and six months. The aim of this project is to improve the health and nutritional status of women and children of 5 Blocks in Hoshangabad Division and 6 Blocks in Bhopal Division.

CARE-India assisted programmes (Food Programme and Non-Food Programmes) are being reviewed by this Department with the State Governments and CARE-India biannually.

ICDS training programme

Training is the most crucial element in ICDS, since the achievement of programme goals depends upon the effectiveness of frontline workers in improved delivery of packages under ICDS. Recognising this, from the inception of the ICDS Scheme itself, the Department of

Women and Child Development formulated a comprehensive training strategy for different functionaries involved in the ICDS, such as the Anganwadi Workers, Supervisors, Additional Child Development Project Officers (ACDPOs) and Child Development Project Officers (CDPOs).

Training is imparted to these functionaries through the National Institute of Public Cooperation & Child Development (NIPCCD) through its three Regional Centres at Lucknow, Guwahati and Bangalore, 36 Middle Level Training Centres (MLTCs) and 392 Anganwadi Workers Training Centres (AWTCs).

Training of Anganwadi Workers

For imparting training of Anganwadi Workers, the grass-root level functionaries, there are 392 Anganwadi Workers Training Centres (AWTCs) in the country. AWWs are given job training immediately on their joining which is followed by a refresher training on completion of two years. During 1997-98, 41,193 Anganwadi Workers were trained. During 1998-99, 15,000 Anganwadi Workers have been trained upto November, 1998.

Training of Supervisors

For imparting training to Supervisors, who are the middle level functionaries of the ICDS, there are 36 Middle Level Training Centres (MLTCs) in the country. They function under the administrative control of NIPCCD and also include the three Regional Centres of NIPCCD, located at Lucknow, Guwahati and Bangalore, which act as MLTCs. Training is imparted to Supervisors to help them acquaint themselves with various components of the scheme, and to develop appropriate skills in supervision an programme management. Refresher training is imparted to Supervisors on completion 0 one and a half years of service. During 1997-98, 921 Supervisors were trained. During 1998-99, 234 Supervisors have been trained upto November, 1998.

Training of CDPOs/ACDPOs

Training of Child Development Project Officers (CDPOs) and Additional Child Development Project Officers (ACDPOs) is conducted by NIPCCD at its headquarters and its three regional centres. On joining service, CDPOs/ACDPOs are given job training followed by a refresher training on completion of two years' service. During the training, efforts are made to familiarise them with various aspects of the Scheme, including, organisational and administrative structures. During 1997-98, 386 CDPCs/ACDPCs were trained. During 1998-99, 265 CDPC)s/ ACDPC)s have been trained upto November, 1998.

Hundred per cent grant-in-aid is provided by this Department to State Governments, NIPCCD and NGCs for conducting various training courses. The entire expenditure on training, except non-recurring expenditure, capital expenditure and rent component, is reimbursed by UNICEF. During 1996-97 and 1997-98, an amount of Rs. 9.94 crore, Rs. 4.29 crore respectively were released under the ICDS Training Programme. During 1998-99, an amount of Rs. 3.97 crore has been released upto November, 1998.

During the last 2 years, the Training Division of the Department - of Women & Child Development and NIPCCD have carried out a comprehensive review of the ICDS Training Programme. Based on this, a new, dynamic, programme called Project UDISHA has been envisioned.

ICDS Training Programme - Project UDISHA

Salient features of the craft proposal - Project Udisha

— Decentralised training

— Concept of 'Training Teams' has been introduced

— Joint training will be held with officials of other departments e.g. health, education and rural development

— Training will be imparted to other groups, e.g. Panchayati Raj members, the community etc.

- There will be an emphasis on advocacy and IEC activities
- There will be a new syllabus and curriculum
- There will be more flexibility, innovations and dynamism in the training programme NIPCCD has been given a very prominent role. It is hoped that it will be the premier institute of child development in the world in the next few years.

— Professional training will be given to all trainers including NIPCCD faculty.

— Each Anganwadi Worker will be given a comprehensive Training Kit which will be in her local language or dialect and will be AWW-friendly.

— All Institutes (NIPCCD, MLTCs, AWTCs) will be upgraded.

— Innovative methodologies for refresher training is being suggested.

Balsevika Training Programme

Balsevika Training Programme was started in 1961-62 to meet the requirements of trained personnel in the institutions implementing welfare programmes for pre-school children. With increased coverage of ICDS, the programme of Balsevika Training was discontinued from 1998-99. During the year, a provision of Rs.20.00 lakh has been provided which will be released to ICCW for spill-over liabilities.

Creches/da centres for children of working/ailing mothers

In the huge subcontinent which is India, it is estimated that there are around 91 million working women; of these, approximately 90% are in the unorganised sector. These women toil hard and long, invariably outside their homes. Most of these women are mothers. Sadly, their children are either taken by their mothers to the work place or left in the care of elder siblings at home. Everyone is familiar with the sight of a small child crying while the mother works nearby. As familiar is the sight of an elder sibling, invariably a girl trying desperately to take care of her younger brothers and sisters. In either case the children involved have lost out on their precious childhood, the heritage which is rightfully theirs. In the latter instance, the enforced care of the little ones frustrates attempts to educate young girls who have to play out an adult role, a role for which they are unequipped.

It is in this scenario that the provision of day care services for children becomes an absolutely crucial service. By helping to look after these children, day care services play an invaluable role in ensuring that children remain in a stable safe environment instead of near any adult work place, and also gives them a semblance at least of a childhood. Equally important is the removal of the burden of child rearing from the fragile shoulders of young girls who become free to go to school.

It was for the purpose of achieving these ends that two schemes were set up, the Creche Scheme in 1975 and the National Creche Fund in 1994. Children in the vulnerable age group of 0-5 and whose parent's total monthly income is not more than Rs. 1800/- p.m. are given essential day care services under these schemes. The parents of these children are usually migrant, agricultural, construction and casual labourers. Children of those women who are sick or incapacitated on account of some sickness or suffering from communicable diseases are also covered. These two Schemes meet the overwhelming requirement in many families of day care services and the facilities provided at these creches include supplementary nutrition, immunisation, medical and health care. While the Creche Scheme is being implemented by three major organisations, the Central Social Welfare Board, the Indian Council for Child Welfare and Bhartiya Adimiati Sevak Sangh, the National Creche Fund provides assistance to registered voluntary organisations and Mahila Mandals throughout the country to run creches. In addition to this, the National Creche Fund Scheme also has a component for converting existing Anganwadis into Anganwadi-cum Creche Centres to be run by the same agencies which run the ICDS Scheme which in most cases is the State Government. All the agencies are given a grant of Rs. 18,.480/ per creche per annum towards recurring expenditure, this includes the honorarium for two creche workers, and a one time grant of Rs. 4,000/- for meeting the initial cost of establishing a creche. Any agency which would like to convert an Anganwadi into an Anganwadi-cum-Creche Centre will be sanctioned a grant of Rs. 8,100/- per creche per annum. The basic idea behind this conversion is that an Anganwadi in a ICDS Centre normally runs for only 4 hours. This time is insufficient to meet the requirements of children whose mothers/parents work longer hours and it is therefore desirable that these Anganwadis are converted into creche centres which run for 8 hours.

A It is estimated that India today requires 8 lakh

creches for its children. Against this, we have been able to set up only 14,925 creches under these two schemes, leaving an enormous gap which should be filled at the earliest. To achieve this, concerted efforts are being made to increase the corpus of the National Creche Fund since the Creche Scheme is a non expanding one.

The Second 'Children of India Concert' was organised by the National Creche Fund on 14th November, 1998 to commemorate Children's Day. The internationally renowned violin maestro Dr. L. Subramaniarn regaled the audience, as did an electrifying performance by a musical troupe from Nigeria.

Physical and financial achievements of the National Creche Fund

The Early Childhood Education (ECE) Scheme was started in 1982 as a distinct strategy to reduce the drop out rate and to improve the rate of retention of children of the age group of 3-6 years in primary schools.

The Scheme is being implemented in nine educationally backward states viz. Andhra Pradesh, Assam, Bihar, Jammu and Kashmir, Madhya Pradesh, Orissa, Rajasthan, Uttar Pradesh and West Bengal. Under the Scheme, financial assistance amount of Rs. 7,980/- per centre per annum is given to voluntary organisations for running the ECE Centres. The Scheme is a non-expanding one and is being continued only in the areas not covered by the ICDS Scheme. During 1997-98, grant to the tune of Rs. 233 lakhs was released to run 2613 ECE Centres in non-ICDS areas in the above states.

Balwadi nutrition programme

The Balwadi Nutrition Programme is being implemented since 1970-71 through the Central Social Welfare Board and four national level voluntary organisations, Bharatiya Adimiati Sevak Sangh, Indian Council for Child Welfare,

Kasturba Gandhi National Memorial Trust and Harijan Sevak Sangh, who extend assistance to local voluntary agencies to implement the programme. The Balwadi Nutrition Programme aspires to meet the very basic nutritional requirement of a child in the age group of 3-5 years by ensuring that she/he is provided with 300 calories and 12-15 gms of protein every day. Apart from nutrition supplement, the Balwadis offer a healthy environment, looking after the social and emotional needs of the children. Under the Scheme, a grant of Rs. 17,220/- is given per Balwadi Centre per annum. This scheme is a non-expanding one, and is being continued only in the areas not covered by the ICDS centres. During 1997-98, a total grant to the tune of Rs. 115.0 lakhs was released to Voluntary Organisations for running 710 Balwadis in non-ICDS areas.

National children's board

The National Policy for Children 1974 envisages a National Children's Board under the chairmanship of the Prime Minister to function as a forum for planning, review and proper coordination of the multiplicity of services aimed at meeting the needs of the children. The National Children's Board was initially set up in December, 1974 with the Prime Minister as its Chairman. The Board is now under consideration for reconstitution.

State recognition for voluntary action

Rajiv Gandhi Manav Seva Award for Service to Children

In pursuance of its policy to support and to encourage voluntary action and in memory of the late Prime Minister Shri Rajiv Gandhi, the Department of Women and Child Development instituted in 1994 the Rajiv Gandhi Manav Seva Award for Service to Children to honour an individual who makes an outstanding contribution in service to children, including care of children with various kinds of disabilities. The award carries a cash prize of Rs. 1 lakh and a citation. Shri Anantrai K. Shah from Bhavnagar, Gujarat has been selected for Rajiv Gandhi Manav Seva Award for Service to children for the year 1998. The Award will be conferred by HRM.

National Awards for Child Welfare

The National Awards for Child Welfare were instituted in 1979 in the International Year of the Child as a state recognition of voluntary action for the cause of the Child. The Scheme envisages awards to 5 institutions and A individuals in a year for the best work done in the field of child welfare.

The National Selection Committee selected the following five institutions and three individuals for the National Awards for Child Welfare, 1998

Institutions:

1. Donyi-Polo Mission School for the Hearing Impaired, Chimpu, Itanagar, Arunachal Pradesh.
2. Seva Niketan Dairy Farm, Junglighat, Port Blair, Andaman & Nicobar islands
3. St. Mary's Convent, Laitumkhrah, Shillong, Meghalaya
4. SOS Children's Village, Aluva, Edathala North, Ernakulam, Kerala.
5. Calcutta Muslim Orphanage, Calcutta, West Bengal.

Individuals :

1. Smt. Shila Barun, President, Kasturba Gandhi National Memorial Trust, Bakthavarpur, Delhi.
2. Smt. Brijabala Nirbheek, General Secretary, Madhu Smriti Sansthan, Ranghbadi, Kota, Rajasthan.

3. Smt. Champa Bahin, Satya Sadha Ashram, Village Pathriya, Sagar, Madhya Pradesh.

The National Awards for Child Welfare 1998 will be conferred on the above mentioned five institutions and three individuals by the President of India.

National Child Awards for Exceptional Achievement

The Government of India instituted an award in 1996 to give recognition to children with exceptional abilities and who have achieved outstanding status in various fields suck as academics, culture, art, sports, music, etc. Children in the age group of 4-15 years are eligible for this award. One gold medal and 6 silver medals are to be given annually.

The Scheme has been revised to increase the number of awards from the existing 7 to 33. In each State/UT, one child with exceptional achievement will now be conferred an award.

The Union Minister for Human Resource Development will confer the National Child Awards for Exceptional Achievement, 1998.

National Bravery Award

The Scheme of National Bravery Award to children for bravery, gallantry and meritorius service was started in 1957. Every year selected children are given National Bravery Award. The National Bravery Award function is organised by the Indian Council for Child Welfare, New Delhi, which is a voluntary organisation of national repute. Since inception of the Scheme, as many as 5,40 children have been awarded. The Department of Women and Child Development supports the Indian Council for Child Welfare financially. A list of National Bravery Award 1998 winners is given at Annexure X.

United nations children's fund

Department of Women & Child Development is the nodal department for UNICEF, which has been associated with India since 19,49 and is now in its fifth decade of cooperation in assisting disadvantaged children and their mothers. UNICEF has its largest programmes in the world, in India.

The Government of India-UNICEF programmes of cooperation is governed and regulated by the Basic Agreement signed in 1949 and executed through the Master Plan of Operations which is normally a five year cycle. Presently, the programme of cooperation between GOI and UNICEF is being executed through a Bridging Programme since 1996-97 which has been extended by another year upto 1998, to enable future preparation for the next MPO cycle 1999-2002. An amount of $ 81.8 million has been committed for the Bridge Programme, 1998 (December).

Traditionally, UNICEF has been supporting India in a number of programmes focusing on Child Development and Women's Development. Preparation for finalisation of the new Master Plan of Operations 19992002 is underway based on the India Country Strategy note considered by the UNICEF Executive Board on January 20, 1997. The major thrust areas would be to assist the government to fulfil its obligations for universalising child rights and achieving the World Summit goals; improving the position of girls and women in society; and strengthening capacities of communities through the agreed strategies of community convergent action; central focus on resolving gender disparities; decentralisation of responsibilities/ authorities and resources to local levels; and forging new partnerships to involve key partners and leverage UNICEF resources.

The last MPO was completed in December, 1995 UNICEF committed an amount of US $ 486 million fo the 1991-95 MPO out of which an expenditure of US $ 308.7 million under GR, SF & Administrative Budget wa made (85.1%).

UNICEF Executive Board in its Second Regula Session held in September, 1998 considered the Indi Country Programme (MPO 1999-2002) and approved th same. A total of US $ 120 million under Genera Resources and US $ 180 million under Supplementar Funds was committed for MPO 1999-2002.

An amount of Rs. 310 lakhs has been released fo India's contribution to UNICEF General Resources fo 1998-99.

National plan for action for children

India is a signatory to the 27 survival and developmen goals laid down by the World Summit on Children, 1990 In order to implement these goals, the Department o Women and Child Development has formulated a National Plan of Action for Children. Each of th concerned Central Ministries / Departments, Stat Governments UTs and Voluntary Organisations dealin with women and children have been asked to take u appropriate measures to implement the Action Plan These goals have been integrated into Nationa Development Plans. A Monitoring Committee under., th Chairpersonship of Secretary (Women and Chil Development) reviews the achievement of goals set in th National Plan of Action. All concerned Central Ministrie

Departments are represented on the Committee Sixth meeting of the IMCC was held under th chairpersonship of Secretary (WCD) on 25 March 1998 a New Delhi.

The Department addressed the Chief Secretaries of states to prepare State Plans of Action on the lines of NPA, specifying their targets for the mid decade goals as well as for 2000 AD and spelling out strategies for holistic child development. So far 17 State Governments have prepared SPACs. They are Andhra Pradesh, Arunachal Pradesh, Bihar, Goa, Gujarat, Haryana, Karnataka, Kerala, Madhya Pradesh, Manipur, Orissa, Punjab, Rajasthan, Tamil Nadu, Uttar Pradesh, West Bengal, National Capital Territory of Delhi. Other States/ UT are in the process of preparing their respective Plans of Action including constitution of a coordination committee to monitor their implementation.

Universal children's day

India observes Universal Children's Day on 14th November every year, the birthday of India's first Prime Minister Pandit Jawaharlal Nehru, who was an ardent lover of children. The Universal Children's Day is observed on different dates in different countries in accordance with the UN General Assembly Resolution of 14th November, 1954. In commemoration of the day, a theme highlighting a specific issue related to children is selected every year. The theme for the year 1998 was "Empowered Girl -Empowered Society". The booklet on the girl child highlights the persisting gender inequalities and existing cultural beliefs and values prevalent in society, and suggests practical strategies that can restore to the girl child her rights and enable her to emerge as an empowered woman of tomorrow.

His Excellency the Vice President of India released a Special Commemorative Postal Stamp and brochure on the theme at a special function organised by the Department on 14 November, 1998 at New Delhi.

UN convention on the rights of the child

India ratified the UN Convention on the Rights of the

Child on 2nd December, 1992 and it represents commitment to provide to Indian children a "'First Call on national resources. India's first periodic report, as State Party to the Convention has been deposited wil the United Nations Committee of Experts on the Righ of the Child, Geneva on 18th March, 1997.

All State Governments / UT administrations hav been requested to take necessary action for th implementation of various Articles and clauses of the Ul Convention and submit reports on the progress made t meet the obligations chartered in the various articles.

SAARC activity

An Inter-Ministerial Meeting under the chairpersonshi of Joint Secretary (WCD) was held on 8th August, 1997 t initiate follow-up on the Ninth South Asian Associatio for Regional Cooperation (SAARC) Summit of the Head of State/Government held at Male during 12th to 14t May, 1997. The meeting considered the proposal for SAARC initiative on nutrition, water and sanitation.

National commission for children (NCC)

A proposal to set up a National Commission for Childre is under the consideration of the Government. Th objective would be to monitor and evaluate the status c safeguards provided to children constitutionally, legall and otherwise and advice the Government from time t time on steps and measures to be taken. The proposal ha been discussed in the Parliamentary Consultativ Committee attached to the Ministry of Human Resourc Development in its meetings on 26 October 1998 and 2 November 1998 under the chairmanship of the Ministe for Human Resource Development. Further action is i progress. Comments of concerned Ministries , Departments and States/UTs have been sought on th revised proposal.

Infant milk substitutes act, 1992

In 1981, the World Health Assembly adopted an International Code on the Marketing of Breast Milk Substitutes. The Government of India recognised this Code and adopted the Indian National Code for Protection and Promotion of Breast-feeding in, December, 1983. To give effect to the provisions of this Code, the Infant Milk Substitutes, Feeding Bottles and Infant Foods (Regulation of Production, Supply and Distribution) Act, 1992 was enacted which came into force w.e.f. I August 1993. The Act provides for the regulation of production, supply and distribution of infant milk substitutes, feeding bottles and infant foods with a view to the protection and promotion of breast-feeding and ensuring the proper use of infant foods and for matters connected therewith or incidental thereto. The Rules framed under the Act also came into force w.e.f. 1 August 1993. In addition to food inspectors appointed under PFA Act, the Central Government has authorised the following four voluntary organisations engaged in the field of child welfare and development and child nutrition to make a complaint in writing against violations of the Act.

Central Social Welfare Board, Samaj Kalyan Bhawan, B-12, Tara Crescent Institutional Area, South of IIT, New Delhi 110 016.

Indian Council for Child Welfare, 4, Deen Dayal Upadhyaya Marg, New Delhi 110 002.

Association for Consumer Action of Safety and Health (ACASH), Room No. 21, Lawyer's Chambers, R.S. Sapra Marg, Mumbai 400 002.

Breast-feeding Promotion, Network of India (BPNI), BP-33, Pitampura, Delhi 110 034.

The efforts made in this direction have placed India

as one of the leading countries in the world having legislation to protect; promote and support breast-feeding. As per UNICEF's 1997 report on the "Progress of Nations", India is one of only 16 countries in the world to have enacted legislation to implement the International Code of Marketing of Breast Milk Substitutes in entirety.

The National Institute of Public Cooperation and Child Development (NIPCCD) is an autonomous organisation with its headquarters at New Delhi. It functions under the aegis of the Department of Women and Child Development, Ministry of Human Resource Develop-ment.

The objectives of the Institute are to develop and promote voluntary action in social development; take a comprehensive view of child development and develop and promote programmes in pursuance of the National Policy for Children; develop measures for coordination of governmental and voluntary action in social development; and evolve a framework and perspective for organising children's programmes through governmental and voluntary efforts.

With a view to achieve the above objectives, the Institute conducts research and evaluation studies, organises training programmes, seminars, workshops, conferences, and provides documentation and information services in the field of public cooperation and child development. The Institute is the apex body for training of functionaries of the Integrated Child Development Services (ICDS) programme. It provides technical advice and consultancy to government and voluntary agencies in promoting and implementing policies and programmes for child development and voluntary action. In addition, it collaborates with regional and international agencies, research institutions, universities and technical bodies.

The General Body and the Executive Council are its two main constitutional bodies, The General Body formulates policies for management and administration of the Institute. The Minister for Women and Child Development is President of the General Body and Chairman of the Executive Council. In addition, there are committees to oversee academic programmes and administrative matters.

The Institute at its headquarters functions through six divisions, namely, Public Cooperation, Child Development, Women's Development, Training, Monitoring and Evaluation and Common Services. The Divisions are grouped under two Departments, namely, the Department of Mother and Child Development and the Department of Training and Common Services.

Recognising that in a country of such vast dimension, an Institute located in Delhi will not be able to cater to the specific field level regional requirements in terms of training, research, consultancy, etc., the Institute has set up its Regional Centres at Guwahati, Bangalore, and Lucknow. It has also identified a number of institutions to cater to the training needs of child care workers in different states and Union Territories.

Programmes and activities

In the pursuance of the recommendations of the committee on reorganisation of the Institute approved by the Executive Council in February 1998, for the prioritisation of its programmes and activities, the central focus of the Institute is the integrated development of the child and the mother in its most comprehensive and varied form. This recommendation of the Committee has been kept in view while planning programmes for the year 1998-99.

The programmes and activities of the Institute may

be grouped under the broad categories of regular programmes of training, research and documentation in the area of Public Co-operation and Child Development; and functionaries.

Regular training programmes

Under regular programmes, the institute organises orientation/training courses for representatives of voluntary organisation and officials of government departments engaged in implementation of programmes of mother care, child development and women's development. The Institute also conducts programmes on subjects of topical interest in these fields to highlight the role of voluntary organisations and government departments in tackling emerging social problems including problems having a bearing on welfare and development of children and strengthening the service delivery system. These programmes are aimed at creating consciousness in the community about the needs of the child and mother and help channelising it into concrete action.

The institute has been consistently trying to maximise the outreach of its regular programmes for officials and non-officials engaged in the area of women and child development with the resources available with it. During the year 1997-98, the Institute organised 75 programmes against the target of 60 programmes. These programmes were attended by 3236 participants against a target of 1800. During the year 1998-99, the Institute organised 77 programmes upto January 1999 against the target of 60 programmes for the year. 2657 participants attended these programmes against the target of 1800 participants for the year. The Institute proposes to organise about 40 more programmes during the remaining year.

In the year 1998-99, the Institute has undertaken several new initiatives in making its training programmes more interesting and effective by laying more emphasis on the participatory method of training. Its training programmes have covered some new areas in terms of subject matter of the courses.

New Initiatives in Methodology and Contents of Regular Training programme.

— Changing family, emerging patterns of care and protection of human development services

— Management of child programmes Laws relating to welfare of children development

— People's participation for sustainability of child welfare and development programmes

— Holistic approach to the development of adolescent girls Prevention and early detection of childhood disabilities

— Early childhood care and education Family life education—emerging challenges Stimulation for children below three years Prevention of Hepatitis B in children

— Training on micronutrients for personnel of voluntary organisations engaged in maternal and child health

— Nutrition and health of young children

— Women's empowerment—their role in governance and decision making Negotiation skills

— Training the faculty of the Institute on application of computer knowledge and techniques

— Qualitative methods in social sciences research

- Training women members of Jilla Panchayats on issues concerning children's rights, needs, problems and management of children in institutions
- Alternate strategies for reaching adolescent girls
- Review training material on Meena— the girl child initiative
- Stress on participatory training method
- Introduction of more skill-based and field-based training and practicals. Emphasis on innovative methods of training such as group discussion, case presentations, mock sessions, etc.
- Greater use of audiovisual aids in training sessions
- Preparation and supply of relevant training material for the participants

Training for ICDS functionaries

As the apex body for the training of ICDS functionaries of Integrated Child Development Services (ICDS) programme, the Institute has been entrusted with the responsibility of planning, coordination and monitoring the training of ICDS functionaries; building up training infrastructure and capabilities of institutions engaged in training of ICDS functionaries; organising training of trainers; designing, revising, standardising and updating syllabi for training of various categories of functionaries; preparation of model programme schedules; and preparation, procurement and dissemination of training materials including audio visual aids. The Institute also provides feedback to the Department of Women and Child Development, Government of India and the concerned departments of State Governments on matters pertaining to the training of ICDS functionaries.

In addition, the Institute is shouldering the

responsibility of training of functionaries of World Bank Assisted ICDS Projects since 1992-93. This includes preparation and revision of syllabi for training of CDPOs, supervisors, Anganwadi Workers and helpers of these projects; training of CDPOs and instructors of AWTCs and MLTCs; and building up infrastructure for training of Anganwadi Workers and middle level functionaries in the states of Andhra Pradesh, Bihar, Madhya Pradesh and Orissa.

The training of Child Development Project Officers (CDPOs) is conducted at the Institute's headquarters in New Delhi and its three Regional Centres located at Bangalore, Guwahati and Lucknow. The training of supervisors takes place at selected training centres known as Middle Level Training Centres (MLTCs) which are located in different states. The Regional Centres of the Institute also function as MLTCs for the states/regions in which these are located. While the training of trainers of CDPOs and supervisors is imparted at the Institute's headquarters, the training of trainers of Anganwadi Workers (AWWs) is given through the MLTCs. The Institute also provides skill specific training in the areas of pre-school education, growth monitoring, nutrition and health education, community participation, 'etc. to trainers of AWTCs and MLTCs.

During the year 1997-98, the Institute imparted job training to 386 CDPOs/ ACDPOs and refresher training to 202 CDPOs/ACDPOs. The number of Supervisors of ICDS who were trained in Job Training and Refresher Training during the above period was 921 and 750 respectively. 278 instructors of AWTCs/MLTCs received training in different courses. A total of 238 senior officers participated in review meets/training programmes during the period under report. 16 Executive Heads of AWTCs were given orientation training, 50 CDPOs attended the orientation course.

New Initiatives in Training of ICDS Functionaries

— Skill training on communication for instructors of AWTCs/MLTCs

— Greater emphasis on making training programmes more participatory, skill-based and practical by using audiovisual aids, role-plan, exercises in groups, demonstrations, etc.

— Adoption of new approaches and strategies such as utilisation of additional training centres, and using alternative methodology for training to minimise the training backlog.

— Revision of curricula and syllabi for training of ICDS functionaries

— Incorporating changing requirements of ICDS programme and its convergence with other schemes such as WILL, IMY, MSY and community based monitoring.

A comparative status of programmes organised by the Institute in 1997-98 and 1998-99 is at Annexure XVII.

A list of training/orientation programmes organised by the Institute and its regional centres in 1998-99 (upto January 1999) is at Annexure XVII.

Research/Evaluation studies and other projects

The Institute undertakes research and evaluation studies as an integral part of its work. It has adopted a policy on research which has the approval of its Executive Council. The following areas identified in the policy provide a broad framework for research work of the Institute:

(a) research for policy formulation and programme development; (b) research and surveys for identification of needs and problems in the areas of voluntary action and mother care and child development; (c) assessment of efficacy and impact of on-going programmes for promotion of voluntary action and mother care and child development and identification of bottlenecks in the implementation and service delivery of various programmes and mid-course corrections; and (d) research, surveys and evaluation studies for identification of training needs in the areas of voluntary action and mother care and child development, development of curriculum and training materials and aids.

During the year 1998-99, the Institute completed the following research/ evaluation studies and other projects:

i) Revision and Translation of the Source Book on Financial Assistance to Voluntary organisations

Voluntary organisations, who have come to play a pivotal role in the process of social development, always face the problem of limited resources which bar them from performing their legitimate role. In this context, the provision of grant-in-aid to voluntary organisations forms one of the important measures for promotion of voluntary action in the field of social development. Today, there are number of Ministries/ Departments of the Central Government which give grants-in-aid to voluntary organisations for carrying out numerous activities for the needy and deprived. In addition, there are number of private funding bodies which, too, provide financial assistance to voluntary organisations for implementing social development programmes. However, information about the availability of such funds is often scattered and not always accessible to voluntary organisations, especially those working in remote parts of the country. With a view to filling up this information gap, the Institute, in 1981, for the first time, brought out a Source Book containing information on various government and non -governmental sources of funding for activities of voluntary organisations. The

Source Book was well received by voluntary organisations and revised editions were brought out in the years 1984, 1987 and 1991. Continuing demand for the Source Book has resulted in the Institute' bringing out the fifth edition incorporating recent changes in the schemes and programmes for financial assistance. This edition contains 50 new entries apart from modification in some of the schemes included in the fourth edition. In all, there are 130 schemes of various Ministries/ Departments, international agencies and other funding agencies whose grant-in-aid programmes have been included in the present edition.

ii) Evaluation of Tamil Nadu Integrated Nutrition Project: A Study

The main objective of this study conducted by the Regional Centre Bangalore was to assess the extent to which the Tamil Nadu Integrated Nutrition Project (TINP) achieved its objectives. The study examined the strategies adopted in accomplishing the objectives of TINP. The study covered 90 villages in 30 blocks spread over 10 districts of Tamil Nadu. A total of 1220 respondents who comprised TINP functionaries and target beneficiaries were interviewed.

Some of the important on-going studies/projects approved by the Academic Committee earlier and which are at different stages of progress are listed below:

i. Girl Child in Adoption - A Study

ii. Child Marriage Restraint Act-A Study of its Implementation in Gujarat

iii. Revision of Guidebook for Creche Workers

iv. Scholastic Problems of Children

v. Information, Education and Communication (IEC) in ICDS Programme: Research And Effectiveness

vi. Evaluation of Utilisation of Medicine Kit provided to Anganwadi Workers

vii. Child Welfare and Development in Post-Independent India - A Profile

viii. A Study of Food Habits and Growth Pattern of Children in the Ecological Context

ix. Child Abuse in Guwahati

x. A micro level study on birth weight and neo-natal deaths of hospital born children in hospitals of Guwahati city

xi. Aggression in Children.

xii. A Comparative Study on Community Participation in ICDS Projects run by a Voluntary Organisation and Government.

Celebration of 50th year of India's independence

To commemorate the 50th anniversary of India's independence, the Institute planned and organised a series of programmes including Consultation Meet, essay competition for children and adolescents, cultural programmes, etc. These programmes were organised by the Institute's headquarters at New Delhi and its three Regional Centres located at Bangalore, Guwahati and Lucknow. Details of these Programmes are given below

Headquarters

Essay competition for children and adolescents in the age-group 10-14 years and 14-18 years. The theme of the essay was "My Vision about India for the year 2000 and beyond".

National Consultation Meet on Women's Empowerment-their Role in Governance and Decision-making.

Initiated preliminary work for bringing out the

publication entitled "Child Development in Post Independent India". The publication will give a comprehensive view of the history of child development in India.

Regional Centre, Bangalore

The Regional Centre, Bangalore celebrated the Golden Jubilee of India's independence. The theme of the celebration was "Folk Media and Mass Awareness". The Regional Centre invited four groups to make cultural presentations which had a bearing on development communication. The first two groups were represented by voluntary organisations, while the remaining groups were represented by the Songs and Drama Division, Ministry of I & B. The other activities included Angavikalana Sutta (Around the Handicapped)-a street play; Hennu Shishu (Girl Child)-a street play; Beesu Kamsale- a folk art presentation, Akashara Vijaya (Yakshagana)- a folk art presentation.

Regional Centre, Guwahati

The Regional Centre, Guwahati celebrated the event by organising a day long programme for children. The activities included organisation of an exhibition highlighting the achievements made by the country in the field of women and child development in the last fifty years, a drawing and painting competition for children, organisation of a Quiz programme on 'India: Land and the People' and a cultural show by the children in the evening.

Regional Centre, Lucknow

The Regional Centre, Lucknow celebrated the occasion at its premises in Lucknow. The theme of the celebration was 'National Integration and Communal Harmony'. The main objective of the celebration was to create general awareness about national integration and communal harmony among participants of training programmes.

The Regional Centre also organised a film show entitled 'Ladki Ke Naam, Kaam Hi Kaam' to draw the attention to the plight of the girl child. A singing competition was organised in which children of different Anganwadi Centres participated. A group discussion for the mothers was also organised to discuss issues suck as breast-feeding, immunisation, hygiene and diarrhoea. A lecture was also organised on detection and prevention of Childhood Disabilities. Participants in the above programme included Anganwadi children, their mothers, Anganwadi helpers, Anganwadi Workers, supervisors and CDPOs.

Documentation

Resource Centre on Children is a specialised research and reference centre on children, women and disadvantaged groups. It is actively involved in development, research and networking activities and provides a comprehensive perspective about the status, and needs of children and women. RCC Data Base has bibliographic details of documents received and indexed. The facility of 'on-line-search' in the Centre provides the users an easy access to information.

During the year 1998-99 (upto January 1999), RCC collected about 310 unpublished documents and added 234 books to the library. It subscribed to 197 journals/magazines and 17 newspapers.

During the year, NIPCCD Newsletter (English) and NIPCCD Samachar (Hindi) continued to cover programmes and activities of the Institute as well as the latest developments in the field of voluntary action and women and child development.

Financial allocation

The expenditure incurred by the Institute during 1997-98 under 'Plan' and 'Non-Plan' heads was of the order of

Rs. 161.20 lakh and Rs. 380.12 lakh respectively. The approved Budget Estimates for 1998-99 under 'Plan' and 'Non-Plan' was Rs.260.00 lakh and Rs.300.00 lakh respectively. The Revised Estimate for 1998-99 under 'Plan' and 'Non-Plan' is to the tune of Rs.2.60 lakh and Rs.4.10 lakh respectively. The expenditure incurred during 1998-99 (upto November, 1998) under 'Plan' and 'Non-Plan' heads was Rs. 173.95 lakh and Rs.372.83 lakh respectively.

A budget provision of Rs.180.00 lakh was approved for the year 1997-98 for project entitled 'Training of ICDS Functionaries and other Tasks connected therewith' and Rs.65.00 lakh for Training of Functionaires of World Bank Assisted ICDS Projects. Upto March, 1998 an expenditure of Rs.126.58 lakh and Rs. 41.51 lakh was incurred against these provisions respectively. The Revised Estimates of Rs.175.00 lakh under 'Training of ICDS Functionaries and other Tasks connected therewith' and Rs.35.00 lakh under 'Training of ICDS Functionaires of World Bank Assisted ICDS Projects and other connected Tasks' were proposed for 1998-99. An expenditure of Rs. 59.42 lakh and Rs.19.14 lakh respectively was incurred till January 1999.

Outstanding audit objections

There are 11 outstanding audit objections from 1990-97. Most of the observations are of procedural nature. The Audit of Accounts of the Institute for 1997-98 by Director General of Audit, Central Revenue has been completed in September, 1998.

Position of reservation

The Institute follows the reservation policy of Government of India for SCs, STs and OBCs.

Meetings of committee working

Academic Committee

This Committee deals with all matters concerning

academic work and programmes of the Institute. The Twenty Sixth meeting of the Academic Committee was convened on 3 June, 1998 to consider proposals of training programmes for the year 1998-99.

Administrative Committee

A Meeting of the Administrative Committee of the Institute was held on 3 December, 1998 to consider various administrative and financial matters. The Committee, inter-alia, reviewed the Annual Report (Volume-1) consisting of information on programmes organised by the Institute during 1997-98, revised estimates 1998-99, budget estimates 1999-2000 and other financial and administrative matters.

The recommendations made by the Committee will be placed before the Executive Council in the forthcoming meeting. The Committee expressed its appreciation for the work done by the institute during 1997-98 and recommended the Annual Report (Volume-1) for 1997-98 for approval by the Executive Council.

Promotion of use of Hindi

In order to promote use of Hindi during 1998-99 several measures were taken by the Institute. These included cash award scheme for officers for giving dictation in Hindi, scheme for incentives allowance to stenographers/ typists for doing their official work in Hindi, nomination of officers for Hindi training, celebration of Hindi Fortnight from I to 14 September, 1998, organisation of two Hindi Workshops from 9 to 13 November, 1998, convening of meetings of Official Language Implementation Committee at the Institute on regular basis and translation of important documents in Hindi.

4

Rights of the Child

Fifty years ago, in the aftermath of the most devastating war in history, UNICEF was created on 11 December 1946 to provide succour to children. Its establishment stemmed from the concern that children would not be adequately protected in the overall relief effort under way in Europe. The international recognition that children required special attention was revolutionary at the time. At the end of the postwar reconstruction period, developing countries emerging from the colonial era invoked the same principle to demand that children be given specific attention in international cooperation. UNICEF's initial relief mandate was enlarged to include the survival and development of children.

Now, the international approach to children has changed dramatically once again. The idea that children have special needs has given way to the conviction that children have rights, the same full spectrum of rights as adults: civil and political, social, cultural and economic.

This conviction, expressed as the Convention on the Rights of the Child, entered into international law on 2 September 1990, nine months after the Convention's adoption by the United Nations General Assembly. Since then, the Convention has been ratified (as of mid-September 1996) by all countries except the Cook Islands, Oman, Somalia, Switzerland, the United Arab Emirates and the United States, making it the most widely ratified human rights treaty in history.

The Convention has produced a profound change that is already beginning to have substantive effects on the world's attitude towards its children. Once a country ratifies, it is obliged in law to undertake all appropriate measures to assist parents and other responsible parties in fulfilling their obligations to children under the Convention. Now, 96 per cent of the world's children live in States that are legally obligated to protect children's rights.

Those rights are comprehensive. The Convention defines children as people below the age of 18 (article 1) whose "best interests" must be taken into account in all situations (article 3). It protects children's right to their full potential, and among its provisions are those affirming children's right to the highest attainable standard of health care (article 12), and to express views and receive information. Children have a right to be registered immediately after birth and to have a name and nationality (article 7), a right to play (article 31) and to protection from all forms of sexual abuse (article 34).

The Convention recognizes that not all governments have the resources necessary to ensure all economic, social and cultural rights immediately. But it commits them to make those rights a priority and to ensure them to the maximum extent of available resources.

Fulfilling their obligations sometimes requires States to make fundamental changes in national laws, institutions, plans, policies and practices to bring them into line with the principles of the Convention.

The first priority must be to generate the political will to do this. As the drafters of the Convention recognized, real change in the lives of children will come about only when social attitudes and which progressively change to conform with laws and principles. And when, as actors in the process, children themselves know enough about their rights to claim them.

The official monitor of this process of change is the Committee on the Rights of the Child. Governments are obliged to report to the Committee within two years of ratification, and every five years thereafter, specifying the steps taken to change national laws and formulate policies and actions.

The Committee, made up of 10 experts, gathers evidence from nongovernmental organizations (NGOs) and intergovernmental organizations, including UNICEF, and these groups may prepare alternative reports to that of a government. The Committee and the government then meet to discuss the country's child rights efforts and the steps necessary to overcome difficulties.

The reporting process has proved dynamic and constructive, with the dialogue established helping to advance children's rights. Unfortunately, however, many countries have missed their reporting deadlines, 28 of them by as much as three years, as of September 1996.

The process of implementing the Convention still remains in its infancy but, as we have noted, the international treaty for children is already beginning to make an impact. As reported in 1996 in UNICEF's annual publication, The Progress of Nations, of the 43 countries whose reports had been reviewed at the time, 14 had incorporated the principles of the Convention into their constitutions and 35 had passed new laws or amended existing laws to conform to the Convention. And 13 had built the Convention into curricula or courses to begin the key process of educating children about their rights.

Around the world, teachers, lawyers, police officials,

judges and care givers are being trained in the principles and the application of the Convention. Inspired by the Convention, Sierra Leone has demobilized child soldiers. In Rwanda, UNICEF, under the Convention's aegis, has been working to move children held in adult detention centres for alleged war offences to special juvenile institutions and has hired lawyers to defend them. And reforms, changes and improvements continue to accumulate around the world.

The monitoring of the Convention and media coverage of the issues have promoted international awareness of gross violations of children's rights. Major initiatives such as the World Congress against Commercial Sexual Exploitation of Children, held in Stockholm in August 1996, and the International Conference on Child's Labour, scheduled for October 1997 in Oslo, derive their impetus from the Convention. Highlighting the problems in this way is an essential first step towards their elimination.

In a positive initiative to involve the media in educating children about their rights, the Asian Summit on Child Rights and the Media, held in Manila in July 1996, included a wide range of participants in four days of discussions on how to educate, inform and entertain children while also taking into account their best interests.

UNICEF itself is at a turning point. In its 50th year, the organization has adopted a mission statement that looks to the Convention as its guiding force.

This new mandate has important implications for the work of the organization. Its efforts for children in the past two decades, including the year 2000 goals established by the international community at the World Summit for Children in 1990, are designed to alleviate the worst aspects of poverty for the majority of the world's children. These goals and agreements must now be pursued in the context of the Convention.

In September 1996, the Secretary General of the United Nations, Boutros Boutros-Ghali, reported to the General Assembly on the progress make in meeting the Summit's year 2000 goals for children as the decade for action passed the halfway mark. Much of the news is good, with millions of children's lives having been saved since 1990.

But much remains to be done. More than 12.5 million children under five in developing countries continue to die each year, 9 million of them from causes for which inexpensive solutions and measures such as immunization and antibiotics have been routinely applied in the industrialized world for 50 years.

As long as preventable death and suffering continue on a large scale in the developing world, child survival must remain the context of the Convention, UNICEF and the world community must not only maintain the commitment to the year 2000 goals but also look beyond them to social protection and other important needs and rights not expressly contained in the World Summit Declaration and Plan of Action. The Convention, by expressing and protecting all the rights of children, expands the scope of action required for children and throws an clear shaft of light on paths that extend beyond the year 2000.

Some of these will involve protecting children and youth in conflict with the criminal justice system; others will ensure the development of the young child, support families, end the use of land-mines and continue to try to bring about a more equitable distribution of resources.

The Convention requires families, societies,

governments and the international community to take action designed to fulfil the rights of all children in a sustainable, participatory and non-discriminatory manner. In practical terms, this means that the poorest, most vulnerable and often the most neglected children in all societies, rich and poor, must have first call on resources and efforts.

The endeavours to touch their lives will be complex and will require a sustained attack on the root causes of poverty and underdevelopment.

In a world where technology and knowledge are available and easy to share, and per capita income has tripled in the past quarter of a century, there can be no excuses: the rights of all children, including those who are most disadvantaged, can be fulfilled.

The international community has tried in this last decade of the 20th century to arrive at a consensus on the way forward on a number of fronts: on human rights, on protection of the environment, on reduction of uncontrolled population growth and on eliminating gender inequality. The avowed aim os sustainable development for all on the basis of social justice and human fulfillment.

Good intentions will now have to be matched with the political will to act and fortified by changes in individual and national attitudes and priorities. An additional $40 billion a year could ensure access for ass the world's people to basic social services such as health care, education and safe water.

Two thirds of this amount could be found by developing countries if they realigned their own budget priorities. Redirecting just one quarter of the developing world's military expenditure—or $30 billion of $ 125 billion—for example, could provide enough additional resources to reach most of the goals for the year 2000. A similar shift in the targeting of development aid by donor countries could generate much of the rest.

This premise is set out in the 20/20 initiative, which calls for developing countries to increase government spending on basic social services from the current average of approximately 13 per cent to 20 per cent, and for donor countries to earmark 20 per cent of official development assistance (ODA).

This kind of shift in the way the world uses its resources is no longer an appeal to the charity of those with the power and the purse-strings but is a matter of rights and obligation. The new era in child rights will still need underpinning by attitudinal change, popular pressure and public demands.

Wherever opinion polls have been undertaken they have shown that people support the ideas and ideals of human rights, child rights and international solidarity. Part of the task, then, is to channel this support into action.

For the past 15 years, The State of the World's Children has mobilized public and political support for child survival and development. UNICEF will continue to mobilize, now with the added power and legitimacy of the Convention, because the need for passionate advocacy on behalf of the world's children has not diminished, even now, half a century after the need for UNICEF was internationally acknowledged.

As Philip Alston, a leading child rights lawyer and activist, states: "In the final analysis, appropriate policies will be adopted... only in response to widespread and insistent public outrage."

5

Child Abuse

Amid all the problems of a world bleeding from continuing wars and environmental wounds, it is nonetheless becoming clear that one of the greatest of all human aspirations is now within reach. Within a decade, it should be possible to bring to an end the age-old evils of child malnutrition, preventable disease, and widespread illiteracy. As an indication of how close that goal might be, the financial cost can be put at about $25 billion a year. That is UNICEF's estimate of the extra resources required to put into practice today's low-cost strategies for protecting the world's low-cost strategies for protecting the world's children. Specifically, it is an estimate of the cost of controlling the major childhood diseases, halving the rate of child malnutrition, bringing clean water and safe sanitation to all communities, making family planning services universally available, and providing almost every child with at least a basic education.

In practice, financial resources are a necessary but not sufficient prerequisite for meeting these basic needs. Sustained political commitment and a great deal of managerial competence are even more important. Yet it is necessary to reduce this challenge to the denominator of dollars in order to dislodge the idea that abolishing the worst aspects of poverty is a task too vast to be attempted or too expensive to be afforded.

To put the figure of $25 billion in perspective, it is considerably less than the amount the Japanese Government has allocated to the building of a new highway from Tokyo to Kobe; it is two to three times as much as the cost of the tunnel soon to be opened between the United Kingdom and France; it is less than the cost of the Ataturk Dam complex now being constructed in eastern Turkey; it is a little more than Hong Kong proposes to spend on a new airport; it is about the same as the support package that the Group of Seven has agreed on in 1992 for Russia alone; and it is significantly less than Europeans will spend this year on wine or Americans on beer.

Whatever the other difficulties may be, the time has therefore come to banish in shame the notion that the world cannot afford to meet the basic needs of almost every man, woman, and child for adequate food, safe water, primary health care, family planning, and basic education.

If so much could be achieved for so many at so little cost, then the public in both industrialized and developing countries might legitimately ask why it is not being done. In part, the answer is the predictable one: meeting the needs of the poorest and the least politically influential has rarely been a priority of governments. Yet the extent of present neglect in the face of present opportunity is a scandal of which the public is largely unaware.

On average, the governments of the developing world are today devoting little more than 10% of their budgets to directly meeting the basic needs of their people. More is still being spent on military capacity and on debt servicing than on health and education. Perhaps more surprising still, less than 10% of all international aid for development is devoted to directly meeting these most obvious of human needs. According to one study, for example, as little as 1.5% of all bilateral aid goes to primary health care, 1.5% of all bilateral aid goes to primary health care, 1.3% to family planning, 3.2% to other health care, and only 0.5% to primary education. Because national aid programmes are not broken down into common or comparable categories, such figures can only be approximate; but 10% is probably a generous overall estimate of the proportion of bilateral aid allocated to such purposes. And as total bilateral aid from the Western industrialized nations is approximately $40 billion a year, this means the amount given for nutrition, primary health care, water and sanitation, primary education, and family planning comes to about $4 billion a year. This is less than half as much as the aid giving nations spend each year on sports shoes.

It could therefore fairly be said that the problem today is not that overcoming the worst aspects of world poverty is too vast or too expensive a task; it is that it has not seriously been tried. With beginning of the 1990s has come new hope that the age of neglect may be giving way to the age of concern.

The evidence for this new hope, amid all the seismic shifts in the political and economic landscape of recent years, is a series of quieter changes which have not made the nightly news but which have affected the daily lives of millions of people. The first of these changes is the entirely new priority that has been given to the task of immunizing the world's children. For a decade, national health services, UNICEF, the World Health organization (WHO) and many thousands of individuals and organizations have struggled towards the goal of 80% immunization coverage in the developing world. In 1990, that goal was reached. The result is the saving of over 3 million children's lives each year and the protection of many millions more from disease, malnutrition, blindness, deafness, and polio. Second, the number of child deaths from diarrhoeal disease has been reduced by over 1 million a year through empowering one third of the developing world's families to use the technique of oral rehydration therapy.

The significance of these achievements goes beyond even the extraordinary numbers of lives saved and illnesses prevented. Eighty per cent immunization means that approximately 100 million children are being reached by a modern medical technique on four of five separate occasions during their first year of life. As a logistical achievement, it is unprecedented; and it shows beyond any doubt that the outreach capacity now exists to put the most basic benefits of scientific progress at the disposal of the vast majority of the world's poor. Secondly, it demonstrates that, with sustained political commitment, progress can now be made towards basic social goals even by the poorest of developing countries; over the last five years, immunization coverage has been lifted dramatically in many nations with per capita incomes of less than $500 a year, including Bangladesh, the Central African Republic, Equatorial Guinea, Myanmar, Nepal, the Sudan, Uganda, Viet Nam, and Zambia. Other advances in knowledge and technique are now lining up outside the door that immunization has unlocked. And the potential remains enormous. Thirty-five thousand children under five die in the developing world every day. Almost 60% of those deaths, and much of the world's illness and malnutrition, are caused by just three diseases-pneumonia, diarrhoea and measles-all of which can now be prevented or treated by means which are tried and tested, available and affordable. Similarly, the vitamin A deficiency which threatens up to 10 million of the world's children with death, serious illness, and loss of eyesight, could now be brought under control at a cost which is almost negligible in relation to the benefits it would bring. Or to take another example, the iodine deficiencies that lower the mental and physical abilities of up to a billion people and are the world's single biggest cause of mental retardation could also now be eliminated at a total cost of approximately $100 million—less than the cost of two modern fighter planes. Even those aspects of poverty which have traditionally been considered the most expensive and the most logistically stubborn-the Declaration and Plan of Action, also agreed to draw up detailed national programmes for reaching the agreed goals. As of September 1992, such plans have been completed in over 50 countries and are nearing completion in more than 80 others. In June of 1992, the United nations Secretary-General reported to the General Assembly that 31 countries have so far indicated they will restructure budgets to increase the proportion of government spending devoted to primary education, basic health care, nutrition, water, and sanitation.

The drawing up and financing of such plans is inevitably a bureaucratic process, and too much should not be expected too soon. But most nations have made a start towards keeping the promises that have made a start towards keeping the promises that have been made to the world's children. Immunization levels have been sustained and in some cases, notably in China, lifted above the new goal of 90% (at which point very significant decreases in the incidence of disease can be expected). Polio has almost certainly been eradicated from Latin America and the Caribbean where a year has now passed since the last confirmed case of the virus. Reported cases of the main vacine-preventable diseases are declining and WHO believes there is a reasonable chance that the 1995 goal of eliminating neonatal tetanus will be met. Countries such as Bangladesh, Bolivia, Ecuador, Malawi, Namibia, Sri Lanka, Tanzania, and possibly Brazil have already begun serious efforts to halve the rate of malnutrition. Similarly, several countries are moving determinedly towards the goal of water and sanitation for all-including Bangladesh, Burundi, China, Ghana, India, Nigeria, Paraguay, the Sudan, Togo, Viet Nam, and virtually all the countries of Central America. And to achieve the Summit goal of empowering all families with today's knowledge about the importance of breastfeeding, hundreds of hospitals and maternity units have begun to change institutional policies and to use their enormous influence to reverse the trend towards the bottle-feeding of infants.

Not least, the promise of the Summit is being kept by the rapid spread of acceptance for the Convention on the rights of the Child, which seeks to lay down minimum standards for the survival, protection, and development of all children. The Convention was adopted by the General Assembly of the United Nations towards the end of 1989 and came into force, with the necessary 20 ratifications, on the eve of the 1990 World Summit for Children. Usually, such conventions require many decades to achieve the stage of widespread international recognition; but in this case, the Summit urged all national governments to ratify as quickly as possible and more than 120 have so far done so. In some nations, the process of translating the Convention into national law has begun. In many nations, it is becoming the accepted standard for what is an is not acceptable in the treatment of the young. In all nations, its mere existence gives citizens; journalists, and non-governmental organizations (NGOs) an agreed platform from which to remind political leaders of their promises and to campaign against the neglect and abuse of children in all its forms.

Finally, it is clear that these promises made to the world's children have now established them selves on the international political agenda. Over the last tow years virtually every major summit meeting of the world's leaders - the Ibero-American, the Islamic States, the Franco- phone countries, the non-aligned movement, the commonwealth, the Organization of African Unity, the south Asian Association for Regional cooperation, the league of Arab States, and finally the United nations Conference on Environment and Development has formally confirmed the commitment to achieving the basic social goals that were agreed at the World Summit for Children. The importance of the Convention, the summit goals, and the national programmes of action that have been drawn up should neither be overestimated nor underestimated. At the moment they remain, for the most part, promises on paper. But when, in the mid 1980s, over 100 of the world's political leaders formally accepted the goal of 80% immunization by 1990, that, too, was just a promise on paper. Today, it is a reality in the lives of tens of millions of families around the world.

One lesson to be learned from that achievement is that formal political commitments at the highest levels are necessary if available solutions are to be put into action on a national scale. But a second lesson is that such commitments will only be translated into action by the dedication of the professional services; by the mobilization of today's communications capacities; by the widespread support of politicians, press, and public; and by the reliable and sustained support of the international community. Most of the countries that succeeded in reaching the immunization goal, including many that were among the poorest and the hardest hit by problems of debt and economic adjustment, succeeded primarily because large numbers of people and organization at all levels of national life became sized with the idea that the goal could and should be achieved. Many developing countries could provide examples, but it will be sufficient to cite the case of Bangladesh: against formidable internal and external difficulties, one of Asia's poorest and most populous countries succeeded in lifting its level of immunization coverage from only 2% in 1985 to 62% in 1990 "Never in the country's history," wrote a UNICEF officer in Dhaka, "had so many groups come together for a single social programme: the President, eight social sector ministries, parliamentarians, senior civil servants, journalists, TV and radio, hundreds of non-governmental organizations, social and youth clubs, religious leaders, film and sports stars and local business leaders all worked successfully towards a common goal."

The question for the years immediately ahead is whether people and organizations in all countries and at all levels are prepared to breathe similar life into new goals that have been agreed on, and into the national programmes of action that have been drawn up for achieving them. Only by this degree of popular participation, by the practical and political energies of literally millions of people and thousands of organizations, will the new commitments and the promises of the 1990s be given a priority in national life. And only by such means will a new age of concern be born. All of these developments, and the hopes to which they have given rise, come at a time of extraordinary change in world affairs. And it is possible to hope that the cause of overcoming the worst aspects of poverty will also draw sustenance, for the long haul ahead, from the changed political and economic environment of the 1990s.

At the moment, that environment remains extremely difficult for most nations of the developing world. There is as yet no sign that the ending of the cold war is leading to any increase in the resources available for development. Indeed, much of the developing world is today facing its worst financial famine of the modern area, starved of resources by its own high levels of military spending, by the continuing debt crisis, by the further falls in commodity prices, by the restrictive trade policies of the industrialized nations by the lingering recession in large parts of the world, by the costs of post-war reconstruction in the Persian Gulf, and by the channelling of new aid, credit, and investment to the nations of Eastern Europe and the former Soviet Union.

But despite all of the these problems, the prospects for progress have been profoundly improved by the enormous political and economic upheavals of recent years: the advance of democracy throughout Latin America; the liberation of Eastern Europe; the collapse of the Soviet Union; The ending of the cold war; the spread of democratic political reform through most of Africa (including the erosion of apartheid); the almost worldwide retreat from the ideology of highly centralized government control over all aspects of economic life; and the growing acceptance of the necessity of joint international action in response to both human-itarian and environmental problems.

WHO estimates that the actual number of polio cases in 1991 was approximately 100,000 worldwide-almost 10 times the number of reported case. The relationship between reported cases and actual cases depends on the merits of the surveillance system. These changes amount to one of the most sudden and fundamental transformations in history. And for all the suffering that is surfacing in the turbulent. Wake of these changes, from

Somalia to the former Yugoslavia, it can still be said that this is a transformation which holds out new hope for world development. If the various forms of free-market economic policies now being adopted are not crushed under the weight of military spending, debt repayment, and trade protectionism, then there is real hope of achieving sustained economic growth. And if the steps now being taken towards democracy do not falter under the assault of continued poverty and social unrest, then there is also real hope that the poor will eventually begin to share more equitably in the benefits of that growth.

These developments are changing the overall environment in which the developing world must earn its living and within which its people must struggle to meet their own needs. Whether those needs are met or not depends, first of all, on whether families have jobs and incomes. Second, it depends on whether governments fulfil their responsibilities for providing the essential services and safety nets to support families so that even the most disadvantaged do not suffer from preventable malnutrition, from disease borne by unsafe water and sanitation, or form the lack of even basic health care and education. The great changes of the last five years by no means make such progress inevitable or automatic; but they do make it more possible and more likely.

This coming together of both general and specific developments means that a new threshold in the struggle to overcome the worst aspects of poverty has been reached in the early years of the 1990s. Broad-scale political and economic change is creating an environment more conducive to a renewal of progress against poverty; and advances in technology, in strategy, and in political commitment to meeting basic social goals have given that challenge both a specific focus and a new impetus.

If there is one area of the development process that is more widely misunderstood than any other it is the relationship between these two factors-between the long-term processes of overall development and the specific, deliberate, targeted interventions such as are represented by the basic social goals that have been agreed. And it is the nature of this relationship which should also give a new urgency to meeting essential human needs.

With sufficient public and political support, it is clearly now possible to control those aspects of poverty that bring the greatest suffering to the greatest number. In particular, it is possible to close some of the most obvious, the most shameful, and the most damaging gaps between today's knowledge and today's needs. Closing these gaps will not solve the problems of economic development; it will not remove the burden of debt or restructure inequitable economic relationships; it will not bring an end to oppression and exploitation or eradicate the many causes of unemployment and low incomes; nor will it meet the legitimate aspirations of hundreds of millions of people in the developing world who are not living in absolute poverty but who do not enjoy the amenities of life that are taken for granted in the industrialised nations. In has therefore sometimes been argued that such specific, targeted interventions address only the symptoms of poverty and leave the causes undisturbed. This is an argument which is no longer deserving of the politeness extended to it in the past.

It is an unacceptable argument on two counts. First, it is an inhuman argument. How much longer must the poorest families wait before it is decided that the world has reached the level of socio-economic development at which a few dollars per capita can be afforded to help them prevent millions of their children from becoming malnourished, blinded, crippled, mentally retarded?

Second, it fails to recognize that frequent illness, malnutrition, poor growth and illiteracy are some of the most fundamental causes as well as some of the most severe symptoms of poverty. It fails to take into account that the pulse of economic development is weakened when millions of children suffer from poor mental and physical growth; that the march toward equality of opportunity is slowed when the children of the very poor drop out of school and into a lifetime of illiteracy; that the productivity of communities is enervated by hours spent carrying water from unsafe sources and by the time, energy, and health that is lost to the diseases it brings; that the prospects of finding a job and earning an income are crushed by preventable disabilities such as polio or nutritional blindness; that a family's capacity to save and invest in the future is the less when a child is born mentally retarded by iodine deficiency; and that the contribution of women to economic development cannot be liberated if women remain chained to long years of child-bearing, long days of attendance on illness, and long hours devoted to the fetching and carrying of water and fuel.

In these and many other ways, the worst symptoms of poverty help to crush the potential of the poor, to reduce their control over circumstance, to reduce their control over circumstance, to narrow the choices available to them, and to undermine the long-term process of development.

The struggle for social justice and economic development, both within and between nations, must continue - just as the poor them selves will continue to struggle, as they have always done, to meet most of their own needs by their own efforts. But it is a tragic mistake not to recognize that those efforts can be enhanced by reductions in disease, disability, malnutrition, illiteracy, and drudgery. Today's advance in knowledge and technology could therefor augment future prospects as surely as they could diminish present suffering. And the argument that making today's advances widely available is dealing only with symptoms is an argument as destructive to the future as it is insensitive to the present.

These links between poverty's causes and effects lend special weight to the case for doing what could now be done to protect young children from the worst aspects of poverty. There are many external causes of that poverty. And the process of development must address all of those causes, whether they be rooted in accidental geographical circumstances or exploitative economic relationships. But one of the most intractable of those causes is the fact that the children of the poor do not usually receive the kind of start in life which will enable them to take advantage of the opportunities that do become available. And one of the main aims of development must be to break into this insidious 'innercycle' of malnutrition and disease leading to poor performance at school and at work: leading to reduced adult capacity for earning an income, initiating change, responding to new opportunities; leading to poor and often large families which are vulnerable to the malnutrition and disease that close the cycle and allow the current of poverty to flow from one generation to the next.

The place at which to make that break is before the child is born and during the early years of his or her life. If the mental and physical growth of the child can be afforded special protection at this time, if families and communities and governments can prevent the worst aspects of poverty from affecting the child's normal growth and development, if special measures can be taken to give those vulnerable months and years something of the protection which is given to children fortunate enough to be born into a higher socio-economic class, then a major contribution to the breaking of the cycle will have been made.

This is the kind of protection for the vulnerable years which millions of parents the world over make sacrifices to provide. From the point of view of those parents, it is special protection given from love and common sense. From the point of view of the effects of poverty on growth and development, it is special protection given in order to artificially and temporarily lift a child to a higher socio-economical level, for the vulnerable early years, so that the poverty into which that child is born will not, as far as is possible, inflict long term damage. To illustrate the thesis still further, this is also the kind of special protection that nature itself tries to provide to those vulnerable years in the form of breastmilk. In almost all circumstances, breastmilk means that during the first six months of life a child is well nourished whether he or she is born into the meanest slum or the most opulent mansion. Nature, too, is here attempting to neutralize the fortunes of birth by providing a standard of nutrition that does not reflect, and is not affected by, the socio-economic level of the family into which that child is born. The capacity for extending this special protection, and for protecting the period of most rapid physical and mental growth from the most damaging aspects of poverty, has now been vastly increased by advances in knowledge and communications capacity. By such means as immunization, growth monitoring and promotion, the proper management of diarrhoeal diseases and respiratory infections, supplementing vitamin A and iodine, targeted food subsides, and low-cost water and sanitation services, it is now possible to broaden and strengthen this basic protection for the most vulnerable years of life.

With today's knowledge and communications power, families, governments, and the international community could now build a shield of basic protection around the early years for all children. And in so doing, a major contribution could be made not only to meeting immediate human needs but to breaking the 'inner cycle' of poverty and underdevelopment.

The present opportunity to meet the most basic and obvious needs of children in the poorest quarter of the world must therefore also be seen in the context of this profound relationship between the physical and mental needs of children and the social and economic development of their societies. "I think it is time," says Professor Muhammad Yunus, founder of Bangladesh's Grameen Bank Movement, "to come out boldly to insist that children should be placed at the centre stage in all development thinking."

To these arguments must be added two other reasons which add weight to the idea that the time is now right for a decisive advance against the worst aspects of poverty. One of the most important common factors uniting today's mans of protecting lives and health and growth is that almost all of them are able to be put at the disposal of families by a community health worker with only a few months of training. A well-trained, well-supervised, and well-supported community health worker can, for example, help to provide family planning information and services; advise on prenatal care and safe birth practices; inform families of the advantages of breastfeeding; organize immunization and record-keeping services; diagnose acute respiratory infections and prescribe antibiotics; teach oral rehydration therapy and the proper management of diarrhoeal diseases; promote home hygiene and disease prevention; organize growth monitoring sessions; promote today's knowledge about the special feeding needs of the young child; organize protection against malaria; distribute the most essential drugs and medicines; provide vitamin A, iodine, and iron supplements where necessary; and refer more difficult health problems to more qualified health professionals. In short, they can demystify today's basic health knowledge and put it at the disposal of communities. And if they are supported in that task by the full range of today's communications capacities, schools and teachers, religious leaders and local government officials, the print and electronic media, retail outlets and professional organizations, NGOs and women's groups, then the trained health worker can be the central span of the bridge between present knowledge and present need.

There are many problems involved in the deployment of large numbers of community health workers-in their recruitment and retention, in their career structure and motivation, in their regular training and supervision, in their regular training and supervision, and especially in the organization of the essential referral services. But such problems can be and have been overcome when the political commitment has been sustained and when the financial resources have been made available.

Above all, it can no longer be claimed that putting a trained health care worker within reach of every family is not a practical and affordable proposition. Assuming a ratio of one health worker for every 200 families, for example, it would require approximately 2 million such health workers to serve the world's poorest 2 billion people (it is not possible, in practice, to reach only the poorest 20%. At an average cost of approximately $ 1,000 per year, to cover salaries and regular in-service retraining, the total cost would be in the region of $ 2 billion dollars a year. Such a sum represents approximately 2% of the amount the developing world now spends every year on the salaries of its soldiers.

For a wider range of services, the point has been elaborated by Amartya Sen, Lamont University Professor at Harvard and former Drummond Professor of Political Economy at the University of Oxford:

> "The question must also be raised... as to whether a poor country should have to wait many decades before it has enough resources generated by economic growth to undertake ambitious public programmes of health care and education. It is not illegitimate to wonder whether a poor country can 'afford' to spend so much on health and education.
>
> "In answering this question we must not only note the empirical reality that many poor countries-such as Sri Lanka, China, Costa Rica, the Indian state of Kerala, and others—have done precisely that with much success, but also under stand the general fact that delivering public health care and basic educational facilities is enormously cheaper in a poor country than in a rich one. This is because both health and education are labour-intensive activities and this makes them much cheaper in poor countries because of lower wages. Thus, even though a poor country is tremendously constrained in expending money on health and education because of general poverty, the money needed to pay for these services is also significantly less when a country is still quite poor".

Fertility rates have fallen in almost every region of the world. In Latin America, the annual number of births has now begun to decline; in Asia, births will reach a peak in the mid-1990s and begin to fall; even in South Asia, a peak will be reached within a decade. Only in Africa will the annual number of births continue to rise until well into the next century. A turning-point in the modern era will therefore soon be reached. For once the annual number of births is stable or declining, any further investment in such services as health and education can be used to improve the quality of the services offered and to increase the proportion of people reached. In other words, the task of providing such services will no longer be case of 'running to stand still', and the goal of meeting basic human needs will no longer be a target that is for ever moving away. As the end of the 20th century approaches, there is therefore an accumulation of reasons for believing that ending the worst aspects of poverty is an idea whose time may finally have come.

New strategies and low-cost technologies are available. Specific goals which reflect this potential have been agreed upon. The commitment to those goals bears the signatures of more Presidents and Prime Ministers than any other document in history. The plans for achieving them have been or are being drawn up in most nations And there is a growing acceptance of the idea that targeting some of these worst effects of poverty, particularly as they affect children, is an essential part of long-term development strategy.

In the wider world, the ground being gained by democratic systems means that the long-starved concerns of the poor may begin to put on political weight; providing basic social services for poor families with the vote is, after all, good politics. At the same time, economic reforms may also create the kind of environment in which a new effort to meet basic human needs would have a much greater chance of success. Meanwhile, the powerful tide of demographic change is also beginning to turn.

For all of these reasons, a new potential now exists for moving towards a world in which the basic human needs of almost every man, woman and child are met. But is equally clear that this attempt will not gather the necessary momentum unless the political commitment sustained and the extra resources begin to be made available.

If advantage is to be taken of the political commitments that have been made, and of the national programmes of action that have been drawn up, then those extra resources must begin to become available in the next 12 months to two years. Some nations have already begun the process of finding the necessary funds from their own resources. In most cases, this is almost certainly going to mean an increase in the proportion of government expenditures allocated to nutrition, primary health care, clean water, safe sanitation, basic education, and family planning services. UNICEF strongly supports the United Nations Development Programme's suggestion that at least 20% of government spending should be allocated to these direct methods of meeting priority human needs. If implemented such a restructuring of government budgets would enable the developing nations as a whole to find several times the $25 billion a year that is needed to achieve the agreed goals.

In practice, such a shift in present patterns of resources allocation will not be easy to bring development in the 21st century. And it is a role that could also provide a focus for the impending reform of the United Nations system and lead to the kind of changes which would make sense to, and meet with the approval of, a worldwide public. Above all, this is an opportunity that must not be allowed to evaporate into the perennial atmosphere of pessimism about the prospects for world development. The necessary task of drawing attention to human needs has unfortunately given rise to the popular impression that the developing world is a stage upon which no light falls and only tragedy is enacted. But the fact is that, for all the set-backs, more progress has been made in the last 50 years than in the previous 2,000. Since the end of the Second World War, average real incomes in the developing world have more than doubled; infant and child death rates have been more than halved; average life expectancy has increased by about a third; the proportion of the developing world's children starting school has risen from less than half to more than three quarters (despite a doubling of population); and the percentage of rural families with access to safe water has risen from less than 10% to almost 60%. Yet even these extraordinary statistics cannot capture the true dimensions of the change that has occurred in only a few decades. Much of the world has also freed itself from colonialism, brought apartheid in all its forms to the edge of extinction, and largely freed itself from the iron grip of fascist and totalitarian regimes. And underlying all of these changes is the slow and even more fundamental change from a world organized almost exclusively for the benefit of a privileged 10% or 20%, in almost all societies, to a world in which the needs and the rights of all people are increasingly recognized. Only a few decades ago, it did not seem a matter of great concern that the poor majority had no right to vote, no freedom of expression or religion, no right to due process of law, or that their children were not educated or immunized and received little or no benefit from advances in hygiene and health care. In many nations, it even seemed natural that the children of the poor could be sold or bonded or made to work 14 hours a day in field or mine or factory. And almost exactly 50 years ago, when more than a million people starved in the Bengal famine, they died in a world which raised no murmur of protest.

Seen from this longer perspective, the fact that two thirds of the world's people now have the right to vote, or that 80% of the world's infants are immunized, or that there is such a thing as a worldwide Convention on the Rights of the Child, is a symptom of a remarkable change. And in the face of such progress, pessimism is a sign less of sagacity than of cynicism. In the decade ahead, a clear opportunity exists to make the breakthrough against what might be called the last great obscenity - the needless malnutrition, disease, and illiteracy that still casts a shadow over the lives, and the futures, of the poorest quarter of the world's children.

It is almost unthinkable that the opportunity to reach these basic social goals should be missed because the political commitment is lacking or because the developing world and the donor nations cannot, together, find an extra $25 billion a year. The technologies and strategies are available and affordable. The outreach and communications capacity are there to be mobilized. The political commitments have been made. And the broader context of political, economic, and demographic change is probably as favourable at this time as it is ever likely to be. The difficulties are enormous. But they shrink beside the difficulties that can be and have been overcome in the course of all the many great achievements of our times.

In the industrialised world, neither recession nor competing claims on resources can justify the failure to find the extra $8 billion a year which would be required to support the developing nations that decide to make meeting basic social goals into a national priority.

In the developing world, underdevelopment is a fast-fading excuse for failure to make that commitment and to begin mobilizing the necessary financial and human resources.

It is time that the challenge replaced excuse. If today's obvious and affordable steps are not taken to protect the lives and the health and the normal growth of many millions of young children, then this will have less to do with the lack of economic capacity than with the fact that the children concerned are almost exclusively the sons and daughters of the poor - of those who lack not only purchasing power but also political influence and media attention. And if the resources are not to be made available, if the overcoming of the worst aspects of poverty, malnutrition, illiteracy and disease is not to be achieved in the years ahead, then let it now be clear that this is not because it is not a possibility but because it is not a priority.

On 5 September 1991, laboratory analysis confirmed that Luis Tenorio Cortez, a two-year-old boy from the municipality of Pichanaqui in south central Peru, had been paralysed by type 1 polio virus. Since then, no further cases of polio have been recorded anywhere in the western hemisphere.

Several more years of vigilance lie ahead. But victory is clearly in sight for the Pan American Health Organization (PAHO), which has led the fight to eradicate polio from the Americas. In the other half of the globe, the virus still paralyses the limbs of over 100,000 children each year. Tragic as this figure is, still represents remarkable progress. A decade ago, the virus claimed over half a million victims a year. Today, polio vaccine has reached 85% of children worldwide. In some countries, the decline has been nothing less than spectacular; reported cases of polio of the Philippines, for example, fell from 1.422 in 1988 to just 82 in 1990.

Three quarters of all new cases of polio in 1989 and 1990 were reported by China and India. But in both, rising immunization levels hold out realistic hope of eradicating the disease by the year 2000. In Africa, where health systems are generally weaker, the position in less hopeful; 14 Africa countries still have immunization coverage levels of less than 50%.

Once high levels of routine immunization have been achieved, the key to eradication is a surveillance system that can immediately detect any new case of flaccid paralysis. While laboratory tests determine whether polio is the cause, the suspected case should be 'surrounded' by immunizing all children in the area. Until all countries are free of the disease, no country can be free. Even in nations with very high levels of routine immunization, the polio virus can be imported and may spread rapidly.

Thousands of people and organizations are now involved in the effort to eradicate polio from the face of the earth by the end of the 20th century—the target set by the 1990 World Summit for Children. National immunization programmes, whose achieve-ments have been one of the great success stories of the last decade, are being supported by WHO and UNICEF as well as by bilateral aid programmes and institutions such as the Rockefeller Foundation and Atlanta's US Centers for Disease Control. In an outstanding example of popular support, Rotary International has raised more than $300 million for polio eradication worldwide and provided thousands of volunteers to assist immunization services. In most countries, the task of informing hundreds of millions of parents about the when and where and the why of immunization could not have been achieved without the support of the mass media, the schools, the religious leaders, and many non-governmental organizations. Two thirds of all costs have been met by the developing world itself.

Eradicating polio from the world will cost approximately $1.4 billion over the next 10 years. But once eradication is confirmed, polio immunization will no longer be necessary. The programme will therefore pay for itself many times over. The savings in vaccines and delivery cots, including savings to the industrialised world, will amount to $500 million a year by the year 2000 and will rise to an estimated $3 billion a year by 2015.

Child-rearing practices considered normal and healthy in one society may seem abusive to members of another group. The common American practice of housing a baby in a separate bedroom and letting her cry herself to sleep is viewed as severe emotional abuse by Native Hawaiians who view close contact as critical for infant well-being. There is wide variation in opinion on the role of punishment in education and in parental discipline. The United States is ranked very high among Western nations in the amount of physical violence directed toward children. Physical punishment is an almost universal method of discipline in the United States. In contrast, parental spanking was outlawed in Sweden in 1979.

Beyond differences in child rearing and techniques of discipline are differences in the culturally meaningful institutions and activities. For example, a variety of rituals and procedures mark maturation and acceptance as an adult member of the community. Westerners react with horror at non-Western initiation rites, such as preadolescent or adolescent circumcision for young men, facial scarring, or deprivation of basic needs. Even broader criticism exists against the practices of female clitoridectomy done without anesthesia, and can result in infection and death. International health conferences have called for the elimination of such practices, yet individuals who value these traditional ways view the prevention of their participation in such procedures as its own form of mistreatment.

Behaviour regarding children

A second level of definition includes standards reflected in public consensus, legal definition, and professional opinion within a culture. Here major deviations from common standards of care are labeled abusive. The term "child abuse" usually denotes this level of definition. Controversy exists over the best ways to define the various subtypes of maltreatment. Different definitions serve different ends. For research and treatment purposes, maltreatment may best be described as a continuum ranging from less than adequate to criminally reprehensible. Within the contexts of social policy and criminal justice, there is a need for categorial definitions. There must be a line between less than ideal but adequate caregiver behavior and practices so harmful they warrant coercive intervention.

Conditions such as poverty, racism, female gender devaluation, poor health care, politically induced famine, international economic inequities, and the terror and disruption of warfare produced more suffering and death among the young than individually inflicted harms. Public and private international relief efforts, relief efforts, religious and charitable agencies, child advocacy groups such as the Children's Defense fund in the United States, national governments, and international leagues such as The United Nations work to eliminate suffering at this level. The 1987 Draft United Nations Convention of the Rights of the Child is an update of the 1924

Geneva Declaration of the Rights of the Child and the 1959 U.N. Declaration of the Rights of the Child. It represents an international effort to define and specify the "special care and assistance" to which children are entitled. Included among the many rights specified in the Draft are the right to adequate nutrition, housing, recreation, and medical services; freedom from punishment for parents' or relatives opinions and beliefs, parental care without separation unless abuse or neglect makes separation necessary; the right to parental and state care that is "in the child's best interest"; the right of disabled children to special care and protections; "the right to the highest attainable standard of health and medical and rehabilitation facilities"; the right to a "standard of living adequate for the child's physical, mental, spiritual, moral, and social development"; the right to education; the right to be protected from exploitation and from work "that is likely to be hazardous or to interfere with the child's education or to be harmful to the child's health or physical mental, spiritual, moral or social development" the right to protection from "all forms of sexual exploitation and sexual abuse"; the right to protection "against all other forms of exploitation prejudicial to any aspects of the child's welfare." Relatively few children in the world recently enjoy the fulfillment of all the rights outlined in the Draft.

Child maltreatment

The mistreatment of children has been documented throughout written history. The tale of suffering is interspersed with periods of reform and efforts to improve the plight of children. First, there is the progression from children as property to children as individuals with personal rights. When treated as property, children have been prostituted, sold as slaves, worked to the point of disability or death, or killed at the discretion of their parents/owners. Efforts to move children from the status of property to that of person have resulted in less abusive treatment of children.

Second, there is progress in meeting the challenge of managing reproductivity. Neonaticide, infanticide, and benign neglect of toddlers have all served as consciously or unconsciously sanctioned methods of after the fact family planning, all at high cost in pain and suffering to the children involved and often to parents as well. These methods of limiting reproduction can be replaced by technological and social alternatives including birth control, abortion, adoption, foster care, and foundling homes or orphanages (the first of which was established in Milan in A.D. 787). The moral and pragmatic values of various methods of birth control and especially abortion continue to be debated.

Third, cultures and historical eras have differed in attitudes toward appropriate discipline in the service of education. Beating students seems to have been common in ancient Greece, Rome, and medieval Europe. The Children's Petition of 1669 was the first time in Britain that legal limits were placed on corporal punishment in schools. It had no influence on common practice. In the United States, New Jersey was the first state to ban corporal punishment in the schools in 1867. In 1980, corporal punishment was legal in 40 states although individual cities and towns may have outlawed it. The U.S. Supreme Court has consistently supported schools' use of corporal punishment even over parental protest. A 1986 Department of Education survey revealed over 1,000,000 instances of school paddling during the previous year; 80% of them occurred in the South. Parents and Teachers against Violence in Education, founded in Australia in 1978, organized a U.S. chapter in

1983. They seek to use voluntary citizen influence to further limit the practice of corporal punishment, in all its forms, in schools.

Finally, the history of human religious and ritual practices includes child sacrifice in various forms, burial of newborns in buildings foundations to improve the durability of the structure, uncomfortable ritual practices, painful discipline for religious purposes, and emotionally disturbing depictions of the horrors of being incorrect in religious belief or lax in religious practice. Debates continue concerning the boundaries between legitimate religious freedom and medical, physical, or emotional maltreatment of children.

During the 19th century a number of influences served to increase child suffering. These included child labor in factories and increased numbers of families living in crowded urban poverty. Early attempts at reform were often made from a religious perspective. They were aimed at limiting the public consequences of individual parental failings. A common intervention was the removal of troubled children to foster care, orphanages, or reformatories established to prevent negative moral development. Civil codes and statutes were later developed to manage these activities on behalf of "dependent children.

There was a turning point in 1873, one of a number of times the popular media has played an important role in altering child-related social policy. That year a New York social worker discovered Mary Ellen Wilson, an 8 year old, who had been beaten, chained, and starved by her foster parents. The laws at the time prevented the child's removal from the family until the caregivers had been found guilty. The case was brought to trial largely through the efforts of leaders in the Society for the Prevention of Cruelty to Animals. Little Mary Ellen was removed to an orphanage and her foster mother served a prison term. The next year the Society for the Prevention of Cruelty to Children was founded in New York. Throughout the rest of the century 160 other Societies were formed, and in 1877 they organized nationally under the name of The American Humane Association. For the next 80 years this organization was at the forefront of child abuse treatment and prevention. Initially, the Societies also served in investigative and enforcement capacities. They advocated the legislative reforms that culminated in the establishment of the Juvenile Courts in many cities during the early 1900s. The Juvenile Courts freed the Societies to return to providing voluntary, direct social services for families who were struggling to cope, yet had not caused enough harm to their children to be the focus of court intervention.

The U.S. Children's Bureau, in the Department of Commercial and Labour, was formed in 1912 as a result of the 1909 White House Conference on Children. The Children's Bureau organized the first registration of infant births and deaths, an important step in addressing infant mortality. In 1921, it sponsored the Sheppard-Towner Infancy and Maternity Act, the first major U.S. program to provide nutritional and health care assistance to mothers and infants in need, and it was instrumental in the eventual prohibition of child labor in 1938. The Social Security Act of 1935 marked an even greater expansion of federal involvement, authorizing federal funds to augment state efforts to provide basic needs and medical care for "dependent children."

Advances in pediatric radiology, during the 1940s, had allowed physicians to review full skeletal X-rays with new precision. Subdural hematomas were detected in combination with multiple long bone fractures, damage at the joints, and injuries to cartilage in various stages of heading. After unsuccessful attempts to define some strange new bone disease, the reality of inflicted injury, perpetrated by caregivers, could not be overlooked. In 1946, John Caffey named the phenomenon the "parent-infant traumatic syndrome" (PITS). Relatively little attention was paid to this syndrome at the time. If one were to ignore the fields of History, Anthropology, and Social Work, and focus solely on the Psychological and Medical literature in the United States, it might appear that child abuse began in the 1960s. Attention from the medical profession, extensively covered by the popular media, propelled physical child abuse into the national spotlight in 1962.

In 1962, Henry Kempe and his colleagues brought extensive media and professional attention to physical child abuse by coining the term "battered child syndrome" in an American Association of Pediatrics symposium and in a related article in the Journal of the American Medical Association. There followed a tremendous professional and public response to the depiction of serious injuries, even death, perpetrated by the very individuals responsible for the children's care. In 1963, the Children's Bureau produced guidelines for establishing state-level child abuse reporting laws. The laws required physicians and professionals in direct contact with children to report known cases of abuse or neglect to designated state agencies. Failure to report known cases carried the risk of fines and imprisonment. To offset mandated reporters' concerns about retribution from reported individuals, the reporting statutes included immunity from charges of libel.

Between 1963 and 1967, all states enacted legislation mandating physicians and many other child professionals to report cases of child abuse. The reporting process plus extensive media education efforts were responsible for an explosion of official reports. Designated agencies were hard pressed to investigate, process, and to serve the avalanche of cases produced by the new policies. Funding had to be provided and then increased to meet the need for services created by the reports.

The Courts have served as arbiters in cases where unwilling parents or children face coercive intervention due to charges of child abuse and neglect. Legal professionals work to ensure due process for accused perpetrators, and to develop evidence gathering and court procedures appropriate for young children. Representation for the children, Guardians ad Litem give legal voice to the child's unique perspective. Innovations in evidence and procedure, such as videotaped child testimony and exceptions to nearsay rule, have been developed to prevent further injury to the child at the hands of the legal processes designed to ensure fair hearing to alleged perpetrators. Research to document these effects is under way. In the midst of this tremendous expansion of the public role in evaluating child-rearing quality, advocates have argued for extreme caution in overriding parental rights, urging that coercive intervention be used in only the most severe situations. They have argued that a mandated report to an inadequate overwhelmed, underfunded child protective agency, resulting in a poorly managed intervention with open-ended separations of children from their families, can produce its own unacceptable harms.

Protective service workers face some of he most difficult demands imaginable. The work is emotionally draining and annual staff turnover rates of 85% are not uncommon. State, federal, and private funding levels determine the degree to which effective programs can be implemented and maintained. The field continues to evolve and improve in investigation, communication with families including clearly delineated treatment plans, and implementing an expanding range of effective case management, treatment, and prevention services. Despite these efforts, critics have come forth to argue that current social policy goes too far to protect children from potential maltreatment and fails to adequately protect adults from false accusations of abuse and neglect. A movement has emerged to substantially limit child protection efforts. Alleged perpetrators of abuse who felt they had been damaged by false reports and the investigatory processes that ensued have organized support and advocacy groups such as VOCAL, Victims of Child Abuse Reporting Laws, founded in 1984. They describe stigma, financial loss incurred in long legal battles, and damage to family relationships. They opposed the acceptance of anonymous reports and argued the rapid expungement of records and reports not substantiated after investigation.

Throughout the first half of the 20th century, state and federal governments passed legislation aimed at eliminating child suffering caused by societal level neglect. In 1974, one hundred years after Mary Ellen Wilson inspired the founding of New York's society for the prevention of Cruelty to Children, the U.S. Congress acknowledged the need for federal involvement by passing The Child Abuse Prevention and Treatment Act. In it child abuse and neglect were defined as "the physical or mental injury, sexual abuse or exploitation, negligent treatment, or maltreatment of a child by a person who is responsible for the child's welfare under circumstances which indicate that the child's health or welfare is harmed or threatened thereby, as determined in accordance with regulations prescribed by the Secretary." Person responsible for the child's welfare includes "any employee of a residential facility; and any staff person providing out-of-home care." Sexual abuse is defined as "the employment, use, persuation, inducement, enticement or coercion of any child to engage in or assist any other person to engage in, any sexually explicit conduct or simulation of such conduct: or the rape, molestation, prostitution or other form of sexual exploitation of children, or incest with children. "The law authorized the establishment of the National Center on Child Abuse and Neglect (NCCAN) which (1) coordinates studies of the prevalence of child abuse; (2) contracts research on causes, identification, treatment, and prevention of child abuse and neglect; (3) funds demonstration projects to support treatment and prevention effort; and (4) provides a clearinghouse to disseminate information.

In the early 1980s, the Regan administration considered eliminating the federal role in child abuse. A National Child Abuse coalition formed to urge Congress to continue federal involvement. Federal involvement did continue and in 1984 the law was amended to expand the definition of maltreatment.

Technological advances in the care of very small, impaired newborns were accompanied by new medical and ethical dilemmas. In 1984, the Child Abuse Prevention and Treatment Act was amended to include the following definition of a new form of child abuse.

> "withholding of medically indicated treatment" means the failure to respond to the infant life-threatening conditions by providing treatment (including appropriate nutrition, hydration and medication) that in the treating physician's or physicians' reasonable medical judgment will be most likely to be effective in ameliorating or correcting all such conditions. The term does not include the failure to provide treatment (other than appropriate nutrition, hydration or medication) to an infant when in the treating physician's or physicians' reasonable medical judgment (A) the infant is chronically and irreversibly comatose; (B)

> the provision of such treatment would merely prolong dying, not be effective in ameliorating or correcting all of the infant's life-threatening conditions, or otherwise be futile in terms of the survival of the infant; or (C) the provision of such treatment would be virtually futile in terms of the survival of the infant and the treatment itself under such circumstances would be inhumane.

Interpreting this law is an ongoing challenge and, as yet, no parents have been punished for withholding extraordinary care.

Some pregnant women have been charged with child abuse in response to their behavioral choices during pregnancy, especially, illegal drug use. A few have been imprisoned in an effort to protect their features. This approach has been strongly criticized. While considerable evidence implicates prenatal smoking and alcohol use as detrimental to the infant outcome, especially for their contribution to low birth weight, the long-term effects of prenatal illegal drug exposure have yet to be established. Illegal drug use is often accompanied by a variety of environmental risk factors, such as poverty, stress, poor nutrition, and the legal use of tobacco and alcohol. A grave concern is that reporting in these cases would deter women with substance problems from obtaining the early and consistent prenatal care they and their babies need. Balancing the rights of parents and their offspring and defining the division between individual and societal responsibility continue to challenge our best thinking in clinical practice and public policy.

The number of sexual abuse cases increased several-fold from 1977 to the early 1980s, as the topic of sexual abuse made a significant move from secrecy into the domain of public discourse. In March of 1984, allegations of sexual abuse of hundreds of pre-schoolers, involving ritualistic abuse, were made against teachers and staff and the McMartin Preschool in southern California. The case received tremendous media coverage for years, becoming the most expensive trial in U.S. history before ending with acquittals for all alleged perpetrators. Allegations in other child care settings followed. The threat of sexual abuse had come closer to the thousands of parents using out-of-home child care.

New research revealed the importance of adolescent perpetrators. Over 50% of molested boys and 15-20% of sexually abused girls had adolescent perpetrators. The number of specialized treatment programs for adolescent offenders grew from 20 in 1982 to 520 in 1988.

Ritualistic abuse, one of the most secretive of all forms of abuse, became the focus of new attention. The Los Angeles-based Resource and Education Network on Ritualistic Abuse estimates that 1 to 5% of all sex abuse cases involve ritual abuse. In a 1988 review of sexual abuse reports in daycare settings, David Finkelhor reported 13% of the cases to be ritualistic in nature. Three types of ritualistic abuse were observed, (1) cult-based where the sexual abuse was in the service of a larger goal, (2) pseudo-ritualistic cases where the sexual experience was really the goal, and (3) psychopathological where the perpetrator was clearly experiencing a psychiatric disorder. Clearly all the aforementioned types of maltreatment carry with them profound emotional effects. In the mid 1980s, James Garbarino pioneered efforts to define independent forms of emotional abuse and neglect. By 1991 an entire issue of the journal Development and psychopathology was devoted to a state of the art review of legal, clinical, research, and social policy perspectives concerning psychological maltreatment.

Current classifications include caregiver behavior which is: rejecting, degrading, terracing, isolating, missocialising, exploiting, or denying of emotional responsiveness. Another approach to definition emphasizes the documentable emotional and psychological effects upon the children including low self-esteem, fearfulness, anxiety, depression, and excessive aggression toward self or others.

The American humane Association tracked the number of U.S. child maltreatment reports from 1976, when 669,000 reports were estimated, through 1986, when over two million reports were recorded. This represents a 212% increase in a decade. In 1990, when the National Center for Child Abuse and Neglect's newly established tracking system made its first estimate, 2.7 million children were named in 1.7 million child abuse and neglect reports. Thus, in 1976 an estimated 1% of the U.S. population under the age of 18 years was reported as maltreated. In 1990 the estimate was closer to 3%. There is generally agreement that the number of reports considerably underestimates the rule instances of maltreatment. Neglect was the most common charge (45%). Twenty-five percent of the cases were reported for physical abuse, 15% for sexual abuse, and 6% for emotional mistreatment. The few remaining cases could not be classified into these categories. Children often experience multiple types of maltreatment. Boys and girls were reported at the same rates except for sexual abuse where 85% of the reports were on female victims. Blacks and whites were reported a similar rates but more whites were reported for physical and sexual abuse while more blacks were reported for neglect.

In 1990, an estimated 42% of reported cases were substantiated after investigation. Lack of substantiation does not necessarily mean the child named in the report did not experience maltreatment. Available evidence may not have been sufficient for a judgment to have been made. Intentional false charges of maltreatment are not common. These may involve custody disputes or disputes between neighbors in which the reporting mechanism is used as a means of harassment. Approximately 2 to 10% of custody disputes include changes of sexual mistreatment of the contested child.

A much greater problem than false reports is that of true cases of maltreatment which go unreported. Research in the area indicates two-thirds of child abuse and neglect cases known to mandated professionals go unreported. There are many barriers to reporting; lack of certainty, embarrassment, fear of retaliation, and fear that the reporting and subsequent intervention may bring stigma and cause more harm than good. Therapists and others in a helping role sometimes believe their continued work with the family would do more good than making the report.

The National Center of Child Abuse and Neglect has produced two national scale incidence studies, one in 1980 and a follow up in 1986. They employed innovative methods to deal with the problem of professional underreporting. In addition to reported cases, the researchers counted cases known to relevant professionals whether or not they had been reported. Strict confidentiality made this technique possible. In the 1986 study, only 44% of the cases serious enough to meet study criteria had been reported and assessed in as in need of protective services.

Cases resulting in demonstrable harm increased by 66% between 1980 and 1986. Abuse increased more than neglect. Physical abuse went up by 58% and sexual abuse tripled. The percentage of fatal or serious injuries did not increase, but moderate injuries did. Levels of neglect and emotional abuse did not rise significantly between the two studies.

Demographics of known Maltreatment

Sixty-three percent of known cases were neglect, with boys and girls experiencing similar rates. Girls were more likely to experience abuse than boys (13.1 cases per 100 children versus 8.4 cases per 1000, respectively). The girls' rate of sexual abuse was four times the boys rate. Boys were twice as likely as girls to have been emotionally abused. Babies under the age of 2 were less likely to have experienced abuse but when they did, the consequences were more likely to be fatal. Older children were at greater risk for all kinds of abuse and to have a moderate injury as a result.

Children from iarger families, defined as four or more children, were more likely to experience maltreatment than children from homes with fewer children. This was especially true for neglect, where children from larger families were more than twice as likely to be neglected as children from smaller families. Type and severity of maltreatment were similar for urban and rural countries in the study. Rates of known maltreatment did not differ significantly by child's race. This finding stands in contrast to finding based on reported cases in which minorities are reported at a rate greater than that expected given their proportion of the population.

Poverty was an important correlate of abuse and neglect. Overall maltreatment rates for children with family incomes of less than $15,000 were more almost seven times as great as rates for children with family incomes above $15,000 The connection between low family income and the onset of abuse is strongest for infants and young children. Low income does not seem to be as important as a risk factor for physical abuse beginning in adolescence or for sexual abuse.

Physical abuse

When individuals are asked in confidence to report acts of violence they have perpetrated, estimates of the prevalence of child abuse are considerably higher than estimates derived from official reports or counts of causes known to professionals. In Murray Straus and Richard Gelles' national representative study of family violence conducted in 1985, parents reported an annual rate of at least one instance of serious abuse for 3% of the boys and 2% of the girls. Blue-collar parents reported twice as much abuse as white-collar workers.

Sexual abuse

Estimates of sexual abuse over the full span of childhood range from 9 to 52% for females and from 3 to 9% for males. The best estimate of female incest comes from a random sample of 930 San Francisco women. Seventeen percent of women who had spent a major part of childhood with a stepfather were molested by them, compared to 2% father-daughter incest among women reared by their biological fathers. One-tenth of a percent of the cases involved a biological mother as perpetrator and there were no causes of incest perpetrated by step-mothers. There is added stigma for males who have been sexually abused so the current estimate of 5 to 15% of male victims may be an underestimate. The first national conference on male survivors was held in 1988. Increased awareness of the issue may improve our understanding of its pervasiveness.

In Kempe's "syndrome" of child abuse, etiological emphasis was on parental psychopathology and personality disorder frequently passed on from parent to child, which would result in abusive behavior under conditions of increased stress. This psychiatric model dominated research in the 1960s. In the 1970s, sociologists countered that such a model ignored the ways in which maltreating parents were themselves victims of greate forces. They supported this "sociological model" wit reviews of reported abuse causes which documented th correlation between child abuse and chronic poverty an unemployment, shrinking labor markets, dysfunctiona family processes, and other forms of social stress.

Also during the 1970, causal models i developmental psychological theory were expanded i two directions beyond main effects parental influenc models to include child and environmental contributo to child outcomes. Children's effects on their caregive were added to theories about the origins of chil personality and mental health characteristics. Studie began to reveal child characteristics that were associate with increased risk of maltreatment. In addition, Uri Bronfenbrenner's "ecological theory of chil development" influenced child maltreatment theory wit its emphasis upon layers of causal influence, includin individual family, neighborhood, and cultur characteristics. James Garbarino first applied these idea in 1976 in an integrated "ecological perspective" on chil maltreatment. Jay Belsky's Ecology of Child Maltreatme published ion 1981 described causal influences at fo levels: the individual parent psychology, family syster proximal environmental context, and overall cultur levels.

In 1981, Dante Cicchetti draw on the "organization perspective" of development and principles fro developmental psychopathology in another integrati model of child maltreatment. He described enduring ar temporary characteristics in the parent, child, an environmental domains that continuously transact influence the quality of caregiving and in extreme cas lead to child maltreatment. He argued that an adequa model had to include both risk and protective factors order to effectively account for maltreatment's occurrence. In the real world maltreatment cannot be predicted by simply adding up the negatives.

High levels of income and valuable social resources act as buffers to stress. Additional protective factors have been identified such as having a warm relationship with a capable adult during childhood, good learning and problem solving skills, and appealing interpersonal or physical attributes. Efforts continue to identify additional protective factors. The bulk of studies accomplished to date have emphasized negative influences or risk factors for maltreatment.

Parent characteristics

Parents of physically abused children tend to be younger at the birth of their first child, unmarried, and relatively less educated than nonabusive parents. Physically abusive parents have been shown to have some distinct biological characteristics such as greater autonomic reactivity (as measured by skin conductance and respiration rates) to children's emotional expressions. They report experiencing both positive and negative social interactions with children as more aversive and stressful than nonabusive parents. Maltreatment parents have more health problems and handicapping conditions. Some of these illness may have psychological origins.

Retardation and lack of information may be related to neglect: however, deficient general intelligence does not seem to be a risk factor for physical abuse. There is evidence for deficiencies in specific abstract reasoning abilities related to child management, coping and problem solving, and limited skills in providing structure and discipline. Abusive parents exhibit overly high expectations and they tend to get caught up in ever escalating, coercive cycles of discipline and negative child reaction. Neglecting parents are characterized more b unresponsiveness and lack of availability. Low sel esteem, low ego strength and resiliency, and externa locus-of-control have been found to be characteristic c abuse and neglect. Physically abusive parents tend t have negative perceptions of their children, attributin more behavior problems to them than independen observers see. In addition, they impute intentionality t their children's misbehavior.

Many abusive parents, especially perpetrators o emotional and sexual abuse, experienced maltreatment a the hands of their own parents. It is a major risk factor However, the "cycle of abuse" is far from inevitable Many maltreated individuals become adequate nonmaltreating parents. The current estimate is 33% o physically abused children repeat the abuse with thei own children. Rates of intergenerational transmission o psychological maltreatment and sexual abuse may be somewhat higher.

Studies indicate that the parents who do not repea the cycle are characterized as having very clear memories of the mistreatment they suffered accompanied by strong emotional responses to it. They are more likely to have supportive interpersonal relationships and the opportunity to confide in at least one other person. As children they were likely to have established a warm and trusting relationship with at least one adult. The marital relationships of physically abusive parents frequently are marked with conflict, especially violent conflict. Abusive family interactions are more negative and less positive than comparisons. Maltreating parents have less supportive social networks beyond their families. Neglecting parents are more likely to be isolated while abusive parents' networks tend to consist of short-term, conflictual relationships.

Despite the early emphasis on parental psychopathology, less than 10% of abusive parents have diagnosable psychological disorders as defined by the American Psychiatric Association standards. Included within the 10% are cases of (a) Munchausen syndrome by proxy, a rare thought and behavioral disorder, named after a famous 28th century German teller of tall tales, in which an adult fabricates a history of illnesses and symptoms for his child, often directly inducing symptoms in the child thorough poisoning or other means in order to experience the attention of the medical response to the child's disorder. The child is subjected to unnecessary tests, hospitalizations, medications and treatments. (b) Antisocial personality disorder, a disorder in which the individual has consistent difficulty operating within the social norms for conflict resolution, honesty and property rights, work, and family responsibility. Child abuse and neglect are defining characteristics. (c) Postpartum psychosis, a rare disorder with a prevalence of one or two cases per thousand births, in which delusions, distorted thinking, and mood states can result in loss of control and harm to the child or the mother. (d) Schizophrenia and manic depression, disorders which include periods during which contact with reality and decision making are diminished. During such times an individual who does not have buffering resources to take over child responsibilities may be neglectful of a child's needs. Distorted thinking and feeling states can be disturbing. These inadvertent consequences of the disorders are a greater risk to children than are direct assaults which are relatively rare.

Abuse and dependence upon alcohol, and illegal drugs are important risk factors for maltreatment. Depression and dysthymia, mood disorders, are characterized by persistent low mood or irritability accompanied by problems with sleep and eating, and disruption in the ability to fulfill role functions such as child management. Depression is particularly common among neglecting parents.

Physical abuses are characterized by difficulties with impulse control and constructive channeling of angry and frustrated emotions more than by full scale psychopathological disorders. They are relatively isolated from other individuals and community agencies which could assist. For sexual offenders the isolation from age-appropriate contacts, combined with a sexual attraction to young children leads to an increase in the probability that the sexual desires will be acted upon.

Child characteristics

Children are not responsible for their own mistreatment. However, there are child characteristics which are associated with increased probability of maltreatment. Some child characteristics are associated with increased child care demands. Prematurity and low birth weight, colic, illness, accidents, and physical and behavioral handicapping conditions all make child care more difficult. Temperamental characteristics such as irritability, persistence, and high activity, especially in combination with maternal depression of high levels of environmental stress, also increase the risk of physical maltreatment.

Mentally retarded individuals are more are risk for maltreatment, especially sexual abuse, than their nonretarded peers. They are viewed as easier targets by perpetrators, and they often spend at least some of their lives in institutional care by nonparental adults. They may not have adequate abilities to defend themselves or report wrongdoing. A recent NCCAN report gave 83% as the estimated lifetime prevalence of at least one instance of some form of sexual abuse in this group

Aspects of child appearance may increase the probability of maltreatment. Some children remind their parent of another disliked individual. Maltreatment can be an unintended result of the resemblance. Careful measurements of the facial characteristics of physically abused and control children have revealed that the physically abused children as a group have facial dimensions more characteristic of older children. This could contribute in subtle ways to inappropriate caregiver expectations.

Numerous studies have documented behavior problems in maltreated children, both within the family and with peers. Some of these studies were based upon parent reports and thus were due to negative parental attributions toward a disfavored child. Teachers and independent observers have also reported elevated levels of behavior problems. Whether or not these problems preceded the maltreatment or are the results of maltreatment, they can contribute to subsequent acts of maltreatment.

Being a stepchild is a risk for maltreatment. Being male is associated with increased risk for physical abuse, and by far most sexual abuse victims are female. Female children continue to be at risk for infanticide or poor care in societies where females are valued less.

Certain developmental phases are harder for parents to cope with than others. The helplessness of infancy is a delight for some parents and a drain for others. Toddlerhood, in which the normal healthy individual experiments with his or her own autonomy, becoming willful and at times contrary, is also the developmental phase during which toilet training is accomplished. This phase can tap the resources of the most patient parent, and it is a high-risk time for toddlers who are in the care of step-parents or whose parents suffer impulse control problems or severe stress levels.

Adolescence is another developmental transition generally considered to be a challenge to the family system. The family has to make room for a new member who has new physical, cognitive, and sexual capacities, is increasingly costly to support, and is increasingly moved by outside influences. The potential for conflict is great. Adolescents experience proportionally more abuse than younger children, especially psychological and sexual abuse. At least half of known abused adolescents were not maltreated during their childhood years, but began to experience abuse during adolescence. Step-parents are even more likely to be part of adolescent onset abuse than is the case for younger children. The etiology of adolescent onset maltreatment differs from the etiology of child onset maltreatment. Poverty and environmental stress are not as important. Parents who begin to maltreat during adolescence are less likely to have a history of maltreatment in their own childhood.

By comparing census tract data with maltreatment report data, James Garbarino found a number of socio-demographic characteristics that characteristics that characterize neighborhoods with high levels of abuse and neglect reports. They are: (1) a high percentage of families living below the poverty level, (2) high unemployment, (3) a high percentage of female headed households, (4) overcrowded housing, (5) a large proportion of racial minorities, (6) low levels of education, (7) frequent moves, and (8) a low percentage of affluent residents. In addition, community leaders describe neighborhoods with particularly high rates of maltreatment as "socially impoverished" as well. They lack a sense of unity. Professional networking is weaker and residents experience less positive neighboring and more stressful day to day interactions.

Some child-related institutional settings have elevated rates of maltreatment. In a 1988 review of reported cases of sexual abuse in child care settings, David Finkelhor discovered that the risk for sexual abuse was lower in day care settings than in a child's own household. The risk was lowest in centers with many teachers and children and in centers where parent were free to come and go easily. forty percent of these perpetrators were female and only 8% of the perpetrators had been arrested previously for sexual abuse.

In 1990, at least 1200 American children died as the result of maltreatment. Twenty-five percent of them were active protective service cases at time of death. Deaths were not distributed uniformly but clustered around the youngest and oldest ages. As with other child abuse estimates this is an underestimate it is, no one know just how great an underestimate it is. No standard protocol exists to differentiate deaths caused by natural illness, accident, or maltreatment.

Violent physical acts often produce harm, Other types of maltreatment can also have physical consequences. Neglect produces inadequate growth patterns, infections, diseases, and accidental injuries due to poor supervision. Sexual abuse is often discovered when a child presents with general disease or injuries to the sexual organs. Emotional mistreatment can also produce physical sequelae. In psychosocial dwarfism or failure to thrive, inadequate caloric intake combines with inadequate parental attention or environmental stresses to produce children below the fifth percentile in size. Upon discovery and hospitalization these children's growth rates rapidly improve. Early studies of maltreatment's consequences to the children lacked control groups, and were based upon clinical judgment rather than systematic and objective observation. Recent studies have employed improved methods and have been theoretically guided. As in other areas of child abuse work assessments of the effects of maltreatment are underestimates. The maltreated children observed in outcome studies have almost all received some intervention from reporting and investigation to extensive individual and family therapy. Ethical standards of research preclude studying maltreated children who have not been afforded whatever level of services are available in their committees, therefore the consequences of maltreatment reported are those that remain after at least some degree of professional intervention, the duration and quality of which are rarely specified.

Commonsense would suggest and research, especially that summarized by Leory Pelton, has confirmed that poverty has profound negative effects on child development. Since a disproportionate number of maltreated children live in poverty, researchers examining the developmental consequences of maltreatment have had to employ demographically matched comparison groups in order to discover maltreatment's unique contributions to negative outcome. Longitudinal studies have demonstrated convincingly that maltreatment does have psychosocial consequences beyond those expected as the result of an upbringing on poverty. Not every abused child experiences these negative effects. The research is not a definite prediction for any one maltreated individual. Group studies can only reveal an increased probability of negative outcome. Buffering and protective factors do exist and they allow some maltreated children to emerge as relatively well adjusted. Prospective studies have documented progressively poor performance on IQ tests among maltreated youngsters and increasing learning disabilities. Neglect and psychological unavailability are particularly detrimental to intellectual development. Maltreatment alters other aspects of cognition as well, altering the very way the victims perceive the world, producing hypervigilence and heightened responsiveness to perceived danger in their surroundings.

Maltreated infants are very likely to develop insecure or "disorganized/disoriented" attachment relationships with their caregivers. An insecure attachment makes successful resolution of subsequent developmental challenges more difficult, e.g., successful negotiation of peer relationships and the ability to relate effectively with care providers and teachers. Maltreated children show language delays, especially in the ways they talk about experiences beyond the here and now and express their inner states and feelings.

Behaviour problems

Maltreated children are described as having more behavior problems than their nonmaltreated peers by parent reports, teacher reports, and objective observation. Parents in maltreating families over report behavior problems, perhaps as a rationalizations for the abuse. Teacher reports and direct observations have shown abused children to be more physically aggressive and verbally abusive to others, both adults and peers.

Studies of children's friendship formation indicate that children who approach new friends with inappropriate aggression tend to be not just ignored but also rejected by those peers. These difficulties, once established, become stable, leading to adjustment problems and isolation in adulthood.

Most maltreated children do not become delinquent and an even smaller number of them advance to criminality. Looking in the other direction we find that juvenile delinquents report much higher rates of abuse and neglect than nondelinquents. Maltreatment contributes to delinquency in a number of ways. It disrupts relationship formation, making the process frustrating and unsatisfying for many children. It sets up a harsh and unfair world view, within which deviant actions and breaking social rules for immediate gain make some sense. Physically abused children are at risk to repeat the aggression. Many runaways leave home to escape maltreatment, especially physical and sexual abuse. Other children's departures from home are involuntary. They are rejected by parents no longer willing to offer even minimal care. Once on the street the probability of illegal involvement, especially prostitution, increases.

Elevated levels of anxiety and depression among maltreated children have been reported during the childhood years. The depression continues for many children and for others produces its own level of suffering and in addition it sets the stage for subsequent those of parenting. Children who have experienced severe severe violence or sexual abuse may show the signs of post-traumatic stress disorder (PTSD), including pervasive sense of fear, sleep disorders, flashbacks, and reenactments are similar to the experiences of victimisation. Some victims of sexual abuse do not experience PTSD because the abuse itself was not a "sudden trauma," but more of a situation, climate, or context. Very young children may have been slowly "groomed" or set up for the abuse in such a way as to reduce the elements of sudden trauma. For these children the impact of their misuse unfolds over a number of years as they become aware of their exploitation.

Dissociative disorders represent some from of mental escape from painful/traumatic experiences. In dissociation certain perceptions and memories are separated from affect, compartmentalized out of the mainstream of psycho-life. These defenses may save the individual from the full immediate impact of a traumatic experience; however, they do so at a price. The dissociation delays or prevents the working through of the experience, producing feelings of confusion and helplessness and, in extreme cases, a fragmented or "multiple personality." This very severe disorder entails a disruption of memory and identity. Two or more personalities, each of which has distinct characteristics and a separate memory of a life history, alternative control of the body. The different ranges of emotions. The person is not usually out of touch with reality but has periods of amnesia or blackouts and becomes increasingly maladjusted over time. Child victims who have a biopsychological predisposition to dissociate come to use this ability in the context of unpredictable extreme trauma at the hands of a person who is at other times a nurturing caregiver. Histories of extensive maltreatment, usually physical or sexual, are present in almost all known cases of multiple personality disorder. Most of the abuse is sexual.

Sexually and physically abused individuals are at greater risk for later abuse and dependence of alcohol and drugs. Victims of sexual abuse, both male and female, often exhibit stress-related symptoms at the time of the abuse or its disclosure including: fear, anxiety, sleep disturbances, depression, aggression, and inappropriate sexual behavior such as explicit words or acts which reveal abnormal sexual knowledge. Long term effects include anxiety, depression or dysthymia, feelings of isolation and stigma, poor self-esteem, and problems in trusting and in establishing satisfying sexual relationships. In some cases these difficulties emerge years after the abuse, after seemingly effective adjustment in the intervening years. Both male and female victims have an increased risk of experiencing sexual dysfunction; however, there is more risk that male victims will become perpetrators of sexual abuse in the next generation.

In addition to the consequences of maltreatment which are directly felt by the victims over the years, is another set of consequences which serve to set up the same risk conditions such as poverty and disrupted family relationships that caused the maltreatment in the first place. A 1989 study of two groups of very poor women (homeless vs those with housing) revealed no difference between the groups concerning history of physical and sexual abuse. Approximately 86% of both groups had been maltreated.

Treatment to stop current abuse

Treatment, or efforts to prevent the recourse of maltreatment once it has already occurred, is also called "tertiary prevention." Different etiological theories and developmental approaches to parenting guide approaches to treatment.

Specific behavioral therapies derived from learning theory focus on family learning histories and the retraining of effective parenting skills. In cases of physical abuse, education concerning escalating coercive patterns of conflict and sound disciplinary alternatives are offered. In addition, self-control skills, especially those directed at anger control, have been shown to be effective in equipping formerly abusive parents with skills to recognize potential conflicts situations, contain their anger through deep breathing or other relaxation techniques, and choose different behavioral responses.

The principles of classical conditioning have been employed in the treatment of sex abuse offenders. The goal in these programs is to override sexual responsiveness patterns and to redirect them to more appropriate targets. Broadly defined parent training approaches are designed to improve parents' coping repertoires especially in the context of child management.

For neglectful parents, behavioral interventions are aimed at increasing the problem solving, organization, and social interactional skills in order to support independence and to develop and maintain support systems in the future.

Therapies within this framework have as their goal the reworking of existing mental models of relationships in order to build more effective ones, either with an individual therapist or in supportive group work. Major treatment goals are to reduce the profound loneliness and isolation, to facilitate a more positive self-evaluation, to provide a hearing for feelings about the individual's relationship with her child, and to offer concrete suggestions on new ways to interact. The comfort, acceptance, and support that develop within the therapeutic relationship become the model for the parent's interaction with her child and family.

Treatments focused on the value of social support include Parents Anonymous for physical abuse and Parents United which addresses sexual abuse. Both these organizations employ many self-help principles, Parents United offers specialized groups for perpetrators, spouses, victims, and siblings, acknowledging that their feelings and perspectives differ.

Integrative, ecological theories of abuse lead to multifaceted approaches such as family preservation. This is an intense, comprehensive involvement which begins when a family is in crisis. It continues for 6 weeks or so. A counselor, with a case load of only one or two other families, is on call 24 hours a day. Intervention is tailored to address the strengths and weaknesses of each family, at the individual, family, and environmental levels. Help in obtaining basic resources such as food, housing, transportation, and medical and legal services is central. The goal is to address the real needs of the family to determine if they can provide adequate care. If they cannot make progress with this intense support, then alternative placements for the child are considered.

The most extensively evaluated treatment approach for abuse and neglect is Project 12-Ways. It, too, is a comprehensive approach which addresses the many sources of difficulty in maltreating families. Treatment includes training in stress reduction, self-control, constructive uses of leisure time, child development basics, and job search strategies. Integration with local substance abuse treatment and employment resources are included. The unique needs of single parents are also addressed.

In its own way the criminal justice system offers an important approach to treatment. Some perpetrators of severe harm are removed from the home through a restraining order or removed from the community through imprisonment. Such action reinforces societal values of nonviolence and the special protection requirements of young children. In less dangerous situations the courts are moving toward alternative sentencing especially treatment which allows a perpetrator to remain in the community and provide support for his or her family. Students of spouse maltreatment have advocated the use of criminal charges and often imprisonment for individuals judged guilty of battering their spouses Child advocates generally have urged a less criminal approach to addressing child maltreatment. Recognizing that spouse and child abuse often occur in the same households, what is needed is a more comprehensive approach to treating family violence in its different forms. Art therapy, imagery, body work, play therapy, individual therapies, and group therapies are employed to reduce the suffering and reduce future negative outcomes among victims. Treatment goals include assisting clients in regaining a sense of control over their lives, improving the sense of self-worth, and teaching new skills for interpersonal relationships. Support groups for survivors work to reduce the sense of loneliness and "damaged goods" feelings that are often a part of the victim experience.

Prevention of maltreatment

Treatment approaches are time intensive and costly. It takes tremendous effort to undo the variety of damage caused by child maltreatment. Much of it cannot be undone. All agree it would be better to prevent maltreatment before it happens. In 1980, few prevention programs received NCCAN funding. By 1990, 50% of NCCAN funding went to prevention. Contributions for preventive programs from individuals and corporations continue to increase as well. Effective new funding approaches combine private and public resources. Between 1980 and 1990 forty-nine states established "Children's Trust Funds," which collectively spent 28 million dollars on prevention programs. The movies come from small fees added to marriage or other licenses and check off boxes on state income tax forms. Federal dollars matched those collected by the states. There has been substantial growth in private efforts to prevent abuse and neglect. Corporations, the media, and private organizations have mounted numerous prevention programs.

Secondary prevention

Two levels of prevention are aimed at parents who have not yet maltreated. Secondary prevention refers to efforts aimed at identified high-risk populations, e.g., families living in poverty, single parents, parents dealings with unexpected or unwanted pregnancies, parents with impulse control problems, depression, or substance abuse, and families in economic or emotional crisis. Specific approaches include: helplines and hotlines for parents in stress; other forms of crisis support such as crisis nurseries in hospitals; ongoing family support services such as assistance with day care, medical care etc.; and self-help support groups such as Parents Anonymous which provide social support and some specific behavioural management techniques to address anger that threatens to go out of control.

Home health services such as early and regular contact with visiting nurses after the birth of a child have been shown to reduce subsequent child abuse and neglect reports during infancy. Evaluation research of such a program designed by David Olds and his colleagues, also revealed enhanced parenting skills such as the expression of affection and providing structure and positive discipline. Visited mothers, especially the youngest, single teen mothers, showed more successful adjustment and satisfaction with their infants than did mothers in a matched control group. In follow-up assessments the visited mothers were the focus of fewer child abuse and neglect reports were less restrictive and punishing with their children and provided more appropriate play materials than similar mothers who had not participated in the program. Babies in the intervention group tended to have higher developmental quotients than the comparison babies and participating mothers waited longer to have their next child than mothers who had not been visited.

Treating victimized children is another approach to secondary prevention. Providing an opportunity to acknowledge past suffering, teaching effective interpersonal problem sylvan and planning strategies and offering situations in which abused and neglected children can increase their self-esteem can serve to reduce the probability of maltreatment in the next generation. Considerable research has been directed at refining methods of assessing adults child abuse potential in order that direct prevention services could be directed to the individuals in most need.

Primary prevention includes activities that exert a positive influence on the whole system, thereby increasing healthy family functioning and eliminating some of the risk conditions that contribute to maltreatment. Included in the scope of primary prevention are; policies that improve educational and employment opportunities for parent; the promotion of family planning in order to avoid unwanted births or births that are too closely spaced; prenatal care for pregnant women in order to reduce the number of premature and low birth weight babies; policies which support new parents during the parental period, such as "rooming in" during the hospital stay, and parental leave with job security; early education interventions such as Head Start with its comprehensive approach to services including parent education and mental health components; economic improvements such as reduction of unemployment through job training programs and placement services efforts to reduce the overall level of violence in the society such as the promotion of violence-free problem solving in general, alternatives to corporal punishment in schools and in homes.

A growing number of preventive efforts, especially those designed to reduce sexual abuse; are now focused on training potential victims to stop or report the abuse. School-based curricula, plays and films," and describe self-protection approaches. They warn children that secrets that make them feel bad are not to be kept. They urge children to seek help from an adult they trust and to persist if they are not believed, urging them to tell and tell again until they find an adult who does hear what they are saying. Evaluation studies of these efforts reveal limited effectiveness in preventing victimization especially among preschoolers who present particular challenges to the creators of these programs. The developmental needs of these young potential victims have not yet been adequately met. Some would argue that we need to direct more prevention efforts toward potential abusers, attacking their misconceptions about the potential for harm their actions entail.

Explicit public education campaigns describe child maltreatment, stressing that it is preventable and treatable. The National Committee for the Prevention of Child Abuse, directed since 1972 by Anne Cohn Donnelly, has produced some of the most extensive public education campaigns. They have used television spots, print, and brief pamphlets directed at parents and children.

6

Status of Woman

Women's work is similarly invisible in providing sustenance and creating wealth for basic needs. Their work in the forest, the field and the river creates sustenance in quiet but essential ways. Every woman in every house in every village of rural India works invisibly to provide the stuff of life to nature and people. It is this invisible work that is linked to nature and needs, which conserves nature through maintaining ecological cycles, and conserves human life through satisfying the basic needs of food, nutrition and water. It is this essential work that is destroyed and dispensed with by maldevelopment: the maintenance of ecological cycles has no place in a political economy of commodity and cash flows.

The existence of the feminine principle is linked with diversity and sharing. Its destruction through homogenization and privatization leads to the destruction of diversity and of the commons. The sustenance economy is based on a creative and organic nature, on local knowledge, on locally recycled inputs that maintain the integrity of nature, on local consumption for local needs, and on the marketing of surplus beyond the imperatives of equity and ecology. The commodity and cash economy destroys natural cycles and reduces nature to raw materials and commodities. It creates the need for purchase and sale to centralized inputs and commodity markets. When production is specialized and for export, surplus becomes a myth. There is only indebtedness, of peoples and nations. The debt trap is part of global commodity production and gale which destroys nurturing nature and nurturing economies in the name of development.

Sustenance, in the final analysis, is built on the continued capacity of nature to renew its forests, fields and rivers. These resource systems are intrinsically linked in life-producing and life-conserving cultures, and it is in managing the integrity of ecological cycles in forestry and agriculture that women's productivity has been most developed and evolved. Women transfer fertility from the forests to the field and to animals. They transfer animal waste as fertilizer for crops, and crop by-products to animals as fodder. They work with the forest to bring water to their fields and families. This partnership between women's and nature's work ensures the sustainability of sustenance, and it is this critical partnership that is torn asunder when the project of 'development' becomes a patriarchal project, threatening both nature and women. The forest is separated from the river, the field is separated from the forest, the animals are separated from the crops. Each is then separately developed, and the delicate balance which ensures sustainability and equity is destroyed.

The visibility of dramatic breaks and ruptures is posited as 'progress'. Marginalized women are either dispensed with or colonized. Needs go unfulfilled, nature is crippled.

The drama of violence and fragmentation cannot be sustained and the recovery of the feminine principle thus becomes essential for liberating not only women and nature, but also the patriarchal reductionist categories which give rise to maldevelopment.

The revolutionary and liberational potential of the recovery of the feminine principle consists in its challenging the concepts, categories and processes which have created the threat to life, and in providing oppositional categories that create and enlarge the spaces for maintaining and enriching all life in nature and society. The radical shift induced by a focus on the feminine principle is the recognition of maldevelopment as a culture of destruction. The feminine principle becomes a category of challenge which locates nature and women as the source of life, and wealth, and as such, active subjects, maintaining and creating life processes.

There are two implications that arise from the recognition of nature and women as producers of life. First, that what goes by the name of development is a maldevelopment process, a source of violence to, women and nature throughout the world. This violence does not arise from the misapplication of an otherwise benign and gender-neutral model, but is rooted in the patriarchal assumptions of homogeneity, domination and centralization that underlie dominant models of thought and development strategies. Second, that the crises that the maldevelopment model has given rise to cannot be solved within the paradigm of the crisis mind. Their solution lies in the categories of thought, perception and action that are life-giving and life-maintaining. In contemporary times, Third World women, whose minds have not yet been dispossessed or colonized, are in a privileged position to make visible the invisible oppositional categories that they are the custodians of. It is not only as victims, but also as leaders in creating new intellectual ecological paradigms, that women are central to arresting and overcoming ecological crises.

Just as ecological recovery begins from centres of natural diversity which are gene pools. Third World women, and those tribals and peasants who have been left out of the processes of maldevelopment, are today acting as the intellectual gene pools of ecological categories of thought and action. Marginalization has thus become a source for healing the diseased mainstream of patriarchal development. Those facing the biggest threat offer the best promise for survival because they have two kinds of knowledge that are not accessible to dominant and privileged groups. First, they have the knowledge of what it means to be the victims of progress, to be the ones who bear the costs and, burdens. Second, they have the holistic and ecological knowledge of what the production and protection of life is about. They retain the ability to see nature's life as a precondition for human survival and the integrity of inter-connectedness in nature as a precondition for life. Women of the Third World have been dispossessed of their base for sustenance, but not of their minds, and in their uncolonized minds are conserved the oppositional categories that make the sustenance of life possible for all. The producers of life alone can be its real protectors. Women embedded in nature, producing life with nature, are therefore taking the initiative in the recovery of nature.

To say that women and nature are intimately associated is not to say anything revolutionary. After all, it was precisely just such an assumption that allowed the domination of both women and nature.

The new insight provided by rural women in the Third World is that women and nature are associated not in passivity but in creativity and in the maintenance of life. This analysis differs from most conventional analyses of environmentalists and feminists. Most work on women and environment in the Third World has focused on women as special victims of environmental degradation.

Yet the women who participate in and lead ecology movements in countries like India are not speaking merely as victims. Their voices are the voices of liberation and transformation which provide new categories of thought and new exploratory directions. In this sense, this study is a post-victimology study. It is an articulation of the categories of challenge that women, in ecology movements are creating in the Third World. The women and environment issue can be approached either from these categories of challenge that have been thrown up by women in the struggle for life, or it can be approached through an extension of conventional categories of patriarchy and reductionism.

In the perspective of women engaged in survival struggles which are, simultaneously, struggles for the protection of nature, women and nature are intimately related, and their domination and liberation similarly linked. The women's and ecology movements are therefore one, and are primarily counter-trends to a patriarchal maldevelopment. Our experience shows that ecology and feminism can combine in the recovery of the feminine principle, and through this recovery, can intellectually and politically restructure and transform maldevelopment. Maldevelopment is seen here as a process by which human society marginalizes the play of the feminine principle in nature and in society. Ecological breakdown and social inequality are intrinsically related to the dominant development paradigm which puts man against and above nature and women.

The underlying assumptions of dialectical unity and cyclical recovery shared by the common concern for the liberation of nature and of women, contrast deeply with the dominant western patriarchal assumptions of duality in existence and linearity in process.

Within the western paradigm, the environmental

movement is separate from the women's movement. As long as this paradigm with its assumptions of linear progress prevails, 'environmentalism' and 'feminism' independently ask only for concessions within maldevelopment, because in the absence of oppositional categories, that is the only 'development' that is conceivable.

Environmentalism then becomes a new patriarchal project of technological fixes and political oppression. It generates a new subjugation of ecological movements and fails to make any progress towards sustainability and equity. While including a few women as tokens in 'women and environment', it excludes the feminine visions of survival that women have conserved.

Fragmented feminism, in a similar way, finds itself trapped in a gender-based ideology of liberation-taking off from either the 'catching-up-with-men' syndrome (on the grounds that the masculine is superior and developed), or receding into a narrow biologism which accepts the feminine as gendered, and excludes the possibility of the recovery of the feminine principle in nature and women, as well as men.

China's patrilineal kinship structure recognizes only male children as descent-group members with rights to the family's property. In the past, and to a large extent today, residence was patrilocal; when a woman married, she left her natal home to live as a member of her husband's family, severing her formal ties with her father's household. Parents considered daughters a liability-as household members who drained family resources when they were children and who withdrew their assets of domestic tabour and earning power when they married. Sons, in contrast, contributed steadily to the family's economic security during its growth and expansion and provided a source of support in old age. Parents strongly preferred male children.

Members of the older generation also favoured arranged marriages. Marriage brought a new member into the household, joined two people in order to produce children and established an alliance between families. The needs of the family therefore took precedence over the desires of the individual in the selection of a mate. When parents arranged marriages, they attempted to recruit women who would be compliant, capable workers who were able to produce heirs for the group and who came from families willing to forge bonds of cooperation and obligation.

The oldest male had the highest status, and women's status, although it increased with the birth of sons and age, was lower than that of any man. The roots anchoring this hierarchy were the mores of the 'three obediences', which required a woman to defer to father, husband and sons, and to the norms of piety (xiao), which obligated offspring to repay parents for nurturing them. Both principles served as forms of social control, perpetuating the family, the subordination of women to men and the domination of the young by the old.

Hsin Hsing is a nucleated village approximately 125 miles southwest of Taiwan's major city, Taipei, and located beside a road that runs between two market towns.

During the 1950s, no significant industries or job opportunities existed locally and land was the primary means of production. Almost all families were agriculturalists, deriving most of their livelihood from two crops of rice, marketable vegetables grown in a third crop and, in some cases, from farm labour hired out for wages. Men, working outside the home in the fields, dominated the public domain. Women managed the house and children, raised poultry, contributed to farm production by weeding fields and drying rice, and, in their 'spare time', wove fibre hats at home to supplement the family income.

By 1979, 85 per cent of resident families' incomes were derived from off-farm employment and almost half of the villagers 16 years or older no longer identified farming as either their primary or secondary activity. The movement of villagers off the land, however, was not limited to men. In 1979 one-half of the married women and four-fifths of the single women in the village worked for remuneration.

The wage employment of single women and men, not surprisingly, was accompanied by modifications in the way marriages were arranged. Parents' monopoly on mate selection disappeared, although the maintenance of family continuity required that parents still be involved in negotiations. Once these were completed, however, dating in the western sense usually occurred. Consequently, women and men married each other frequently after having already developed an emotional commitment.

The cruelty of a Chinese mother-in-law toward her daughter-in-law is common knowledge and, during the 1950s, an older woman's treatment of a younger woman in Hsin Hsing was no different. Women today frequently speak of the bitterness of their early years of marriage, when they were saddled with work under the close supervision and scrutiny of their mothers-in-law.

Many describe the capricious ways in which the older woman exerised her authority, by cursing, harassing and even, on occasion, beating. A young woman had to be socialized and integrated into the household and, in the division of labour, this task fell to her mother-in-law. To enforce obedience, and perhaps in retaliation for her own lifelong subjugation, an older woman might well resort to physical abuse of a daughter-in-law with whom she was dissatisfied.

Any number of women reported that men also had beaten their wives to keep them in line. These men had acted as agents of their mothers, who had demanded they bend their wives to the older women's will. One might ask why an older woman would find it necessary to impose her authority through her son. Enforcing compliance was considered to be the mother-in-law's prerogative; a daughter-in-law did not have sufficient power as an individual to defy her mother-in-law or disobey her commands.

The explanation for a mother-in-law's abrogation of authority to her son must, then, lie elsewhere. In Hsin Hsing, the most likely reason was rivalry for the affections of the son. An older woman had first come as a stranger to her husband's family and the birth of her son had improved her status within it and guaranteed her old age insurance. She had spent years nurturing her relationship with her son and tying him firmly to her. She saw the young wife as a competitor for claims on him, someone who would deprive her of his loyalty and support.

Older women had witnessed cases in which, despite the mother's stratagems to protect the filial bond between her son and herself, a real compatibility or unity of interest had developed between the husband and wife, so that the husband had listened to his wife's views and had accepted her advice. From the perspective of the mother, such an alliance represented a powerful and significant threat to her relations with her son, because the younger woman could use her husband to remove the older woman from the family.

To counter this threat, then, the mother-in-law

enlisted her son as an ally in the abuse of his wife. Because he had been taught that the goal of marriage was the continuation of the family, and because he had close emotional ties with his mother, the man sacrificed his personal feelings toward his wife and beat her. The effect was that his acquiescence to his mother's demand reaffirmed and strengthened his solidarity with her, while his wife's resentment toward him for the beating negated and weakened his solidarity with her. The invigoration of filial ties and erosion of marital bonds contributed to the maintenace of the undivided family and the older woman's future economic and social security.

Undoubtedly, the ability of a mother-in-law to work her will so successfully reflected a young bride's lack of recourse. The husband was expected to and, as we saw, did side with his mother in dealings with his wife. Her neighbours were reluctant to interfere; 'husband-wife violence... [was] regarded as something "to shut the door on and listen to". Nor could her father and brothers be counted on to intervene on her behalf.

The inaction of her relatives, in part, was due to the fact that they did not see her that often: marriage was usually village exogamous; people were poor; transportation facilities were not well developed; and visiting revolved primarily around village-based religious events. Unless the abuse of a woman was extreme, her natal family probably was not aware of a beating until long after the incident had occurred.In part, however, their inaction was also due to the fact that most affines were unwilling to jeopardize a meaningful and utilitarian relationship; ties of affinity served as an important foundation for economic activities and were a source of support which supplemented that which was derived from patrilineal kin. It was therefore not in the family's interest to support a female relative who 'belonged' to a unit from which it hoped to elicit assistance.

An abused wife, then, had but two alternatives available to relieve her misery. She could endure it and look to the time when she would assume the role of the wife of the head of the house, or she could escape it by committing suicide. I do not know specifically whether any woman from Hsin Hsing chose this alternative, but Margery Wolf has pointed out that 'for peasant women suicide was... and still is... a socially acceptable solution to a variety of problems that offer no other'.

Given this situation, did the pattern of wife abuse and the reasons that underlie it change with the transformation of the village's economy? One way to begin to answer this is to look at the way brides were integrated into the households of their husbands in the 1970s. In the 1950s, young women had few resources with which to contest the authority of their mothers-in-law. In the 1970s, in contrast, young brides were not as helpless in dealing with their mothers-in-law as the older women had been with theirs, because they brought decided emotional and economic advantages to the relationship.

First, the mutual affection that a young couple developed during the betrothal period represented in marriage a serious challenge to the mother-son bond on which an older woman depended to subjugate her daughter-in-law.

Second, by 1979 the value of a young woman's sai-kbia (private money)-funds which represented a sizeable portion of the seed money for the conjugal family she and her husband would eventually establish and which he would head-outweighed the resources a man's mother had at her command. An older woman, then, was no longer assured of the loyalty and support of her son in confrontations with his wife. Perhaps for this reason, mother-in-law undertook with moderation the integration of a new bride into the household. Although older women complained frequently about their daughters-in-laws' failings, they tended to avoid direct confrontations with them. It was better to side- step an issue than pit a son's ties to his mother against those to his wife, since at best, a son might remain neutral and withdraw from the fray, but at worst, he might defend his wife.

Ironically, it was the material resources which allowed young women to negotiate the new role relationship with their mothers-in-law that precipitated the following beating in 1979. The couple involved in the incident had been married about seven years and the husband drank and gambled heavily. Although he and his wife were members of a joint family, the woman knew that division of the large unit was inevitable and that, when it occurred, she would not be able to depend on her husband, certainly not as a stable source of support for their conjugal family

It was in her interest, therefore, to guard her sai-kbia-to invest and cultivate it for future use. Consequently, when her husband demanded that she give him her private money she refused. Unable to extract the money from her through verbal abuse, he resorted to physical violence and beat her. Despite this, the young woman remained uncowed. She had very practical reasons not to give up her sai-khia: the future prosperity of her family, and, more importantly, the future prosperity of her two sons-which would determine the nature of her life in old age depended on this money.

Like her counterparts in the 1950s, however, the young woman had little recourse to escape her husband's abuse. Divorce was not really a viable option; customary law required that sons remain with their father upon dissolution of a marriage and, without sons, who would take responsibility for her in her old age? Her father and brothers also were unlikely to offer protection or a haven to which she could retreat. The increasing importance of affinal ties in the world of a cash economy meant they would place their family's interests before her needs. Indeed, her natal family did not intercede to demand that her husband stop his abuse. Recognizing the delicacy of affinal ties, her father acted as his son-in-law's agent and also beat her. To reinforce his own family's security, he forced her to give her sai-kbia-her bulwark against her future insecurity-to her husband. On face value, it would appear that, in the absence of a well-developed social-security system, women's attempts to ensure their old-age security underlie wife abuse in Hsin Hsing.

This explanation masks, however, the fundamental cause of wife abuse in the village and constitutes victim-blaming. The perceived coalition of a young woman with her husband and the refusal of a wife to relinquish her private money were not the cause of wife-beating, though they provided significant excuses for it. In the cases described, young women were considered to have stepped outside the bounds of the cultural definition of femininity by challenging the traditional authority of both the older women and the man. To strengthen and sustain the hierarchical structure of subordination within the family, therefore, beating was believed to be justified.

We in India give our women a special place of honour and dominance in the home and family life; we respect our women. Encounters with variants of the above self-satisfied pronouncement have forced upon me the realization that, as feminists, we urgently need a cross-cultural examination of the control over female sexuality. Most Indian women would say that while, perhaps, we are not made to feel we are sex objects in the same manner as women in the West, we are certainly made constantly aware of ourselves as embodiments of sexuality. Whatever the justification for this, the implications for the restrictions on women's mobility, dress, behaviour or interpersonal ties are very similar in many parts of the country. What we have then is the following interesting duality. In the West, the female body is constantly used as an advertising medium for the sale of commodities-jeans, automobiles, washing machines, airlines-every consumer product where the choice of brand is believed to depend on the extent of sexual arousal of the consumer. The effect is to reinforce the objectification of woman as a purely sexual creature; all other human attributes are submerged. In India, on the other hand, use of the female anatomy for the purpose of selling commodities, while growing, is not quite so prevalent. Women are not turned into sexual objects principally via the commodity form. Sexual objectification is more direct and personal, its social roots lying in the historical antecedents of a peasant society.

In such a society, production has historically been privatized on the basis of patriarchal family units using family labour complemented by nonfamily labour. Patrilocality and patrilocality are the norm. Women of the landholding classes are secluded and their sexuality guarded not only as a mechanism to recruit and control their labour to the productive and reproductive tasks of the family, but especially to ensure the paternity of children. Children represent labour potential and are the heirs of the next generation.

It is an interesting puzzle why the patriarchal family should be so concerned about the precise paternity of the children borne by its female members. If the concern of the patriarchs is over children as potential labourers or as heirs, what does it matter who the biological father is, so long as the children are socially recognized as belonging to the patriarchal family? One possible answer is the tension among brothers or between males of different generations within the family. Control over children may be a crucial aspect of such intrafamily struggles for domination among males. It is possible, however, that a more fundamental basis of the tension over biological paternity may lie in the relations between men and women. We have been accustomed to viewing paternity tensions as tensions among men, viz., 'to which man does this child belong?' However, if we examine the social origins of such 'appropriation' and treat it as historically evolved, we come to a different hypothesis about the social meaning of struggles over paternity.

This hypothesis states that in earlier, more egalitarian societies, it is most likely that women had both responsibility for and control over children. This would have been reinforced by the fact that, until recently, the only biological certainty in most societies was maternity, not paternity. However, as patriarchal household structures developed concomitant with the growth of economic surplus and the development of the state, the control of children (as over inanimate means of production) passed from women to some (if not all) men. This 'appropriation' of children by patriarchs occurred through the sexual control over women and was strongly reinforced by social and religious glorification of the 'chaste' woman. Indian religious mythology, for example, is full of stories of such embodiments of female 'chasity'; it is my hypothesis that many of these myths arose with the growth of patriarchal religious, cultural and economic domination over prior, more egalitarian, communities. Tensions over paternity therefore represent an ongoing assertion by patriarchs of their control over children. The expressed tension is really that between women and men, and only secondarily among men themselves.

It would be a mistake to infer from this that al women are in identical positions within the hierarchica structure of the patriarchal peasant household. Clearly, i is the sexuality of young women, daughters-in-law and daughters that is most in question. Even here, the position is not symmetrical; daughters-in-law must be sexually controlled in the interests of reproducing the patriarchal hierarchy within the household.' Control o daughters on the other hand is undertaken to ensure their recruitment to other households via marriage, and thus to ensure the reproduction of the household within the nexus of the community's social life. The strictes guardians of the sexuality of young women are older women, mothers and mothers-in-laws, whose own relative position within the hierarchy is based on their ability to recruit and channel the labour and sexuality o younger women so as to reproduce patriarcha domination.

It would be a great mistake to imagine that the control of women's sexuality is as rigid within the kin network as it is outside. The extent to which sexuality is expressed within the family varies in different regions o India, but its existence is undeniable. The best known example is the relationship, involving a considerable degree of emotional and physical intimacy, between the daughter-in-law of the house and her husband's younger brothers in parts of North India. Much of this sexuality within kinship is unacknowledged as such, but there is a definite awareness among kin members about its nuances, the subtleties in tabooed relations, forms, etc Sexuality is not therefore totally suppressed. Rather, it is channelled by and through the networks of the patriarchal family.

The role of men in such channelling is to dominate and control the public space. This control takes the form of a more or less aggressive occupation of the space in which women, especially young women, are tolerated only within very rigidly defined and strict limits of movement, dress and action. Any transgression of these limits by a woman brings down swift and sometimes harsh retribution in the form of physical, often sexual molestation. Men police the limits, furthermore, by making women constantly aware of themselves as sexual objects, through looks, gestures, laughter and ribaldry. Harkening back to the duality with which we began, women then are no less sexual objects in India than they are in the West, but the form of objectification is different.

In India, for the most part, sexual control is very direct and only peripherally through the commodity form. The economic and cultural conjuncture of a peasant society that is turning capitalist throws up strange and highly contradictory ideological forms. The messages transmitted by Indian cinema, for example, about women and sexuality are a fascinating study in inconsistency, as they attempt to interpret and glamorize life in the cities for the benefit of a largely rural and small-town audience.

The growth of the film image of Indian woman-as-sex-object presents a paradox for our argument that the commodity form is less responsible here for the sex objectification of women. There is a rapidly growing use of female nudity, molestation and rape to titillate and attract male audiences, as well as a sharp increase in pornographic film during the last decade. Commercial Indian film has been using female sexuality precisely in order to sell a commodity-itself. But the apparent paradox is easily resolved when we note that cinema, while a commodity, is of a very unusual type. It is what we may call an 'ideological commodity'. At its most successful, it draws out and mirrors the cultural unconscious of its audience. For better or worse, whether we as feminists like it or not, male control of the public space is part and parcel of the Indian male's image of his world today. And it is this peculiarly male vision of gender relations, with its corollaries of direct, personalized sexual control of women, that is projected on the Indian screen. The example of film therefore buttresses, if anything, our argument about the personalized nature of sexual objectification and control in India.

The direct control of women's sexuality in India, arising as it does from the social relations of patriarchal, family-based production, has its roots in the economics and culture of the landed classes. Is sexual control unimportant then among those with no land? Women's experience appears to indicate otherwise. While seclusion and restrictions on mobility may not be as rigid among the class of landless wage-earners, they are not totally absent. Women agricultural labourers, construction workers or petty traders experience a degree of sexual control over their mobility that affects their entry into the market for wage labour and income earning. Within the home and community of the landless, female chastity and female virtue are preponderant values guarded, as among the landholders, by older women and by men, young and old, in the public spaces. The relatively high incidence of free unions without formal marriage, or of wife-initiated separation bespeaks a degree of female autonomy within the conjugal bond; but this in no way implies an absence of sexual control.

To what can we attribute this concern with women's chastity in a situation where inheritance is largely irrelevant? Srinivas's theory of Sanskritization hypothesizes an attempt by those at the lower ends of the social, particularly caste, hierarchy to move upwards through the adoption of upper-caste norms, values and practices. A variant of this concept, of special relevance to women, is the idea that as agricultural households acquire more land or other access to income, they imbibe 'middle-class' values and withdraw their women from work outside the home, and even from work on the family farm.

A counter theory is the orthodox Marxist one that the dominant ideology is that of the dominant class. Control by the ruling classes of the material means for the production of culture allows them to dominate and manipulate the ideas, beliefs and consciousness of the ruled. Such a domination fosters a more effective reproduction of the social hierarchy. Thus the two theories can be seen to approach the problem from opposing directions, the orthodox Marxist seeing the problem as one of domination and imposition, while Srinivas sees it as one of emulation and upward mobility.

Neither approach grants sufficient autonomy to the production of culture and beliefs by the ruled themselves. Neither can tell us enough about the material referents of the sexual control of women among the landless rural population in India. The orthodox Marxist theory of ideology cannot be simply applied in this case, since it is not at all clear what landholders have to gain from the sexual control of women among the landless. Arguments that it promotes divisions within the working class, thus lowering wages and militancy, are too general (perhaps tautological), and tend to confuse causality with factual assertion. Srinivas's theory of cultural assimilation, on the other hand, presumes an emulative pattern in the beliefs and culture surrounding sexuality that does not dissect the implicit hierarchies based on gender. The real question is who believes and who emulates, and why?

And why do poor, landless women submit to sexual restriction in a situation where they do not, indeed cannot, rely on men for economic survival?

The answer to these questions must be two-fold. Male interest in the control of sexuality is probably rooted deep in the psychological make- up of oppressed manhood Common experience tells us that sex between human beings (like perhaps all human interaction) has dual, possibly dialectical, aspects-control appropriation versus communication. To the extent that male control of a woman's body is the dominant aspect (as opposed to the reciprocity inherent in communication), the sexual act is itself intrinsically linked to the transformation of woman into sexual object, not subject.

Though no formal studies have been done in India, the sharing of women's experiences tells us that such control/appropriation is the norm not only among the middle and upper classes, but also among poor people. For the latter, the absence of communication is compounded by very material problems such as lack of space and over- crowding. Perhaps, in addition, the extent of their oppression and subservience based on caste and class leads poor men to control and appropriate in the only sphere possible to them, the sexual. Be that as it may, the consequent sexual objectification and control is experienced by poor women at various levels, from the conjugal bed to the village street. Sexual objectification and control in the public space has its counterpart, perhaps its roots, in objectification within the sexual act itself.

But why do poor, labouring women submit to this control? Responsibility for children under conditions of acute poverty makes women willing to submit to male sexual control in return for some economic resources, however meagre. Connection to a man also means a degree of protection, socially sanctioned and itself reflecting the community's control and channelling of women's sexuality, against sexual harassment by other men of the community. Such protection is much less effective against sexual molestation by members of the landed classes, a subject to which we will now turn.

Sexual demands by men from landed households are a regular and systematic aspect of the lives of poor women, Such oppression may take the form of regularized rape of women who are employed as casual agricultural labourers or as bonded permanent labourers on the owner's land. It may take the less onerous but no less demeaning form of undesired physical intimacy from landowners and supervisors who consider the women who work under them to be 'fair game'. The threat of joblessness and the ever-present spectre of hunger work effectively to ensure women's acceptance of molestation, unless there is a conscious attempt to organize against it.

This type of oppression is heightened during periods of class and caste tension. During times of militancy and organized resistance by either landless labourers or poor peasants, landowners and their hired goons often counter with organized orgies of gang rape and mass sexual violence. For poor women, their class is enmeshed with their gender in an unmistakeable way, since class violence here takes precisely the form of sexual violence. It punishes the militant women in the most direct and brutal manner, and it violates the militant men by appropriating the only arena in which they exercise authority-'their' women. The class nature of sexual violence in India has been noted before. Brutal as it is, the existence of such violence perpetrated by the ruling classes is perhaps easier to acknowledge than the sexual control inflicted by poor men upon the women of their own class. A socialist-feminist perspective does not allow us, however, to be blind to either, and even forces us to search out the links between the two.

In the course of organizing work among the women agricultural labourers in a district of Tamilnadu activists who were themselves village women found the medium of role-plays to be very useful in raising the consciousness of women in the village.

One such play dealt with the theme of sexual oppression by landowners. In the discussion that followed a debate ensued about the meaning and relevance of female chastity when it was a well-known, if unacknowledged, fact that such sexual impositions were fairly common. Some young village men on the periphery of the audience intervened, hotly demanding of the women how they could dare question 'chastity', and whether they all wished to be 'immoral'.

What had affected the men most was not the idea of the women having to face the violence of the landlords but the idea that the women might begin to question the notion of female 'virtue', thereby undermining their own, male, control over the women's sexuality.

The theory of labour-market segmentation has been adopted without much modification to explain Indian women's 'secondary' position in [that] market. In a Third World context, the explanatory power of theories developed for labour markets in the West is limited. For women workers, in particular, restrictions to mobility arising from the control of sexuality play a crucial role in defining their secondary place.

Two examples will illustrate this argument, Women agricultural labourers are traditionally considered among the freest and most mobile of women workers. Given that many of them are casual labourers who have to search for work, sometimes on a daily basis, it has been assumed that they are free to move considerable distances and to accept work with little restriction.

In fact, the picture above is a rather roseate version of reality. Women labourers generally tend to work fairly close to their homes, or in work situations where co-workers are other women, or men from their own family/community. Women tend to work more in the 'private' or 'semi- public' spaces, and do few tasks considered demeaning to modesty. The private space is defined, in the context of Kerala, as the house-site or owner's garden-area, while semi-public space is that which involves a short walk from home. Only part of this work definition is based on considerations such as proximity to child care since most labouring women have either an older child, a neighbour or an older family member to look after small children. A significant part is the women's own, socially defined perceptions of 'virtue', and the importance they attach to it. Working in proximity to strange men often carries a moral stigma and a suspicion of promiscuity. Gulati documents such a perception for women construction workers in Kerala. Gangs of migrant labourers, who travel a great deal during the harvest periods, are often hired by contractors on a family basis. Usually, this is the only way in which women can be made to travel long distances from home.

A second illustration is derived from research on women petty traders in Madras city. Quite apart from the handicaps of insufficient capital and connections needed to obtain a stall in the market, women suffer significantly from the control of sexuality. Their inability to travel, to associate easily with male wholesalers, or to be in the market late at night, all act as barriers to their income-earning capacity. This is compounded by the daily sexual harassment faced by these women as a consequence of their being in the public space. The effect of the sexual control of women on their labour-market position and income-caring capacity needs to be taken more systematically into account. Certainly such phenomena are not entirely unknown in the history of industrialization in the West. Our conceptual concern is that sexual control is such a 'normal' and accepted part of the work life of women that it has achieved the status of an axiom. Our task as feminists is to raise it to the level of a practical and theoretical problem.

In India today, the progressive feminist movement has two sections. Those who focus mainly on the economic and class problems of poor women, and those who focus more attention on issues like dowry and bride-burning which seriously affect middle- and upper-class women. While neither side underplays the importance of the work done by the other, and while there are many points on which the two sides come together, there is an unease in the alliance around the issues of class and of the control of sexuality.

Impact of economic crisis

The economic crisis has made it extremely difficult for families to survive on a single wage, forcing additional women into the labour force to meet, the rising cost of living and the decreased wage-earning capacity of men due to unemployment or wage cuts, or due to their absence as a result of migration. At the same time structural adjustment policies are forcing families to absorb a greater share of the cost of survival as a result of the cutbacks in social services, such as health and education, and the elimination or reduction of subsidies on food, transportation and utilities. By shifting more responsibility for survival from the state to the household, structural adjustment policies are increasing the burden on the poor, especially women. We shall examine the impact of the economic crisis and structural adjustment policies on poor women and their households in the Caribbean, focusing on Jamaica and the Dominican Republic, two of the countries most severely affected, In order to deal with balance of payments difficulties, both governments signed standby agreements with the International Monetary Fund (IMF): Jamaica in 1977-78, 198 1 and 1984-85, and the Dominican Republic in 1983 and 1985. Similar structural adjustment policies were instituted in both countries, including cutbacks in social services, continuing devaluation of the national currency, liberalization of regulations regarding imports, removal of food subsidies and price controls on basic consumer goods, and the promotion of non-traditional exports.

As a result of the crisis in the external sector, austerity measures and high debt-servicing payments, GDP per capita declined in both countries, but more precipitously in Jamaica than in the Dominican Republic, since the economic crisis generally has been more severe and of longer duration in Jamaica. In 1988, per capita Gross Domestic Product (GDP) in the Dominican Republic was US $1509, below that of Jamaica, which was $1843, Jamaica's GDP per capita in 1988 was, however, lower in real terms than it had been in either 1980 or 1970. The resulting economic crunch has dramatically highlighted the structures of female subordination and exploitation which have long characterized both countries.

The impact of the crisis and structural adjustment policies has been devastating for poor women due primarily to three factors: (1) a sharp fall in wages and rising female unemployment; (2) the unequal burden which the rising cost of living imposes on women; and (3) the reductions in public spending for services on which women rely. The combined effect of the rising cost of living, particularly rising food prices, and decreased health care is that malnutrition as well as mortality from curable diseases is on the rise. UNICEF has documented the often dramatic changes in consumption and dietary patterns induced by the crisis, with severe implications for health and nutrition. There is a growing concentration on cheap sources of calories such as rice or yucca in the diet, and declining intakes of protein, such as milk or meat. Women and young girls are the family members most likely to be affected by declining food consumption, since preference is given to male wage earners.

In Jamaica, a decline in the nutritional status of children under the age of four years, with the percentage of malnourished rising from 38 per cent in 1978 to 41 per cent in 1985, sums up the effects of these policies This trend was confirmed by hospital admissions; the proportion of children under five admitted to the Bustamante Children's Hospital for malnutrition and malnutrition/gastroenteritis, for example, rose from 2.7 per cent of all admissions in 1980 to 8.4 per cent in 1985. In addition, the percentage of pregnant women screened at prenatal clinics who were deemed anaemic rose from 23 per cent in 1981 to 43 per cent in 1985. Moreover, the infant mortality rate has increased from 16 per thousand in 1980 to 18 per thousand in 1987.

In the Dominican Republic, despite dramatic improvements in mortality and life expectancy rates starting in the 1950s, infant mortality in 1987 still stood at 65 per thousand, a figure which is surpassed only by Haiti. The rate of infant mortality tends to be generally under-reported and is considerably higher in rural areas and among the lowest income groups Maternal mortality, which also differs significantly in urban and rural areas and by income group, stood at 56 per 100,000 in 1980. In one major maternity hospital in the capital of Santo Domingo, maternal mortality, while much lower than in rural areas, increased from 15 to 22 per 100,000 from 1981 to 1985.

According to a study conducted by the Central Bank in 1976-77, 90 per cent of the Dominican population consume less than the recommended minimum of 2300 calories and 60 grams of protein per day, with the poorest significantly below this minimum standard. Among children aged one to four, the level of malnutrition in 1984 reached 40.8 per cent.

A 1981 US Agency for International Development (AID) study found the highest prevalence of malnutrition among infants aged five to eight months. The authors attribute this to a variety of causes: the abrupt cessation of breast-feeding as mothers are forced by economic circumstances to return to work, dilution of baby formulas to make them stretch, and lack of potable water used in infant feeding. It is estimated that one-fourth of all babies born in the Dominican Republic are children of malnourished mothers. In 1983, one-fourth of all children admitted to a major children's hospital in Santo Domingo died, not of incurable diseases but of the combined effects of poverty, ill health and poor health care.

Caribbean women are not simply victims of economic hardship; they and their families are devising innovative strategies for dealing with it. Four main strategies can be detected:

1. women are entering the labour force in increasing numbers particularly as workers in export-processing industries;
2. along with men, they are engaging in a wide variety of activities in the informal sector;
3. households are diversifying their survival strategies, changing living and consumption patterns; and

4. women are joining, and even predominating in, the international migration stream, especially to the United States.

All of these constitute important economic and social changes of the last decade.

At first glance the growing number of women in the labour force may appear contradictory in view of increased unemployment and under- employment in the Caribbean generally. However, women are forced into the labour force precisely because of increased unemployment among men and because real wages of employed household members are decreasing, contributing to an overall reduction in household income. Women are able to find jobs even when men are not, because they work for lower wages, because the labour market in the Caribbean (as elsewhere) is highly segregated by gender, and because a high percentage of women work in the informal sector.

Several factors in the development process in the Dominican Republic have favoured the dramatic increase in the number of women entering the labour force (from 11 per cent in 1960 to 37.5 per cent in 1980), including urbanization, the growth of the service sector and the growth of export-processing industries. At the same time, changes have taken place in the female population in the last two decades which have made them more employable, including a rise in educational levels and a marked decline in fertility it would seem that many of these same factors help explain the high percentage of Jamaican women in the labour force. In the English-speaking Caribbean, however, women's participation rates have traditionally been high, and in Jamaica in 1985 stood at 62 per cent for women over 14 years of age.

Export manufacturers have shown a preference for

women workers because they are cheaper to employ, less likely to unionize and have greater patience for the tedious, monotonous work involved in assembly operations. Although Jamaica was initially targeted as the showpiece of the Caribbean Basin Initiative (CBI), export manufacturing never took off on the scale anticipated. The bulk of employment created in export manufacturing in Jamaica in recent years has occurred, not through the CBI (which excluded textiles and garments from its duty-free provisions) but through the preferences created by US Tariff Code 807 for apparel assembled overseas from US components. Between 1981 and 1985, an additional 6800 women found employment in the manufacturing sector, so that the proportion of women employed in manufacturing rose from 7 to 8.7 per cent of the female labour force, the majority presumably employed in apparel production.

While data are unavailable on whether the increased number of women employed in export manufacturing are located in formal vs. informal- (domestic homeworkers) sector jobs, there is some evidence that garment manufacturers appear to be turning to the use of domestic homeworkers as a way of cutting their labour costs. By contracting out to homeworkers, they avoid the payment of fringe benefits and the costs of factory installations as well as any possible threat of unionization. Moreover, homeworkers offer manufacturers considerable flexibility in managing the size of their workforce, which can be scaled up or down with market fluctuations, clearly offering these women workers little stability of employment. The bulk of these manufacturers appear to be Jamaican nationals who are linked to US companies through subcontracting arrangements. Free-trade zones in Jamaica have had less appeal to US firms than have their counterparts in Haiti or the Dominican Republic.

A study done for AID of the apparel industry in Jamaica revealed that US firms see unions as a major obstacle to investment, although only one of the twenty-two factories in the Kingston Export Free Zone is unionized. Nonetheless, fear of labour unrest may explain the preference of US firms for subcontracting because there have been frequent public protests against such work abuses as low pay, excessive and forced over-time, occupational health hazards, arbitrary suspension and dismissal for protesting, and absence of trade union representation. Such complaints are common among workers employed in export manufacturing, and have also been voiced in the Dominican Republic.

The Dominican Republic has seen a dramatic growth in export manufacturing in recent years. The greatest increase has taken place precisely during the years of structural adjustment, when the number of firms in the free-trade zones increased from 103 in 1983 to 224 in 1988, and the number of employees more than quadrupled, reaching an estimated 85,000 in 1988. The overwhelming majority (84 per cent) of these workers in export manufacturing are women.

One of the reasons for the explosion of export manufacturing in the Dominican Republic is the general wage reduction resulting from devaluation. Between 1981 and 1984 there was a 17 per cent reduction in the average real wage in manufacturing, despite increases in the minimum wage. At the rate of exchange prevailing in August 1986, the average wage in free-trade zones was approximately US $90 monthly In addition, succumbing to pressure from industrialists in the free-trade zones, the Dominican government granted them access to the parallel currency exchange market, which enabled them to buy local currency at an even more favourable rate. This new exchange-rate policy lowered operating costs by approximately 30 per cent, and is another major factor behind the rapid growth in activity in the zones in the last few years. Because of devaluation, average hourly wages are now at approximately the same level as in Haiti, the poorest country of the hemisphere.

In addition to low wages and various government incentives, the weakness of the labour movement in the Dominican Republic attracts US investors to the free-trade zones. There are no unions in the zones and workers are fired and blacklisted with other plants if any union activity is detected. Women who have tried to take complaints of mistreatment or unjust dismissal to the government Labour Office have generally been rejected in favour of management. Workers complain of the lack of public transportation, proper eating facilities, adequate medical services and child care. Labour turnover is high, since many workers cannot with-stand the pressure of high production quotas, strict discipline, sexual harassment and a 44 hour work week, with overtime sometimes imposed in addition.

In a study of Dominican free-trade zones conducted in 1981, it was found that most of the workers are under 30 years old, but in a departure from the global pattern of young, single women, over one-half are married and one-fourth are female heads of households. Their need to work is demonstrated by the fact that nearly three-fourths of the female heads of households and nearly half of the married women claim they are the principal breadwinners for their families. In fact, employers in the Dominican Republic indicate a preference for women with children because they feel their need to work ensures greater job commitments.

While growth in demand for female labour has been greatest in manufacturing, women in the Dominican Republic have also been employed as wage labourers in the new agro industries that have flourished recently due to the CBI. A 1985 study of rural women revealed that wages in these industries are even lower than in manufacturing, averaging three to six pesos daily in 1985, and the work is very unstable, concentrated in the harvest season. Many women also work as unremunerated family labour on small farms, some of which produce for agribusiness on a contract basis.

In short, the growth of employment for women in domestic home-work, in the free-trade zones and in agribusiness represents strategies by industries to reduce production costs at a time of intense international competition. The growth in export manufacturing employment also represents the adaptation by poor women to the need to augment their earnings. But while export promotion has increased the demand for female labour, it has also taken advantage of women's inferior position in the labour market and reinforced their subordination through poorly paid, dead-end jobs.

Women workers in the free-trade zones of both the Dominican Republic and Jamaica have received little or no support from their governments in their efforts to achieve better wages and working conditions. Both governments have attempted to control labour unrest in order to attract foreign investment. Under these circumstances it is understandable why workers have not organized nor protested more vehemently, although in March 1988 there were widespread strikes among Jamaican garment workers in favour of higher wages and better working conditions. Thus the failure to improve working conditions lies more with the lack of support women workers receive from government, political parties and unions than with the women themselves. At present, these women workers have no adequate vehicles to express their grievances or to transform their sense of exploitation (which is very real) into greater worker solidarity. These difficulties are compounded for women employed in the urban and rural informal sectors.

Despite its disadvantages, most women still regard jobs in export processing, particularly the free-trade zones, as preferable to work in the informal sector. The informal sector in the Caribbean still includes a high percentage of domestic servants and petty vendors, as well as other self- employed workers whose activities range from food preparation for sale on the streets to home repairs and other services, as well as artisan production. Working in this sector generally provides no labour protection, minimum wages, social security or other benefits, but for growing numbers of men and women there is little alternative.

In Jamaica, the 38 per cent of women working in the informal sector is much higher than that of men (12 per cent). Undoubtedly this reflects the high percentage of Jamaican women who work as 'higglers' or petty vendors, trading in homegrown foodstuffs and local manufactured goods. Women's involvement in the marketing of foodstuffs for the domestic market dates back to the days of slavery, and has traditionally provided them with the flexibility needed to manage their dual roles and a certain degree of independence. Studies on higglers in the English- speaking Caribbean suggest that women comprise over 80 per cent of the population engaged in trading and commercial activities.

In recent years the role of higglers itself has been transformed, as some women now travel internationally, buying clothing and other consumer goods in Miami to sell in Jamaica or selling Jamaican goods in Haiti and other areas. The complex web of inter-relationships in which these women engage at different levels and their creativity in managing their business is quite impressive-

finding loans, identifying 'sure sells', bargaining wholesale purchases, devising book-keeping and accounting systems, learning the intricacies of air and boat travel, and learning new languages.

In the Dominican Republic, the economically active population in the informal sector has grown from 39 per cent in 1980 to 45 per cent in 1983, with men outnumbering women. Unemployment in the 1980s would surely have been much higher were it not for the growth of this sector. Nevertheless, jobs in the informal sector pay 60 per cent less on average than those in the formal sector. Seventy per cent of women in the urban informal sector earn less than the estimated poverty level of income The majority of women working in the sector are employed in domestic service, which pays the lowest wages and has practically no labour protection. The growth of the informal sector in the Dominican Republic may also reflect state policy, since international development assistance has increasingly been encouraging the growth of micro-enterprises in Latin America and the Caribbean. Because of their capacity for absorbing labour and their very low costs, micro-enterprises have been identified as enjoying a comparative advantage in a highly competitive international market. Micro-enterprise development has thus been getting increasing support from both the public and private sector in terms of credit, access to raw materials and foreign exchange, and other privileges formerly reserved exclusively for the formal sector.

The increasing informalization of Caribbean economies has brought the household to the limelight, as it is here that strategies for generating incomes are conceived and coordinated by men and women, and across generations. In the context of the economic crisis, the household has acquired new importance as a centre for small-scale entrepreneurial activity, as women and men prepare foods for the market, organize and package agricultural produce, sew and embroider, do macrame and craft jewellery, grow and sell ornamental plants, collect aluminium cans and, as we have noted, engage in industrial homework for garment, electronic and computer industries. Women in poor Caribbean households have always sought to stretch family income by producing goods at home rather than purchasing them in stores and by making use of extended family and neighbourhood networks. The economic crisis has obliged women to intensify these activities in order to cope with declining household income, increasing prices and cuts in government services.

An understanding of Caribbean concepts of 'family' and 'community' is important here in understanding women's responses to the crisis. The structures of the family and of the community have emerged out of the history and culture of the region, They represent reconstructions of human communities out of the dehumanizing experience of slavery, the destruction, reconstruction and resistance of the African family, and the specific realities and requirements of the local economy For the majority of the black, working-class population of the Caribbean, the concept of family often extends beyond the household unit or nuclear family, beyond the neighbourhood or village, and even beyond the country, to encompass a network of mutually supporting members. Similarly, the concept of 'community' may transcend spatial dimensions to include people who are linked together in communities of interest-savings groups, the sports club or closely knit religious groups.

The persistence of these networks and associations has been important in building links among different social classes and in enabling women to respond creatively to the current crisis. For a central feature of women's survival strategies is the extent to which they draw on networks of family and community in times of hardship. These networks provide both a mode of survival and a source of affirmation-crucial for emotional support as well as for the empowerment of women.

However, by providing a retreat from an exploitative system, Caribbean forms of the family and community also facilitate the continuation of exploitation and the inequitable distribution of resources. It appears that governments have in fact taken advantage of women's ability to draw on traditional networks of support to introduce policies which have been particularly devastating to women and those for whose care they have been traditionally responsible-children and the elderly.

In Jamaica, for example, women have extended household exchange networks, which increases the amount of goods, services and occasion- ally cash that flows among relatives, friends, and neighbours. Many women have taken advantage of commissaries at their place of work to purchase scarce items such as dairy goods or baby-care products whether or not they need them themselves in order to exchange them for food, child care or other needed services. Rural and urban kin have linked up, with higglers providing their urban kin with fresh vegetables in return for manufactured goods such as flashlight batteries. A conscious attempt is made to avoid market transactions because of the increasing scarcity of cash.

Survival strategies vary with household composition, and one emerging response to the crisis is to increase household size. Expanding the number of people living in a household potentially increases the number of income earners as well as those available to undertake chores and child care. Dominican sociologist Isis Duarte believes that the incorporation of additional members into the household as a survival strategy may be one explanation for the continued large size of households in the Dominican Republic, which has remained at about 5.3 persons since 1920, despite the sharp decline in fertility levels since the 1960s. Large households generally consist of extended families, among whom 69 per cent have five or more members. Extended families continue to account for approximately 30 per cent of all households, and the percentage is higher in urban than in rural areas, which runs counter to most demo- graphic expectations. The increasingly high cost of housing may be one factor that forces families to double up and results in severe overcrowding among the urban poor.

In a 1981 study in Kingston it was found that there was a greater tendency among female-headed households than among those headed by a stable co-residential couple to incorporate additional kin into the household. These are added for two reasons: they free women from some domestic chores and child care so that they can be full-time workers, and they often contribute to household income through informal-sector activities. Whenever possible, new household members are expected to help with the payment of rent and utilities; this is particularly expected of men joining households, whether they are stable partners or boyfriends in visiting unions, or fathers of one or more of the woman's children. However, because of the high rate of unemployment among men, particularly in the urban areas, many men are unable to fulfil these traditional financial obligations. In this study, less than a quarter of the women living in visiting unions and none of the single women then living alone with their children received regular support from their boyfriends or the fathers of their children. While a series of sexual partners may have been a traditional means by which Jamaican women sought financial support, it would seem that the devastating decline in male earning capacity in recent years has made women even more reliant on their own wages and other sources of income. In the study just cited, over 80 per cent of the women who headed households were directly responsible for all major household expenditures; 63 per cent of those in the stable unions also assumed this responsibility. Throughout the English-speaking Caribbean, women express the need to be economically 'independent' as one central to their lives.

In the Dominican Republic, although women have been joining the workforce in increasing numbers, the role of the male breadwinner has remained more intact. The 1981 study of Dominican free-trade zones referred to earlier found that husbands are still considered the principal economic provider in many if not most households, and are responsible for providing such basic items as food and housing. However, the great majority of working women also maintain that their families could not survive without their wages, suggesting that their wages are not just supplementary, but rather, crucial to the household's well-being.

Nonetheless, women's contribution to the household economy is greatest among female heads of household; as mentioned previously, the proportion of such households has been increasing since the 1970s. While the 1981 Census puts the figure at 20.6 per cent, other estimates reach as high as 33.5 per cent it may be that the increased difficulties men are facing in fulfilling their roles as economic providers are partly responsible for this increase. Although female heads of household have higher rates of labour-force participation than married women, they are a particularly vulnerable group, with lower incomes, higher rates of unemployment and twice as likely to find employment as only occasional labourers as are male heads.

The relocation of manufacturing industry from developed to developing countries by multinational corporations engaged in 'offshore sourcing' is part of a new international division of labour and pattern of trade in manufactures.' This is the direct result of two developments in the world capitalist economy which began in the 1960s. First, growth in international trade intensified inter-capitalist competition among the developed nations. In particular, the ascendancy of Japan as a major industrial power and its rapid and highly successful penetration of western consumer markets led American and European manufacturers to invest in developing countries as a means of reducing costs in competition with the Japanese.

In the 1970s, the slowing down of growth in western and world markets further intensified these competitive pressures. Second, the accelerating development of capitalist relations of production in a number of developing countries resulted in some of their indigenous entrepreneurs manufacturing for export to western markets, beginning in the 1960s. This placed them in direct competition with western manufacturers, who were forced to relocate to these same countries in order to be cost competitive in their own home markets. This trend continued through the 1970s on an ever larger and wider scale, particularly in Asian countries like Hong Kong, Taiwan, South Korea and Singapore, whose larger local firms have themselves become multinationals operating offshore manufacturing plants in other developing countries.

The crucial factor in the competition was and is the cost of production, which differs between mature and developing capitalist economies according to their stage of development. In the 1960s and early 1970s, the mature western economies experienced tight domestic labour markets-low unemployment rates, high wages and chronic labour shortages in many industries. Labour-intensive manufacturing industries-those which employ large numbers of workers in generally unskilled or low-skilled jobs-were the most affected, and these countries began to lose their international comparative advantage in industries such as garments, shoes, plastic toys and electronics assembly. The developing countries, on the other hand, had relatively abundant supplies of labour, reflected in the rural-urban migration of surplus labour off the farms; high urban-unemployment rates; and low wages. Cheap labour, combined in many cases with government-subsidized capital costs, including tax holidays and low-interest loans from government banks, gave these countries a comparative advantage in world trade in labour-intensive products.

It is labour-intensive industries, then, that tend to relocate manufacturing plants to developing countries, becoming multinational in their operations. This is a rational competitive response to changing international comparative cost advantages. In a free world market, factors of production like capital and labour will tend to move to locations where they are most scarce and can command the highest returns from the employment in production. Through the nineteenth and early twentieth centuries, this was reflected in fairly free international migration of labour, but subsequent restrictive national immigration policies together with transportation costs and imperfect market information have increasingly inhibited the mobility of labour across international boundaries, except for the legal and/or illegal immigration of 'guest workers'. Capital, however, remains internationally mobile, especially from the developed to developing countries, a flow encouraged by policies of the latter's governments that offer profit tax holidays, duty-free imports and exports, unrestricted remittance of profits and repatriation of capital.

Imperialism—the system of military, political, economic and cultural domination of the Third World by its former colonial masters-was historically the outgrowth of capitalist development in the West. In the economic sphere, it is characterized by the exploitation of natural and human resources in the Third World by western capitalist enterprises. Although bourgeois economists were in agreement with classical Marxists-including Lenin, Luxemburg and Marx-that imperialism, or western investment in developing countries, would be an agent of capitalist development in the Third World, modern-day theorists of imperialism—including dependency theorists and 'world-system' analysts following Andre Gunder Frank and Immanuel Wallerstein- argue that it retards such development.

Most of the latter analysis has been applied to the sectors of primary production for export and import-substituting industrialization in developing countries. But manufacturing for export by multinational subsidiaries also has its critics. It is pointed out that workers' wages are much lower and their working conditions worse than in the multinationals-home countries; that few transferable skills or industrial linkages are generated; that there is heavy dependence on foreign capital, technology, skills, inputs and markets; that few taxes are paid in the host country; and high profits that accrue only to foreigners are mostly remitted overseas.

Although the above are true in most situations, it

should be noted that manufacturing for export in developing countries is not the sole preserve of multinationals. Many local firms are also involved, and in some countries-such as Hong Kong, Taiwan and South Korea-and industries, such as garments, they may outnumber the multinationals. In general, Third World enterprises engaged in manufacturing for export to western markets are smaller, less capital intensive and more labour intensive than multinational subsidiaries and are concentrated in simple- technology industries with competitive markets and relatively low profit margins. Wages are usually lower and working conditions worse, some- times much worse, than in the multinational sector. Skills are low, and there is dependence not only on foreign markets, to which access is less easy than for the multinationals, but also on foreign technology and inputs purchased on the world market. Tax payments and reinvestment rates may be higher than for multinational subsidiaries; but since earnings are less, absolute contributions may be lower.

Comparisons between multinational subsidiaries and local firms in export manufacturing in developing countries suggest that the former may contribute more to the host economy in terms of market access, output growth, total wage-bill, and skill and technology acquisition. Local firms may, however, contribute more to the national development of capitalist relations of production in the long run, in developing a class of indigenous entrepreneurs in the manufacturing sector. They may rein- vest more, since they do not remit profits overseas and are less likely to transfer operations. But competition with multinational subsidiaries in factor, input and output markets may inhibit the development of independent indigenous enterprises and entrepreneurs. A complementary relationship is possible, but it tends to maintain local firms in the dependent position of subcontractors and suppliers to foreign firms and markets.

Despite the validity of many of the criticisms against it, manufacturing for export does enhance the development of capitalist relations of production in developing countries, mainly by spurring the growth of industrial wage labour and an indigenous industrial capitalist class. Multinationals and local firms make somewhat different contributions to this process. Two more questions remain: What are the long-run prospects for a multinational-led, export-manu-facturing sector in a developing country? Is this likely to lead to the development of an independent national capitalism in the developing country?

One of the criticisms commonly levelled at manufacturing for export by multinational corporations is that it is likely to be only a temporary phenomenon in developing host countries. Multinationals that relocate manufacturing capacity in these countries are 'footloose' because they are not bound to any particular location by a need for local markets or local input sources other than labour, which is abundantly available everywhere. Therefore, it is argued, they will tend to move away from a location if labour-market conditions or government policies change to make it less competitive. Although this has happened in individual firm cases, it has not yet threatened the viability of an entire export-manufacturing sector in any country.

On the contrary, in the less developed countries where most of the export-oriented multinational subsidiaries are concentrated-Hong Kong, Taiwan and Singapore-changing comparative costs, particularly the appearance of tight labour markets, have resulted in an upgrading of the industries producing for export.

Multinationals, encouraged by host government policies, have begun relocating more capital-intensive, technology-intensive industrial products and processes from their home countries to these locations. Labour-intensive processes are replaced or shifted to more labour-abundant locations as comparative advantages continue to change between developed and developing countries and among developing countries themselves.

This suggests that, at least in some developing countries, the multinational-led export-manufacturing sector does mature over time, further developing capitalist relations of production. Wages rise, working conditions improve, more skills are imparted, more local linkages generated, more taxes paid and more profits reinvested locally. Although the countries where this is happening are still a minority in the Third World, they are the ones that have had the longest experience with multinational subsidiaries in manufacturing for export.

But what about local firms and the development of an independent national capitalism? As the multinational subsidiaries continue to grow and to upgrade and diversify their products, they generate more local linkages, make more input purchases from local suppliers and subcontract some of their simpler products and processes to local manufacturers. This may stimulate the growth of indigenous enterprises, though these remain in a dependent position vis-a-vis the multinationals. From the point of view of enhancing capitalist development, dependence may not be a problem if it results in accelerated growth and the emergence of an indigenous industrial capitalist class.

A nationalist industrial policy that excludes multinationals may result in more independence but less growth and thus a smaller indigenous capitalist class since the advantages multinationals possess in stimulating supply sources and in providing technical and managerial training would be lost.

Although dependency theorists and others who argue that multinationals retard the development of capitalism in developing countries are right with respect to their criticisms of the early stages of labour-intensive manufacturing for export, the experience of some important developing countries suggests that bourgeois economists and classical Marxists alike might be right in the longer run, that multinationals do foster the development of capitalist relations of production and are often more successful in this than indigenous firms. The relocation of industry between countries continues if firms behave rationally in response to changing comparative advantages. Although multinationals may shift labour-intensive industries out of some developing countries as comparative costs change, so do national firms in these countries (as in the case of Singapore firms that shifted to cheaper-labour countries like Malaysia, Indonesia, Sri Lanka and Bangladesh); so long as new industries and processes are moved in, capitalist relations of production continue to develop and mature. Patriarchy is the system of male domination and female subordination in economy, society and culture that has characterized much of human history to the present day. In the economic sphere, it is reflected first in the sexual division of labour within the family, which makes domestic labour the sole preserve of women. Their involvement in production activities outside the home varies with different societies and different stages of development, but is, particularly in those countries where capitalist development has penetrated, often accorded inferior status and reward compared to the activities of men.

In the pure capitalist model of 'bourgeois'

economists, conditions of perfect competition prevail in the labour market, where workers are hired solely on the basis of their marginal productivity. Competition and the progress of capitalist relations of production should eventually eliminate any differences between the sexes in the labour market.

This model is clearly invalid in the real-world capitalist labour market. Not only is participation in the wage-labour force lower for women than for men, but women are concentrated in a narrow range of occupations characterized by low wages, low productivity, low skill levels, high turnover, insecurity of tenure and limited upward mobility. Productivity differences between male and female workers are one explanation for this phenomenon, but they themselves reflect differential access to the determinants of productivity, such as education and skill training and different levels of technology in the jobs to which they are assigned. In addition, there is an element of pure discrimination by employers, discrimination unrelated to any productivity differences between male and female workers.

Patriarchal institutions and social relations are responsible for the inferior or secondary status of women in the capitalist wage-labour market. The primacy of the sexual division of labour within the family has several consequences for the woman who seeks wage employment. Socialized to accept this sex role in life, she has little motivation to acquire marketable skills; is often prevented by discrimination from acquiring such skills; and even after she has acquired them may be prevented by discrimination from achieving the employment or remuneration that those skills would command for a man.

Discrimination itself is based on the patriarchal

assumption that woman's natural role is a domestic one and that she is therefore unsuited to many kinds of wage employment, either because her productivity will 'naturally' be lower than a man's in the same employment or because it will be affected adversely by her domestic responsibilities.

It is this comparative disadvantage of women in the wage-labour market that gives them a comparative advantage vis-a-vis men in the occupations and industries where they are concentrated. In the manufacturing sector of mature capitalist economies, women are concentrated in labour-intensive industries where the wages earned are often insufficient to support a family. It is assumed by employers and in general that women work only for 'pocket money' for luxuries or to make a secondary-income contribution to families where the principal breadwinner is a male.

Both the demand for and supply of female labour arc determined by the culture of patriarchy, which assumes woman's role in the family as natural and consigns her to a secondary and inferior position in the wage-labour market. Even where women are acknowledged to be more productive than men, they are often paid less, and prevailing wages ark, always lower in female-intensive than male-intensive industries and occupations, even at equivalent skill levels. This is contrary to the prediction of neoclassical economic theory that higher productivity means higher, not lower, wages.

The industries in which women manufacturing workers are concentrated in mature capitalistic economies are the very industries that are losing their comparative cost advantage to newly industrializing countries. It is likely that these labour-intensive industries maintained their comparative advantage as long as they did because they employed the lowest-paid workers in those countries-women, often women of minority races. Thus it is female-intensive industries that have the greatest propensity to 'run away' from the developed countries and relocate manufacturing facilities in the Third World, where wages are even lower than those of women in the developed countries. In the developing countries as well, traditional patriarchal social relations ensure that women occupy a similarly secondary and inferior position in the wage- labour market and so are the preferred employees of multinational and local employers in labour-intensive export industries.

Although the relocation of manufacturing industry from mature to developing capitalist countries reflects changes in world capitalism, the employment of women in these industries reflects the influence of patriarchy on the female labour market in both mature and developing countries. Women's comparative disadvantage in the capitalist wage-labour market enhances the comparative advantage of firms that employ them in labour-intensive industries producing for the world market. This disadvantage-reflected in low wages-is greatest for women in countries where capitalist relations of production are least developed, since there they have the fewest opportunities for wage employment and the weakest bargaining power in the labour market. Patriarchal social relations are also strongest and most restrictive of female wage-employment where precapitalist modes of production, e.g. feudalism, persist. Thus, female employment in export manufacturing industries is most prevalent in those developing countries where capitalist relations of production are developing most rapidly, but traditional patriarchy is sufficiently strong to maintain women in an inferior labour-market position.

All workers employed in capitalist enterprises are

exploited to produce profits for their employers, but the degree of exploitation differs among different groups of workers. In addition to being paid less than the value of the output they contribute, Third World women workers in multinational export factories are paid less than women workers in the multinationals' home countries and less than men workers in these countries and in their own countries as well, despite the fact that in relocated labour-intensive industries their productivity is frequently acknowledged to be higher than that of either of these other groups. Thus, Third World women workers are the most heavily exploited group of workers, relative both to their output contribution and to other groups. Although all are subject to capitalist exploitation, Third World women workers are subject additionally to imperialist and to patriarchal exploitation.

Imperialist exploitation—the differential in wages paid to workers in developed and developing countries for the same work and output-arises from the ability of multinationals to take advantage of different labour-market conditions in different parts of the world-a perfectly rational practice in the context of world capitalism. Patriarchal exploitation-the differential in wages paid to male and female workers for similar work and output-derives from women's inferior position in the labour market.

Although multinational employers in developing countries practice all the above forms of exploitation, they do so only in response to labour- market forces, specifically the international and sexual segmentation of labour markets. Differences in the degree of development of capitalist relations of production and natural restrictions on the international mobility of labour are responsible for differential wage rates between countries, whereas patriarchal institutions and attitudes limiting the employment opportunities open to women are responsible for differential wage rates between the sexes. Multinationals may consciously attempt to preserve these differentials from which they benefit, but in general they merely take advantage of [their existence].

It may be argued that the activities of multinationals in labour-intensive export manufacturing in developing countries might in the long run contribute to a reduction of national and sex wage differentials-in other words, a reduction of the imperialist and patriarchal components of capitalist exploitation of Third World women workers. To the extent that these [firms] contribute to the development of capitalist relations of production, particularly to the growth of demand for wage labour and to the upgrading of skills, wages will rise in the developing countries. If at the same time the relocation of industry from the developed countries reduces demand for labour in those countries, wage increases there will decline. Both factors will reduce over time the wage differential between the developed and developing countries-that is, the degree of imperialist exploitation.

Because multinationals engaged in export manufacturing in the developing countries employ mostly women workers, they increase the demand for female over male labour. Female wages will rise relative to male wages, and female unemployment rates will fall. Sex wage differentials will narrow. In some countries governments have already expressed concern about the lack of employment creation for men-whom they consider to be the principal breadwinners-in multinational export firms. So far the narrowing of national and sex wage differentials has been imperceptible in most cases. In most developing host countries, multi- nationals manufacturing for export constitute too small a sector of the economy to have a significant impact on the national labour market. Even where, as in a handful of Asian countries, they are an important sector of the economy and have contributed to rising wages, wages have increased just as rapidly in the developed countries with generalized inflation. Furthermore, the relocation of industry has not reduced the overall demand for labour in the developed countries, where capitalist development continues in different sectors. With respect to sex wage differentials, although female wages have risen, high turnover of labour and the short average working life of women factory workers keeps their average wages low. The countries in which female wages have risen most rapidly are also those where male employment creation has been proceeding apace, and male wages have often increased even more rapidly in other sectors of the economy. Continued imperialist and patriarchal exploitation in multinational factories in developing countries does not, however, imply that the women employed in these factories are worse off than they would have been without such employment. On the contrary, the vast majority are clearly better off, at least but not only in a narrow economic sense, for being subject to such exploitation. Wages and working conditions are usually better in multinational factories than in alternative employment for women in indigenous capitalist enterprises. Although in the relative economic sense defined previously they may be more exploited in the multinationals, in an absolute sense their incomes tend to be higher, This is true also when compared with women's traditional economic roles as housewives and unpaid family labour in farms and shops.

In developing as in mature industrial economies, the state of development of capitalist relations of production defines the employment opportunities available to wage labour. Patriarchal social structures and cultures divide these opportunities by sex, typically limiting female wage labour to a narrow range of inferior jobs. In this situation the entry of labour-intensive export manufacturing industries and of multinational corporations in particular into sex-segregated local labour markets has two somewhat contradictory effects. On the one hand, multinational and local employers can take advantage of women's inferior position to employ them at lower wages and poorer working conditions than exist for men in the same country and for women in developed countries. Both local firms and multinationals benefit from the gap between workers' wages in the developing country and final product prices in markets of developed countries. On the other hand, in however limited a way, the availability of jobs in multinational and local export factories does allow women to leave the confines of the home, delay marriage and child-bearing, increase their incomes and consumption levels, improve mobility, expand individual choice and exercise personal independence. Working for a local or foreign factory is for many women at least marginally preferable to the alternatives of staying at home, early marriage and child-bearing, farm or construction labour, domestic service, prostitution or unemployment, to which they were previously restricted. Factory work, despite the social, economic and physical costs it often entails, provides women in developing countries with one of the very few channels they have of at least partial liberation from the confines and dictates of traditional patriarchal social relations.

Given their lack of access to better jobs, women usually prefer multi- nationals as employers over local firms since they offer higher wages and better working conditions and often have more 'progressive' labour practices and social relations. Indeed, the more multinationals there are in any one country and the longer they have been established, the stronger becomes the workers' bargaining position. Exclusive employment of female production workers in labour-intensive export industries creates occasional labour shortages, resulting over time in rising wages, greater job security and improved working conditions for women in indigenous as well as multinational enterprises Greater competition for female labourers will tend to reduce the degree of exploitation found in women's work.

Whether or not market forces alone will expand women's employment alternatives beyond the traditional 'female ghettoes' of low wage, low skill, dead-end jobs depends on the state and rate of development of capitalist relations of production in the economy as a whole. In an economy that is rapidly growing, diversifying and upgrading itself in all sectors, high demand for labour might eventually propel women into skilled industrial and non-industrial jobs from which they have previously been excluded by custom, education or employment discrimination. This will improve the wages and working conditions of women who remain in factory employment as production workers, given the reduction in the numbers of women available for work,

So far, such a situation is an exceptional one among the many developing countries that host multinational corporations in female-intensive industries. Even where rapid growth occurs, employers may escape the tightening tabour market by importing migrant [workers], by automation and by shifting labour-intensive processes to other countries, as they have done in the home countries of the multinationals and are now doing in rapidly developing countries like Singapore. In [Singapore], growth in other industries and sectors has prevented these actions from having a depressing effect on wages, and the government's high-wage policy has forced firms to shed or shift their labour-intensive activities. Also, when women ascend the job hierarchy, it is usually to take jobs vacated by male workers who have since advanced even higher in the hierarchy of skills and incomes. That is to say, although rapid growth may enable women to improve their position in the tabour market in absolute terms, relative to men they remain in an inferior position,

Capitalism cannot wipe out patriarchy, though exploitation in capitalist enterprises can provide some women with an at least temporary escape from traditional patriarchal social relations.

Many of the studies of female employment in multinational export factories in developing countries focus their criticism on the multinational corporation as chief perpetrator of all the forms of exploitation that these women workers are subject to. Although the multinational does take advantage of national and sexual wage differentials and sometimes reinforces them, it is not responsible for creating them and cannot by its own actions eliminate them. National wage differentials are the result of differences in the development of capitalist relations of production between nations, whereas sex wage differentials originate in indigenous patriarchy.

Removing the multinational will, in the absence of a credible alternative form of development, drastically reduce employment opportunities for women in developing countries. This will weaken their tabour-market position and subject them to even greater exploitation by indigenous capitalists and continued subordination to traditional patriarchy. A less radical solution-attempting to reduce imperialist exploitation by imposing reforms on the multinational or local employeris unlikely to succeed even if host governments were willing. Export manufacturers operate in highly competitive international markets with generally elastic supply and, in important industries like garments and shoes, inelastic demand. Host governments and workers can neither demand nor enforce better wages and working conditions in profit-oriented multinationals that are mobile between countries. Local firms are often less competitive than multinationals in the world market and with their lower profits, are unlikely to be able to absorb the costs of such reforms.

Another possibility for reducing imperialist exploitation is through international action to restrict multinationals from exploiting market wage differentials between nations-for example, by standardizing certain terms and conditions of work in particular industries or occupations. This is clearly unrealistic, given the different stages of development of capitalism. Furthermore, workers in developed and developing countries tend to have opposing interests vis-d-vis the relocation of manufacturing industry. National interests inhibit the development of international tabour solidarity. For example, protectionist groups of employers and tabour unions in the multinationals' home countries have furthered their own self-interest by citing exploitation of women workers overseas as a reason why goods made by these workers should be prevented from reaching their destined markets by means of tariffs, quotas and other restrictive trade practices. This has the effect of pitting workers in mature and developing capitalist countries against each other.

Because patriarchal social relations are at the bottom of women's subjection to imperialist exploitation, it is logical to turn to an attack on traditional patriarchy as a means of improving the position of women. The successful elimination of patriarchal institutions and attitudes, discrimination, differential socialization by sex and the sexual division of tabour within the family would equalize male and female employment opportunities and incomes. In developing countries, national identity is bound up with a traditional, often feudal, patriarchal culture. An attack on traditional patriarchy may be construed as an attack on national identity and thus arouse the forces of a reactionary nationalism against the liberation of women. Indeed, one of the dangers of multinational exploitation of Third World women workers is that it arouses local anti-imperialist sentiment that becomes identified-as in fundamentalist Islamic ideology in Iran-with traditionalism and opposition to wage employment by women.

Even if traditional patriarchy is undermined successfully and equality in the capitalist labour market achieved, women workers will remain subject, together with male workers, to capitalist exploitation in a capitalist economy. Capitalist employers themselves are unlikely to be indifferent to the elimination of sex differences in the tabour market. Although employers of predominantly female workers may be expected to oppose sex equalization because it would reduce the supply and thus raise the wages of women workers in low-skill, labour-intensive and dead-end jobs, employers in male-intensive industries where tabour is scarce may welcome the entry of female tabour as a means of increasing the tabour supply and reducing wages. The balance between these opposing interests, and the attitude of male workers themselves, depends on the state and rate of development of capitalist relations of production. A nation that is rapidly growing and upgrading into high- skill, high-wage industries and occupations, and experiences rising demand relative to supply of tabour is likely to have greater sex equalization in the tabour market than one which is growing only slowly or stagnating, with high unemployment and a dependence on low-wage, labour-intensive industries. In other words, rapid capitalist development is more conducive to sex equalization in the tabour market but by itself cannot bring about such equalization.

Elimination of worker exploitation altogether can occur only if capitalism itself is eliminated. This presents enormous difficulties for the small developing country in a world dominated by capitalism and imperialism. Domestically, a necessary precondition is the unity of the working class, which is hampered by sex, race, regional and other differences. So long as patriarchal relations of production persist, male and female workers remain divided by occupational segregation and by the tendency for male workers to assume the position of a labour aristocracy. If development is slow and mainly in low-skill industries, male unemployment and low wages will limit this aristocracy to a small segment of the male workforce, rather than creating a male elite that opposes female workers. Thus, the elimination of patriarchy would facilitate the elimination of capitalism itself. The elimination of capital exploitation does not, however, necessarily facilitate the elimination of patriarchal exploitation. In some cases, the struggle against a capitalism identified with imperialist exploitation can lend itself to a reinforcement of traditional patriarchy and opposition to women's participation in the labour force.

Within the existing structure of economy and society, pro-capitalist and pro-imperialist strategies-for example, encouraging maximum investment by labour-intensive multinational factories-may serve an anti-patriarchal aim by increasing the demand for female tabour and raising female wages absolutely and relative to male wages where, as in many developing countries, male wage employment is growing more slowly. Multinationals generally offer a better employment alternative to women than local enterprises in modern and traditional sectors of the economy and also provide a limited escape from the domestic roles imposed by traditional patriarchy. But there are limitations to the success of this strategy in raising women's wages permanently. Because female employment-creation in multinational factories is based on patriarchal exploitation, the elimination of these conditions may well bring about an elimination of the jobs themselves, given the international mobility of multinational capital and the availability of exploitable female labour in other countries. A similar limitation faces attempts to impose reforms on the multinationals through government policy actions or worker organization and labour-union activity on an enterprise, national or international scale. In the larger national context, a pro-capitalist, pro-imperialist strategy on behalf of women workers can generate a 'backlash' from traditional patriarchy, making a general and genuine liberation more difficult. It also weakens worker solidarity where anti-imperialist and anti-capitalist struggles exist. On the other hand, these struggles are unlikely to succeed so long as the labour force and labour market remain divided by sex; these struggles would be strengthened by the undermining of patriarchal relations of production. Ultimately, it is the existing structure of the economy and society that has to be changed if the exploitation of women in the labour force is to be eliminated. Capitalist market forces and employment based on imperialist exploitation cannot liberate women from patriarchal exploitation that is the very condition for their entry into wage labour in multinational factories producing for the world market. In the long run, capitalism and imperialism only perpetuate and may even reinforce patriarchal relations of production, which in turn reinforce capitalist and imperialist relations of production.

Women and AIDS

The biggest impact of AIDS on women's lives had been until recently as carers for people with HIV disease or AIDS. However, more women are now becoming infected and the number is likely to increase in the next few years-in New York AIDS is already the leading cause of death in women between 25 and 34.1 In Africa and some parts of Latin America, mainly the Caribbean, HIV has always been transmitted predominantly through heterosexual sex, and in these areas AIDS has affected women and men equally. Yet women have received, until recently, little attention in the AIDS literature and when they are referred to it is usually only in their role as transmitters of the infection. There has been little focus on women as sufferers from AIDS.

Prostitutes especially have been singled out as a high-risk group, and have even been portrayed as being responsible for the spread of the Hiv and AIDS epidemic in some places. The word 'prostitute' means different things in different cultures. In some countries prostitutes are an easily identifiable group, whereas in others they are much less visible. Where prostitutes form a definable group they are accessible and easy to study and have become the focus of research in some cities of Africa They have been found to have a higher rate of HIV infection than the rest of the population.

A common assumption in much of the AIDS literature is that prostitutes are always female. In some countries this is not the case and male prostitutes may be common. Yet women, particularly prostitutes, are frequently referred to as AIDS transmitters. While they may constitute a pool of infection, the role of their clients in transmission is rarely mentioned. Gabriella Leite, a prostitute in Brazil, put it bluntly:

As for AIDS, official bodies, society, attempt to define it in terms of people: prostitutes, homosexuals, the promiscuous, drug users. The political question is, what about the people who frequent prostitutes? They are not regarded as a high-risk group... Sure AIDS kills, but so do many other things. Prostitutes have always been at risk of diseases and the government and health services have never lifted a finger before

The concern with prostitutes is as transmitters of AIDS, not as sufferers. This is not new or limited to AIDS. An article from Brazil draws a comparison with what happened previously with syphilis and gonorrhea. This in spite of the fact that female-to-male transmission of gonorrhoea is documented to be around 20-25 per cent after a single exposure, and from male to female 50-80 per cent.

The possibility that a prostitute may catch HIV from an infected customer is rarely considered. For example, a study in The Lancet on the effectiveness of condom promotion and health education among prostitutes in Kenya concluded. We believe that this programme has prevented the transmission of a large number of HIV infections in men ... In view of the sexual activity of these women and their high prevalence of HIV, every day approximately 3750 men are sexually exposed to HIV through contact with them. The phrasing makes one wonder whether the researchers were equally concerned about the health of the women. In the Philippines 'hospitality girls' have identified this risk for themselves and together demanded testing for the men from the army who are frequent clients.

Men infecting women is never highlighted. However, in fact, the little information that is available on heterosexual transmission seems to suggest that male-to-female transmission is slightly higher than the other way around Also, in many African countries, men who have acquired the infection in the cities then return to their wives in rural areas and possibly start a new cycle of infection. There are anecdotal reports from some countries where HIV is prevalent in urban areas that some men are now looking for younger women in rural areas for the exchange of sexual favours, thinking that such women are less likely to be infected with HIV.

'Sex tours' for Western businessmen are well-known, particularly in some Asian countries, yet this group is not usually mentioned as a high- risk group. A study of prostitutes in London showed that they were more likely to use condoms with their clients than with their own partners, even though these partners often engaged in high-risk behaviour such as intravenous drug use.

Harsh economic realities push women into prostitution, particularly in developing countries; for poor women on their own in urban areas there may be few choices other than becoming domestic servants or prostitutes. Often, they have been abandoned by a partner and have children to support. Women refugees also frequently end up resorting to prostitution, sometimes illegally, as their only survival strategy. With little education or access to other resources, their opportunities are non-existent, and it is unrealistic to blame prostitutes and single them out for education and other programmes without offering them some kind of economic alternative. While education may help them to protect themselves, for many of these women abandoning prostitution would mean destitution.

Projects which aim to support women in prostitution

or women sex workers should not limit themselves giving health education; condoms need to be mac available at an affordable price. General health service including access to birth control, are also important. It also essential to explore alternative income-generatir activities with these women and to provide the relevai assistance, as well as to explore other social an economic needs they may have. The number of wome infected with HIV in some African countries is higl particularly in certain urban areas. The female-to-ma ratio is approximately one to one i.e. at least 50 per cen or sometimes slightly more, of those infected are wome The peak incidence of infection for women in Africa between 20 and 29 years while for men it is between 2 and 39, probably reflecting an earlier start of sexu activity for women. Yet few AIDS-control programm have considered women's particular needs; neither thos of urban women nor of the wives of men returning to th rural areas bringing HIV with them.

AIDS cannot be separated from the extreme povert lack of resources and the heavy burden of work women. For women the possibility of transmission their babies is a cause for additional concern and when occurs it adds to the guilt and worry. Women hav traditionally been the carers for children, the sick and th elderly and have already experienced the problem caring for partners or others with AIDS. Who will tak over this role for women when they themselves need be cared for?

A research project in a capital city of an Africa country is following a sample of 1500 women for fiv years. The study, concerned with more than the researc itself, has expanded to provide a valuable education service, condoms and spermicides, and counselling fo the women as well as offering counselling and testing fo their partners. Testing was carried out, with informed consent and appropriate counselling. Approximately 25 per cent of the women were found to be seropositive. Marital conflict arising after disclosure of a positive result and the role of counselling in helping to overcome this have been particularly relevant.

This study exemplifies many of the problems faced by women in relation to HIV infection and AIDS. Many of these women were single and had little in the way of social or economic support. It is a generalized assumption that in Africa the extended family provides support and care for the sick. However, among the group of HIV seropositive women interviewed, 60 per cent of them said they would not be able to rely on husband or family for support. Support from self-help groups, particularly with an income-generation component, was very relevant to these women.

The same study identified the needs of women with AIDS. The provision of child care, food and funeral services were major areas of concern to them, For women who were seropositive but asymptomatic, housing and employment assistance were a higher priority, although another important consideration was concern about preparing for the future in the event of illness or death. It is important to identify priorities and needs with the women themselves and to support projects which allow them to have more control over their situation and improve their economic status whenever possible. Many of the women experience feelings of terrible isolation after being told they are seropositive, stigmatization is real and many have been abandoned by friends, relatives or lovers; nurses and health workers have been known to refuse care. Hopefully, this rejection will decrease with appropriate information and education. Meanwhile, in the words of 'Rosie' (a pseudonym), a sick woman in Zimbabwe.

Aids and children

The majority of women with HIV or AIDS are of chil bearing age. HIV can be transmitted from an infecte mother to her child, either during pregnancy or at birt There have been eight reported cases so far whe transmission has been possibly related to breast-milk, a of them in special circumstances.

The risk of a baby being infected is still not know with certainty. Results from different studies vary fro less than 10 per cent to 30 per cent, and the risk transmission appears to be associated with the stage the disease. The problem is bigger in those places i Africa and the Caribbean where a large number women may be infected. In the West, women with HI are advised to avoid pregnancy or to consid termination of pregnancy but for most women i developing countries these are not options.

The debate on whether women should be offere testing for HIV as part of antenatal care is an ongoir one. In a survey in one African country about half th women said that knowing their HIV status would n affect their decision to become pregnant. In a clinic London when women were offered a confidential test, 9 per cent of them declined. In some developing countri women have been tested without their knowledge. In th USA some reports suggest that women, mainly fro deprived or minority groups, accept testing because the fear they will be denied access to health care if the decline. It is imperative that confidentiality b maintained if one is to encourage those women most need of counselling and support to come forward. Eve though it is now well-recognized that pre- and post-te counselling is an essential part of testing for HIV, many places it is often lacking. Doctors often have n informed patients of their diagnosis because they la counselling skills and feel unable to provide the necessary support.

The above discussion has relevance to health and health-education policies. Women's needs are different from men's and policy-makers have to take this into consideration.

Women should be offered appropriate information and education so that they can make informed choices. This should take into account their particular social and economic circumstances, as information is not enough if women are not in a position to have control over their own lives and bodies. The messages will be different depending on which women are being addressed. Sex workers, women in stable relationships or adolescent girls about to start sexual activities need to be approached with messages that are relevant to their particular situation. In the case of prostitutes it is important not to make them scapegoats. Health education should be aimed at their clients as well. Education on prevention of HIV infection/AIDS and other sexually transmitted diseases should ideally be in the context of education and information on sexuality. There is a need for sex education which empowers women and encourages them to feel more confident to express their own needs and to negotiate over condom usage with a partner. Education with men on these aspects is necessary as well. Participation of the male sexual partner in an education and testing programme in, Rwanda positively affected change to lower-risk sexual behaviour. Access to family-planning services offering appropriate choice and to early treatment of other STDs is also important.

The experiences of women who are beginning to organize themselves and to come up with their own solutions for support, sharing of child care and income-generating activities need to be taken into account. In relation to income-generating activities, particularly for prostitutes, it is important to ensure that activities are genuinely productive. 'Traditional' income-generating projects like jam-making, knitting, weaving, etc., do not usually generate much money and large-group activities are not profitable in most cases. It is difficult to find successful income-generating projects but access to credit through revolving credit schemes could be explored. Access to child care remains an important issue on which self- help groups could, with some external support, organize their own schemes.

There are various groups which are attempting to deal with the problems of women in a different way. Some of these are particularly concerned with helping women sex workers. Empower is one such group in Thailand. It is an association of bar workers set up to help women working in Patpong. They have staged shows on safer sex aimed not just at sex workers but at their clients and bar and brothel owners. They also have a drop-in centre which gives information on AIDS and other STDs, nutrition, safe drug use and family planning, and they provide education for the women. The main problems they face are discriminatory attitudes towards sex workers who often get beaten up when they insist on the use of condoms. Yet women are still blamed for transmission.

Another example of positive activities is those undertaken by Gabriela, a national coalition of Filipino women's groups. This group has been involved in demanding the dismantling of US military bases in the Philippines and the compensation by the US government for 'hospitality women' infected with HIV. It has drop-in centres and provides information and education for sex workers. It has also formed a Task Force on AIDS to do advocacy work and attempt to educate people in the media and general public about the problems of AIDS in particular and the sexually prostituted in general.

Ecofeminism embodies within it several different strands of discourse, most of which have yet to be spelled out fully, and which reflect, among other things, different positions within the western feminist movement (radical, liberal, socialist). As a body of thought ecofeminism is as yet underdeveloped and still evolving, but carries a growing advocacy. Disentangling the various threads in the debate, and focusing on those more clearly articulated, provides us with the following picture of the ecofeminist arguments:

1. There are important connections between the domination and oppression of women and the domination and exploitation of nature.
2. In patriarchal thought, women are identified as being closer to nature and men as being closer to culture. Nature is seen as inferior to culture; hence, women are seen as inferior to men.
3. Because the domination of women and the domination of nature have occurred together, women have a particular stake in ending the domination of nature, in healing the alienated human and non-human nature.
4. The feminist movement and the environmental movement both stand for egalitarian, non-hierarchical systems. They thus have a good deal in common and need to work together to evolve a common perspective, theory and practice.

In the ecofeminist argument, therefore, the connection between the domination of women and that of nature is seen basically as ideological, as rooted in a system of ideas and representations, values and beliefs, that places women and the non-human world hierarchically below men. It calls upon women and men to reconceptualize themselves, and their relationships to one another and to the non-human world, in non-hierarchical ways.

We might then ask: in what is this connection between nature and women seen to be rooted? The idea that women are seen as closer to nature than men was initially introduced into contemporary feminist discourse by Sherry Ortner who argued that 'woman is being identified with-or, if you will, seems to be a symbol of-something that every culture devalues, defines as being of a lower order of existence than itself... [That something] is 'nature' in the most generalized sense... [Women are everywhere] being symbolically associated with nature, as opposed to men, who are identified with culture. In her initial formulation, the connection between women and nature was clearly rooted in the biological processes of reproduction although, even then, Ortner did recognize that women, like men, also mediate between nature and culture.

Ortner has since modified her position which was also criticized by others (particularly social anthropologists) on several counts, especially because the nature-culture divide is not universal across all cultures, nor is there uniformity in the meaning attributed to 'nature', 'culture', 'male' and 'female'. Still, some ecofeminists accept the emphasis on biology uncritically and reiterate it in different ways. An extreme form of this position is that taken by Ariel Kay Salleh who grounds even women's consciousness in biology and in nature. She argues: 'Women's monthly fertility cycle, the tiring symbiosis of pregnancy, the wrench of childbirth and the pleasure of suckling an infant, these things already ground women's consciousness in the knowledge of being coterminous with nature. However tacit or unconscious this identity may be for many women... it is nevertheless "a fact of life". Others such as Ynestra King and Carolyn Merchant argue that the nature-culture dichotomy is a false one, a patriarchal ideological construct which is then used to maintain gender hierarchy. At the same time they accept the view that women are ideologically constructed as closer to nature because of their biology.

Merchant, however, in an illuminating historical analysis, shows that in pre-modem Europe the conceptual connection between women and nature rested on two divergent images, coexisting simultaneously, one which constrained the destruction of nature and the other which sanctioned it. Both identified nature with the female sex. The first image, which was the dominant one, identified nature, especially the earth, with the nurturing mother, and culturally restricted 'the types of socially and morally sanctioned human actions allowable with respect to the earth. One does not readily slay a mother, dig into her entrails for gold, or mutilate her body... . The opposing image was of nature as wild and uncontrollable which could render violence, storms, droughts and general chaos. This image culturally sanctioned mastery and human dominance over nature.

Between the sixteenth and seventeenth centuries, Merchant suggests, the Scientific Revolution and the growth of a market-oriented culture in Europe undermined the image of an organic cosmos with a living female earth at its centre. This image gave way to a mechanistic world-view in which nature was reconceived as something to be mastered and controlled by humans. The twin ideas of mechanism and of dominance over nature supported both the denudation of nature and male dominance over women.

Today, Merchant proposes, juxtaposing the egalitarian goals of the women's movement and the environmental movement can suggest 'new values and social structures, based not on the domination of women and nature as resources but on the full expression of both male and female talent and on the maintenance of environmental integrity'.

Ecofeminist discourse, therefore, highlights

a. some of the important conceptual links between the symbolic construction of women and nature and the ways of acting upon them (although Merchant alone goes beyond the level of assertion to trace these links in concrete terms, historically);

b. the underlying commonality between the premises and goals of the women's movement and the environmental movement; and

c. an alternative vision of a more egalitarian and harmonious future society.

At the same time the ecofeminist argument as constructed is problematic on several counts. First, it posits 'woman' as a unitary category and fails to differentiate among women by class, race, ethnicity and so on. It thus ignores forms of domination other than gender which also impinge critically on women's position. Second, it locates the domination of women and of nature almost solely in ideology, neglecting the (inter-related) material sources of this dominance (based on economic advantage and Political power). Third, even in the realm of ideological constructs, it says little (with the exception of Merchant's analysis) about the social, economic and political structures within which these constructs are produced and transformed. Nor does it address the central issue of the means by which certain dominant groups (predicated on gender, class, etc.) are able to bring about ideological shifts in their own favour and how such shifts get entrenched, Fourth, the ecofeminist argument does not take into account women's lived material relationship with nature, as opposed to what others or they themselves might conceive that relationship to be. Fifth, those strands of ecofeminism that trace the connection between women and nature to biology may be seen as adhering to a form of essentialism (some notion of a female 'essence' which is unchangeable and irreducible). Such a formulation flies in the face of wide-ranging evidence that concepts of nature, culture, gender and so on are historically and socially constructed and vary across and.within cultures and time periods.

In other words, the debate highlights the significant effect of ideological constructs in shaping relations of gender dominance and forms of acting on the non-human world, but if these constructs are to be challenged it is necessary to go further. We need a theoretical understanding of what could be termed 'the political economy of ideological construction', that is, of the interplay between conflicting discourses, the groups promoting particular discourses, and the means used to entrench views embodied in those discourses. Equally, it is critical to examine the underlying basis of women's relationship with the non-human world at levels other than ideology (such as through the work women and men do and the gender division of property and power) and to address how the material realities in which women of different classes/castes/races are rooted might affect their responses to environmental degradation. Women in the West, for instance, have responded in specific ways to the threat of environmental destruction, such as by organizing the Greenham Common resistance to nuclear missiles in England and by participating in the Green movement across Europe and the United States.

A variety of actions has similarly been taken by women in the Third World. The question then is: are there gendered aspects to these responses? If so, in what are these responses rooted?

Vandana Shiva's work on India takes us a step forward. Like the ecofeminists, she sees violence against nature and against women as built into the very mode of perceiving both. Like Merchant, she argues that violence against nature is intrinsic to the dominant industrial/ developmental model, which she characterizes as a colonial imposition. Associated with the adoption of this developmental model, Shiva argues, was a radical conceptual shift away from the traditional Indian cosmological view of (animate and inanimate) nature as Prakriti, as 'activity and diversity' and as 'an expression of Shakti, the feminine and creative principle of the cosmos' which 'in conjunction with the masculine principle (Purusba)... creates the world'. In this shift, the living, nurturing relationship between man and nature as earth mother was replaced by the notion of man as separate from and dominating over inert and passive nature. 'Viewed from the perspective of nature, or women embedded in nature', the shift was repressive and violent. 'For women... the death of Prakriti is simultaneously a beginning of their marginalisation, devaluation, displacement and ultimate dispensability. The ecological crisis is, at its root, the death of the feminine principle...

At the same time, Shiva notes that violence against women and against nature are linked not just ideologically but also materially. For instance, Third World women are dependent on nature 'for drawing sustenance for themselves, their families, their societies'. The destruction of nature thus becomes the destruction of women's sources for 'staying alive'. Drawing upon her experience of working with women activists in the Chipko movement-the environmental movement for forest protection and regeneration in the Garhwal hills of northwest India-Shiva argues that 'Third World women' have both a special dependence on and a special knowledge of nature. This knowledge has been systematically marginalized under the impact of modern science: 'Modern reductionist science, like development, turns out to be a patriarchal project, which has excluded women as experts, and has simultaneously excluded ecology and holistic ways of knowing which understand and respect nature's processes and interconnectedness as science.

Shiva takes us further than the western ecofeminists in exploring the links between ways of thinking about development, the processes of developmental change, and the impact of these on the environment and on the people dependent upon it for their livelihood. These links are of critical significance. Nevertheless her argument has three principal analytical problems. First, her examples relate to rural women primarily from northwest India, but her generalizations conflate all Third World women into one category. Although she distinguishes Third World women from the rest, like the ecoferninists she does not differentiate between women of different classes, castes, races, ecological zones and so on. Hence, implicitly, a form of essentialism could be read into her work, in that all Third World women, whom she sees as 'embedded in nature', *qua women* have a special relationship with the natural environment. This still begs the question: what is the basis of this relation- ship and how do women acquire this special understanding?

Second, she does not indicate by what concrete processes and institutions ideological constructions of gender and nature have changed in India, nor does she recognize the coexistence of several ideological strands, given India's ethnic and religious diversity. For instance, her emphasis on the feminine principle as the guiding idea in Indian philosophic discourse in fact relates to the Hindu discourse alone and cannot be seen as applicable for Indians of all religious persuasions Indeed, Hinduism itself is pluralistic, fluid and contains several coexisting discourses with varying gender implications But perhaps most importantly, it is not clear how and in which historical period(s) the concept of the feminine principle in practice affected gender relations or relations between people and nature.

Third, Shiva attributes existing forms of destruction of nature and the oppression of women (in both symbolic and real terms) principally to the Third World's history of colonialism and to the imposition of western science and a western model of development. Undeniably, the colonial experience and the forms that modern development have taken in Third World countries have been destructive and distorting economically, institutionally and culturally. However, it cannot be ignored that this process impinged on pre-existing bases of economic and social (including gender) inequalities. Here it is important to distinguish between the particular model of modernization that clearly has been imported/ adopted from the West by many Third World countries (with or without a history of colonization) and the socio-economic base on which this model was imposed. Pre-British India, especially during the Mughal period, was considerably class/caste stratified, although varyingly across regions This would have affected the patterns of access to and use of natural resources by different classes and social groups. Although much more research is needed on the political economy of natural resource use in the pre-colonial period, the evidence of differentiated peasant communities at that time cautions against sweeping historical generalizations about the effects of colonial rule.

By locating the 'problem' almost entirely in the Third World's experience of the West, Shiva misses out on the very real local forces of power, privilege and property relations that predate colonialism. What exists today is a complex legacy of colonial and pre-colonial interactions that defines the constraints and parameters within which and from which present thinking and action on development, resource use and social change have to proceed. In particular, a strategy for change requires an explicit analysis of the structural causes of environmental degradation, its effects and responses to it. Women's and men's relationship with nature needs to be understood as rooted in their material reality, in their specific forms of interaction with the environment. Hence, insofar as there is a gender and class/caste/race-based division of labour and distribution of property and power, gender and class (caste/race) structure people's interactions with nature and so the effects of environmental change on people and their responses to it. And where knowledge about nature is experiential in its basis, the divisions of labour, property and power which shape experience also shape the knowledge based on that experience.

For instance, poor peasant and tribal women have typically been responsible for fetching fuel and fodder and in hill and tribal communities have also often been the main cultivators. They are thus likely to be affected adversely in quite specific ways by environmental degradation. At the same time, in the course of their everyday interactions with nature, they acquire a special knowledge of species varieties and the processes of natural regeneration. (This would include knowledge passed on to them by, for example, their mothers.) They could thus be seen as both victims of the destruction of nature and as repositories of knowledge about nature, in ways distinct from the men of their class. The former aspect would provide the gendered impulse for their resistance and response to environmental destruction. The latter would condition their perceptions and choices of what should be done. Indeed, on the basis of their experiential understanding and knowledge, they could provide a special perspective on the processes of environmental regeneration, one that needs to inform our view of alternative approaches to development.

In this conceptualization, therefore, the link between women and the environment can be seen as structured by a given gender and class (/caste/race) organization of production, reproduction and distribution. Ideological constructions such as of gender, of nature, and of the relationship between the two, may be seen as (interactively) a part of this structuring but not the whole of it. This perspective I term 'feminist environmentalism'. In terms of action such a perspective would call for struggles over both resources and meanings. It would imply grappling with the dominant groups who have the property, power and privilege to control resources, and these or other groups who control ways of thinking about them, via educational, media, religious and legal institutions. On the feminist front there would be a need to challenge and transform both notions about gender and the actual division of work and resources between the genders. On the environmental front there would be a need to challenge and transform not only notions about the relationship between people and nature but also the actual methods of appropriation of nature's resources by a few. Feminist environmentalism underlines the necessity of addressing these dimensions from both fronts.

7

National Commission for Woman

The National Commission for Women (NCW) was constituted by the Government of India on 31st January 1992 as a high-powered autonomous body at national level in pursuance of National Commission for Women Act 1990. The Commission was constituted to safeguard the interest of women, gaining for them equality in status and elimination of any discrimination against them. The Commission consists of a Chairperson, five Members an one Member Secretary.

During the period under report, Ms. V. Mohini Giri was Chairperson of the Commission till 20th July, 1998 thereafter Ms. Vibha Parthasarathy took over as Chairperson of the Commission from 18th January, 1999. Ms. Indira Basavaraj, Ms. Sukeshi Oram, Ms. Syeda Saiyidain Hameed and Ms. Binoo Sen continued to be Members and Member Secretary respectively of the Commission whereas Ms. Vijay Daksh and Ms. Poornima Advani took over as Members of the Commission in place of Ms. Kokila Vyas who expired and Ms. Kailash Pati who completed her tenure as Member.

In order to review the strength and weaknesses of the NCW and assess its contribution, a conference "Crossing the Bridge" was organised. The Chief Guest at the conference was Smt. Suman Krishan Kant. The key note address was delivered by Smt. Margaret Alva, who emphasised the need for NCW to have financial autonomy and status equivalent to NHRC. She was alsc of the view that NCW should be free from bureaucratic control; there was also a need to have transparency in selection of

Chairperson and Members, which should be free from political considerations.

Activities of the commission

The Commission took extensive tours in various states, in order to acquire a first hand knowledge of the problems and plight of socially and economically oppressed groups of women, women in custody, women belonging to SC/ST and other special groups. A number of seminars, conferences and workshops were organised or sponsored to deliberate on various socioeconomic and legal issues relating to women's empowerment.

During the period under report, the Commission concentrated on consolidation of the activities initiated in the preceding year. A resume of the main activities of the Commission undertaken during the period, 1st April 1998 to 31st December, 1998 is given below:

Safeguarding Women's Rights

The main function of the Commission, according to the NCW Act, is to safeguard the rights of women in the country. The Commission noted with great concern that the women were increasingly being denied their rights. With a view to make women aware on this aspect, the NCW has initiated a multi-pronged strategy consisting of:

i) Legal Awareness Programme

A country wide legal awareness programme for women has been initiated by the Commission aiming at dissemination of the knowledge of legal rights and safeguards provided to them in law. The Commission sponsors NGC)s and women's colleges conducting the programme. During the period under report 10 legal awareness generation programmes were held.

ii) Complaints, Prellitigation and Counselling Cell

The functions of the Complaints and Prelitigation Cell are to look into complaints and take suo-moto notice of matters relating to (i) deprivation of women's rights, (ii) non- implementation of laws enacted to provide protection to women and also to achieve the objective of equality and development, (iii)non-compliance of policy decisions, guidelines or instructions aimed at mitigating hardships and ensuring welfare and (iv) providing relief to women and taking up issues arising out of such matters with appropriate authorities, which include the law enforcing agencies and police departments.

During the period under report, nearly 1752 complaints had been lodged with the NCW.

In certain specific cases, the Commission investigates the complaints under section 10(l)(4) of the Act for the purpose of summoning and enforcing the attendance of any person against whom the complaint has been lodged, for the purpose of making an in-depth enquiry into the allegations made by the complainant. As per the provision, the Commission made the following enquiries and investigations regarding atrocities on women:

Reports were received from Gundupatti village at Kodaikanal in Tamil Nadu, regarding unleashing of violence by the police on women and children as a sequel to abstinence from voting by the villagers. The villagers were protesting against the Government for not providing them basic necessities. The inquiry report of the Commission was forwarded to the State Government of Tamil Nadu and also to the Inquiry Committee set up by the Government for their consideration. On receiving a report that the village health nurses of Perambalur

District of Tamil Nadu were being harassed by the doctor of the Primary Health Centre at Poyyur, the Commission inquired into the incident and submitted its report to the State Government. In their recommendation, the NCW suggested that the doctor who was guilty of harassing the nurses should immediately be transferred to the General Hospital; also, the Supreme Court judgement regarding Sexual Harassment to Women at Work Place be translated into Tamil and pasted on the notice board of all the primary health centres to prevent innocent women from being victimised.

During their visit to Madhya Pradesh, the NCW team were approached by several women's organisations to look into the indiscriminate violence unleashed at villagers, and molestation of women by police. The women were peacefully demonstrating as part of the "Narmada Bachao Andolan" against the Makeshwar Hydra Project in Khargaon District. One of the Members of the Commission, alongwith an investigating team, visited the areas, carried out investigations and forwarded their recommendations to the Madhya Pradesh Government. The Commission also urged the State Government to stop all construction at the Maheshwar Hydra Project until the task force constituted to look into the grievances of the villagers, submitted its report.

iii) Sexual Harassment of Women at Work Place

The Commission sponsored a study on "Sexual Harassment of Women at Work Place". For this study, a survey was conducted in States of Andhra Pradesh, Maharashtra, Madhya Pradesh, Uttar Pradesh and West Bengal, covering a sample of 1,211 women. It was found that 50 percent of the women in the sample faced sexual harassment. Among these, 85 percent were not even aware of the Supreme Court Judgement regarding protection of women from sexual harassment at work place. More problems are reported from women in the unorganised sector compared to those in the organised sector.

The Commission also formulated a code of conduct in accordance with the directions given by Supreme Court Judgement on Sexual Harassment to be implemented at Work Place. According to this code, all organisations, both government and private, are required to set up "complaint committees" for investigating charges of sexual harassment. These committees should investigate the charges within a limited period of time. The code has been widely circulated to Central and State Commissions, public sector organisations, banks, media and apex bodies of private sector like FICCI, CII, etc.

iv) Parivarik Mahilla Lok Adallats

The fact of hundreds of cases remaining pending with courts, causing undue delay in justice delivery and sometimes no justice at all, had been a cause of anguish for the Commission. The desire to provide speedy justice to women led to the development of the innovative concept of Parivarik Mahila Lok Adalats (PMLAs) by the NCW. These adalats are organised on the lines of the Lok Adalats with the help of NGOs and the Legal Aid Boards at state and district levels. The effort has been very successful in getting justice delivered to women in respect of family disputes. The types of cases which are handled by the PMLAs are : pending cases, prelitigation cases, legal advice in respect of legal/judicial matters such as matrimonial disputes, criminal cases, labour, motor accident cases and dowry harassment, etc.

v) Review of Laws and Legislative Measures

The Union Government had referred a list of 39 legislations which have a direct bearing on women, for review by the National Commission for Women. During the year under report, the Commission reviewed the following 11 legislations and forwarded their comments to the Government for consideration.

1. Amendment to the Commission of Sati (Prevention) Act.
2. Amendment to the Dowry Prohibition Act.
3. Amendment to the Hindu Marriage Act.
4. Medical termination of pregnancy Act.
5. Child Marriage Restraint Act, 1929 (19 of 1929)
6. Family Courts Act, 1984 (66 of 1984)
7. Foreign Marriage Act, 1969 (A of 1969)
8. Guardian and Wards Act, 1869 (A of 1869)
9. Indian Succession Act, 1925 (39 of 1925)
10. Immoral Traffic Prevention Act, 1986
11. Indecent Representation of Women (Prohibition) Amendment Bill, 1998

New Bills/Laws prepared by NCW

During the year under report, the NCW proposed 2 new Bills for the consideration of the Government of India. These are:-

— Draft SAARC Regional Convention on Prevention and Combating Trafficking in Women and Children.

— Framing of rules under Section 9(b) and Section 10 of the Dowry Prohibition Act 1961.

Activities Reguarding Legal Rights

Campaign against gender based violence in south Asia

The NCW was a partner in the Indian context to the 16

days global campaign launched by the UN Development Fund for Women and other UN agencies, NGC)s and educational institutions. The beginning of the campaign coincided with the International Day for Elimination of Violence Against Women, November 25. Various awareness building programmes for people formed a part of the campaign. The campaign culminated in a Global March on 10th December, 1998 which coincided with the Human Rights Day.

Dahei Mukti Abhiyan

The NCW has launched the Dahei Mukti Abhiyan so that the country marches into the 21st century without the social stigma of dowry. For bringing about awareness even at the formative stages, essay, painting and poster competitions would be organised through State Governments for different age groups from 6 years to 25 years.

Abuse of the girl child

A public inquiry was sponsored by the Commission on "Sexual Abuse of Girl Children in Kanyakumari District", Tamil Nadu. This event was organised by All India Democratic Women's Association at Nagarcoil. Eleven cases of child rape were presented before the jury during the inquiry. It was noted that all the victims belonged to the working class and were extremely poor. During the hearing, the DSP and the District Collector were also present.

A Some of the recommendations made by the NCW, adopted at the end of the hearing are :

— Child rape cases should be covered by a separate law ;

— The definition of child rape should be widened to involve a wide range of sexual abuse and violence.

— Minimum punishment for child rape should be 10 years.

— Child rape cases should be disposed of within a period of six months.

— A special fund for rehabilitation of rape victims should be created.

Special social groups

Carrying forward the activities undertaken for the Special Social Groups like widows, women in custody, and the mentally ill women, the Commission took up the issue of the development of these groups. The important activities undertaken by the Commission in this regard are as follows

i) Women Belonging to Muslim Community

During their visits to cities like Kolhapur, Jabalpur, Aligarh, etc., the Commission met groups of Muslim women who had expressed a number of grievances and requested for the following:

— Divorced women should start getting maintenance as in the past under the Criminal Procedure Code 125.

— A law should be enacted for disallowing oral one sided divorce.

— The single wife law applicable to Hindus should be extended to Muslims also.

— A Commission should be established for rehabilitation of divorced women and their children.

Taking note of the above, the Commission decided to study the problems of minority communities in greater depth. An Expert Committee was set up by the Commission to study the problems of the development of women belonging to minorities. The Expert Committee came to the following conclusions regarding the problems of Muslim women and ways of resolving them:

— Effort should be made to win the confidence of Muslim women and work should be done through these women for their own benefit.

— Priority was necessary for educational development of Muslim women.

— There was a need to organise seminars and conferences, etc., to generate awareness among Muslim women.

— Dialogue may be initiated with Muslim Personal Law Board to bring about reforms.

— Public hearings may be arranged at the regional level to bring to the fore, the grievances of Muslim women.

— A standard Nikahnama may be prescribed for marriages.

The Commission participated in a Seminar on Muslim Personal Law organised by the Centre for Study of Society and Secularism and the Institute of Islamic Studies. At this seminar, two major problems were identified viz. : Muslim Personal Law (Triple Talaq) and multiple marriages.

On the basis of the recommendations of the Expert Committee, public hearings were organised at different places to hear the grievances of minority women. Such hearings were held at Chennai, Mumbai, Lucknow, Hyderabad and Jabalpur.

During a discussion between the Commission and the Muslim Personal Law Board, it emerged that there is no religion which accords as much rights to women as

Islam. The Muslims, in fact, extrapolate from it only that which is convenient or useful to maintain men's superiority over women. The question is how to change the mindset and how to show the Muslims that this mindset is harming their image.

The public hearing for minority women, sponsored by NCW and organised by the Jabalpur Centre of the All India Womens Conference was attended by more than 300 women including Muslims, activists and other minority communities. Some of the important suggestions made at this event are:

— Divorce of Muslim women should be registered with some recognised Muslim organisations so that influential persons can intervene and settle family disputes,

— Maintenance should be increased to Rs. 3000/-p.m.

— A woman should have the right to file the case at the place of her choice.

ii) Scheduled Caste/Scheduled Tribe Women

The Commission has been deeply concerned about the empowerment of women belonging to SC/ST communities. The Commission visited a number of states and the tribal areas therein to study the problems faced by tribal women. The Commission visited the State of Orissa and attended a Parivarik Mahila Lok Adalat (PMLA) held at the Angul TD area. The Commission also visited the Tribal Research Institute in Orissa and viewed the research work done by the Institute relating to tribal women. The Institute has done complete ethnographic studies of 12 out of 62 tribes in the state.

During the Commission's visit to Kodaikanal in Tamil Nadu, the Commission interacted with a group of women who came to attend the Adivasi and the Dalit

Women's Conference organised by one of the NGOs. Addressing the group of women, the chairperson pleaded for formation of micro level groups at all villages in the area. Such core groups will ensure total empowerment of women particularly Adivasi and Dalit women and make them economically independent. The women in the gathering narrated their suffering to the Commission and submitted petitions. The Commission requested the State Commission to form a two member committee to study their problems and submit a report.

The Commission during their tour of Andhra Pradesh visited a housing colony developed at Guntur, by one of the NGOs, with the cooperation of HUDCO. Women belonging to this colony were being provided with training in vocations like stitching, leather work, etc., apart from literacy. A dairy' unit was inaugurated by the Commission in the colony.

A conference of the Directors of Tribal Research Institutes in various states was organised by the Commission to discuss the ways and means of evolving an institutionalised mechanism for generating comprehensive data and information regarding tribal women and fill the existing gaps.

The above conference was followed by a conference of State Tribal Commissioners to deliberate on implementation of women specific programmes within the Tribal Sub Plan and orientation of general programmes to suit the needs of the female population in tribal areas.

iii) Mentally ill women

The Commission sponsored a documentary film on mental health of women. The film was made by Counter Point. It portrays the conditions prevailing and services provided in various institutions in the country providing mental health care.

The report of a study of mentally disabled women who have been separated or divorced, which was sponsored by the Commission in the preceding year and conducted by Schizophrenia Research Foundation in India, Chennai was released at the "Regional Conference on Rehabilitation and After Care of Women Mental Patients" organised by Indian Women Council for Social Affairs at Chennai.

iv) women in Custody

Under section 100)(k) of the NCW Act 1990, the Commission is required to inspect or cause to be inspected a jail, remand home, women's institutions or other places of custody and take up with the concerned authorities remedial action. Accordingly, the Commission inspected a number of jails and took up the emerging issues with the concerned authorities. During the period under report the Chairperson and Members of the Commission visited nine jails in five states viz. Bihar, Karnataka, Madhya Pradesh, Orissa and Uttar Pradesh.

The general observations in these jails were :

— Most of the prisoners were undertrials in cases related to dowry.

— The prisoners were not produced in the courts for long periods for various reasons causing prolonged detention.

— Majority of the undertrials had no work to do.

— Generally the food provided was not according to the required norms.

At Bellary, the Commission met three women prisoners who had murdered their husbands under grave provocation. The Chairperson requested the jail authorities to release them.

Apart from the prisons, the Commission visited other custodial institutions. One of the important institutions thus visited was Liluah Home in Calcutta. The Home appeared to be overcrowded and lacked medical facilities. The Commission found inhuman conditions in the Home which accommodated as many as 715 inmates though it had capacity for only 350. The Commission wrote a letter to the Chief Justice of Calcutta High Court who treated this letter as a writ petition. The Court issued notice to the Judicial Secretary and the Secretary to the West Bengal Social Welfare Department to show cause as to why appropriate direction should not be issued for the release of these inmates and why compensation should not be paid to those who might have been illegally detained.

After a hearing, a Division Bench of the Calcutta High Court ordered setting up of a five member committee to examine the conditions of the undertrials in the Liluah Home. The report of the Committee is awaited.

The Commission also met, wherever necessary, the Governors of States in connection with problems faced by women prisoners languishing in jails.

Interaction with NGOs and Masses

Apart from the women of special groups and the custodial institutions, the Commission interacted with a number of NGOs and groups of men and women during their state visits. During these meetings, fruitful discussions were held regarding various women's issues and ways of tackling them.

During their tour of Bihar, a visit was paid to A.N. Sinha Institute at Patna, where a prolonged discussion with a gathering of 500 women, including a number of NGOs, took place regarding the strategies of empowerment of women. A meeting with Bihar Women Lawyers' Association brought out a number of legal issues facing the women in the state. The Chairperson of the Commission was also the Chief Guest at the meeting of the Bihar Chamber of Commerce. She also participated in a meeting of police officers and emphasised in her speech the need for their sensitisation regarding the problems of women. She also addressed a gathering of women and men lawyers of the Bar Council in Patna. One of the Members of the Commission paid a visit to 'Aditi, an NGO in Bihar and appraised herself of the work done by the organisation, particularly in regard to female foeticide in Sitamarhi and Katihar.

The Commission also met Officer of Dalmia Cement where the labourers were suffering immensely on account of a lock out. The Commission and the Labour Officers had received a number of complaints from the women, who were particularly suffering due to the lock out.

During the state visit to Maharashtra, the Commission visited the Maharashtra Council of Agricultural and Educational Research (MCAER), which is an apex Institution coordinating six agricultural universities in the State. It was noted that the MCAER had taken a decision and reserved 33 percent seats for rural girls for courses of agriculture graduation, since most of the women are involved in agricultural work. The Research Institute has also developed a training module on single window system for sensitising senior level officers of Agricultural Department. Each topic in this module has a gender component.

The Commission had a discussion with the DCP, Pune, who looks after the women's cell and discussed the need for sensitisation of police personnel. The chairperson also paid a visit to the Maharashtra Women's

Development Corporation. A fruitful discussion with Pune Shramik Patrakar Sangh was held by the Joint Secretary, during the course of which some important issues were suggested to be taken up by NCW such as improvement of facilities in women's railway coaches and for undertrials in jails; study of family courts, etc.

The Commission during a visit to Ranchi in Bihar, had a meeting with district officials. It was noted that community mobilisation through Self-Help Groups was quite successful in the State. The minority community in the State had also developed Self-Help Groups engaged in economic empowerment of women and improvement of basic services as well as availability of credit for women. Major social problems were witchcraft, lack of land rights for women, domestic violence and alcoholism.

Sensitisation of police officials

The National Commission for Women conducted the first in a series of sensitisation programmes for police officials from the IG to the ASI level in Ranchi and Hazaribagh. At the request of the DGP, the NCW prepared a special module and conducted the first workshop on 'Gender Sensitisation' for nearly 200 police officials at Ranchi and a similar workshop at Hazaribagh. The DIGs and Dy.Commissioners of Police right upto the level of Sub-Inspector and Asstt. Sub-inspectors, and members of the Judiciary participated in the workshop. The sensitisation programme was welcomed by the police officials which emphasised the need for the law enforcement agencies to have a human face, for creating confidence in the community.

Voluntary agencies came forward with offers to help the police in curbing violence against women and to help in tackling social problems. The police in turn came up with deep insights into the reasons which led to atrocities against women such as witchcraft.

Political participation

The NCW sponsored a National Project on "Women in Panchayati Rai", coordinated by Professor Susheela Kaushik, which covered States of Madhya Pradesh, Orissa, Rajasthan, Tamil Nadu and Uttar Pradesh. During the study information was gathered on :

— The extent of political awareness of the elected women based on family background, their notions on politics and Panchayati Rai, on political structure of the village community and identification of the community needs and priorities.

— Their self-image as women's power and limitations,

— Their views on women's development and rights.

The Commission organised workshops "Listen to Women Vote" in Jaipur, Mumbai, Chennai and Chandigarh jointly with the British Council. The keynote address was given by the Chairperson, National Commission for Women. The main issues discussed were public accountability of politicians and strategies to raise women's awareness. It was noticed that the women wanted a change in the culture of politics. They do not want politics of war, but politics to resolve conflict.

The NCW has set up a Core Committee on "politics and women" which met on 1 6th and 20th July and on 9th September, 1998. The Committee discussed the constitutional aspects of the 84th Amendment Bill and also the strategies to generate awareness among people. The Committee was of the opinion that:-

— There should not be any dilution of the Bill

— Indian women should not be divided on the lines of religion, caste, etc. It was decided that:

— Efforts for mobilisation of women and masses in

general, to demand introduction of the Bill in the Lok Sabha should be intensified.

— Regional conferences should be held in Gujarat, Guwahati, Hyderabad, Chandigarh, and Chennai for raising awareness on the issue of reservation for women in the Parliament.

— A rail yatra may be organised to mobilise public opinion.

As per the decision of the Core Group, the NCW supported and encouraged the "Rail Chetna Yatra" financed by the CSWB and the Joint Action Front for Women. The main objectives of the yatra were :

— To mobilise public opinion in support of Reservation Bill

— To prevent violence against women

— To make women aware of their rights

The Yatra passed through nine states viz. Delhi, Haryana, Uttar Pradesh, Maharashtra, Madhya Pradesh, Andhra Pradesh, Tamil Nadu, Kerala and Karnataka, creating mass contact with passengers, meeting people at stations and several women activist groups *en route*. Regional conferences were arranged by the state commissions, State Social Welfare Boards and NGOs at Ernakulam and Chennai..

The campaign succeeded in reaching out to the people on issues of growing violence on women and girl children. The goal of obtaining a million signatures from supporters of the Women Bill on a 100 yard long cloth was achieved after discussion with the signatories and going through the pamphlets.

A delegation of the NCW met the Minister for

Parliamentary Affairs regarding the Women's Reservation Bill and pleaded for introduction of the Bill in the Winter Session of the Parliament. The bill was finally introduced in Parliament on 14 December 1998.

The Commission also sponsored various seminars/ workshops relating to women, girl child, family, etc during the year under report.

8

Central Social Welfare Board

The development of welfare services and the growth of the voluntary sector in India from the early years after Independence have increased almost in tandem, as it was recognized that governmental intervention alone would not be able to provide succour and relief to all the deprived and disadvantaged sections of society.

The growth of the Central Social Welfare Board has kept pace with the development of the welfare and voluntary sectors in India since 1953, when it was first established.

In the words of Jawaharlal Nehru, the first Prime Minister of India, "This attempt that we are making to encourage social welfare activities, is in a sense, rather unique. It is not some central authority which is doing it all by itself, nor does the burden of this fall on the local social welfare organisation. It is a certain combination of the two, where the Central Social Welfare Board comes in as a helper and advisor and at the same time the local welfare organizations who are best suited for it, undertake the work. In this way we can utilise the energy, enthusiasm and initiative of vast numbers of persons all over the country."

Although founded on 13th August 1953 by a resolution of the Government, the Central Social Welfare Board was registered as a Charitable Company under the Companies Act, 1956 in April 1969.

The stated objectives of the Central Social Welfare Board indicate inter alia the following thrust areas:

— To-promote social welfare activities for the general public such as welfare of the family, women children and the handicapped and give assistance in cases of unemployment, old age, sickness, disablement and other similar cases.

— To render technical and financial aid, when necessary, to deserving institutions or organisations including Panchayati Rai institutions.

— To promote the setting up of voluntary organisations in places where they do not exist and to promote additional organisations wherever necessary.

— To study the needs of Social Welfare organisations from time to time and to evaluate the programmes and projects of the aided agencies.

— To organise emergency relief measures in times of calamity.

— To organise and promote training in social work and to organise pilot projects whenever necessary.

The objectives of the Central Social Welfare Board are sought to be translated into reality by the implementation of various schemes and programmes for women and children. The Central Social Welfare Board receives grants for the purpose from the Department of Women & Child Development, Government of India.

Programmes of the Board

The programmes and activities of the Central Social Welfare Board have undergone several changes from time to time in order to make them responsive to society's changing needs. Within the broad objective of empowering women and providing for the needs of children, the Board is implementing specific programmes.

Empowerment through education

The schemes of Condensed Courses of Education and Vocational Training Programme for needy women in rural, hilly and tribal areas were started in 1958 and 1975 respectively. These schemes were revised in 1988-89 in order to provide relevant educational qualifications and skills so that women can become eligible for paying work opportunities. The revised scheme is being implemented from 1990-91.

Under the Scheme of Condensed Courses, voluntary organisations are given grants to conduct courses of one to 2 years duration to enable women of the age of 15 plus to pass Matric/Secondary, Middle and Primary level examinations. Under the vocational training programme, grants are provided to give training to needy and deserving women in different vocations suck as dress designing, computer courses, handicrafts, batik, hand-loom weaving, nursery teacher training, stenography, etc.

During the year 1998-99, a total of 70 courses were sanctioned and an amount of Rs. 20.79 lakh has been released upto December 1998.

Awareness Generation Programme (AGP)

In order to raise the general awareness of rural and poor women, the Awareness Generation Programme was introduced by the Central Social Welfare Board in 1986-87. The broad aim of this Programme is to create awareness among rural and poor women on various social issues so that they can realise their potential in the family and society. Since 1993-94 special emphasis is being given to the participation of women in Panchayati Rai institutions and their role in national integration and communal harmony. Under this scheme, NGO's are provided with grants to hold awareness camps for women. An NGO can conduct camps of varying duration in each area according to local needs. The local panchayats are also involved in conducting the camps. The Central Social Welfare Board's emphasis has been on involvement of genuine grass-root level activist organisations in the implementation of the awareness programme. During the year 1998-99, Rs. 18.30 lakhs has been spent on the programme uptil December 1998.

Economic empowerment

Socio Economic Programme (SEP)

Under the Socio Economic Programme, initiated in 1958, women's organisations are given financial assistance to take up a wide variety of income generating activities which include the production of industrial components in ancillary units, handlooms, handicrafts and fishery and self-employment ventures like vegetable or fish vending, etc. During the year 1998-99, an amount of Rs. 7.93 lakhs has been spent under the Programme uptil December 1998.

Support services

The provision of support services to women is a major thrust area of the Central Social Welfare Board which has the following schemes under which different types of services are provided to working women:

— Creches for Children of Working and Ailing Mothers

— Working Women's Hostels.

Creches

The programme of Creches for Children of Working and Ailing Mothers provides day care services to the children of upto 5 years of age of mothers from lower income group families who are working or ailing. Financial assistance upto Rs. 18,480/- as recurring grant is provided per unit of 25 children. Continuation units are given Rs. 2,000/- every five years for equipment. In the year 1998-99 an amount of Rs. 777.77 lakh has been released for a total of 9225 creches.

Hostels

In order to provide accommodation for women who are working away from their homes, the Board gives assistance to voluntary organisations for running women's hostels. Under this programme, the Board assists in the expenditure on the salaries of a matron, and chowkidar, for provision of recreational facilities and for rent subsidy (for a hostel in a rented building). The annual grant to NGO's under this scheme varies from Rs. 40,000 to Rs. 50,000 to a unit, depending on the class of city or town. An amount of Rs. 43.65 lakh has been sanctioned as grant for 108 hostels in 1998-99.

Social empowerment

The main objective of the Voluntary Action Bureaux and Family Counselling Centres is to provide services to women (and children) who are victims of family maladjustments and atrocities.

The FCC program has served a vital function in mending family relations through systematic counselling. The Board provides assistance In the form of grants, which cover honorarium for counsellors and other contingencies. Grants upto Rs. 1 lakh can be provided to an NGO for running a FCC. During 1998-99, the Central Social Welfare Board has so far released grants of Rs. 136 lakhs for 290 FCCs.

Family Counselling Centres in Collaboration with Police Departments

The Central Social Welfare Board had also decided to assist Family Counselling Centres in police stations to handle cases. During 1998-99, 15 Family Counselling Centres have been sanctioned in 15 States/ Union

Territories. These are Andhra Pradesh Assam, Gujarat, Karnataka, Manipur, Meghalaya, Orissa, Sikkim, Tripura, Uttar Pradesh, West Bengal, Del h I Goa, Maharashtra and Pondicherry.

During the year 1998-99, an amount of Rs.16.41 lakhs was sanctioned and Rs.7.83 lakhs was released for these Family Counselling Centres.

Since training forms an integral component of the Scheme, intensive orientation training is given to all new counsellors within six months of their joining the Centre, while trained counsellors are imparted refresher courses annually to update their professional skills. Training is also conducted for office-bearers of the institutions. 2.6.4 A need has been felt for professional monitoring and evaluation of the functioning of FCCs and also for regular training of counsellors posted in the FCC's.

Schools of Social Work have been involved in the implementation of the scheme as nodal agencies to provide monitoring, evaluation and training services. 17 nodal agencies were identified in different states and a sum of Rs. 3.53 lakhs has been released to them for this professional service.

Mahila Mandal Programme

The Mahila Mandal Programme came into being in 1961-62 to take up welfare services for women and children. These groups of women form an entry point for comprehensive welfare services at the grass-root level. Out of the total expenditure on Mahila Mandals, 75% is borne by the CSWB and the remaining 25% by the organisations themselves. This is a decentralised programme of the Board and it is being run by State Social Welfare Advisory Boards. For 1998-99 an amount of Rs. 217.06 lakhs was sanctioned and Rs.91.80 lakhs has been released to the various State Boards uptil December 1998 to cover 722 centres and 76,163 beneficiaries.

Area Projects

These schemes were started by the Board in the 50's and 60's. The provision of integrated services for women and children is being facilitated by CSWB through a number of specific area projects. The Welfare Extension Projects are multi-purpose projects that extend services such as pre-primary school education, craft activities for women, maternity services and recreational facilities in rural areas. At present there are 44 such projects in five States. Expenditure on the Projects is shared between the CSWB and State Governments in the ratio of 2:1. In 1998-99 an amount of Rs.53.89 lakhs has been released to the State Boards for the implementation of these projects uptil December 1998.

Expenditure on the Border Area Projects is also shared by the CSWB and the State Government in the ratio of 2:1. This scheme was initiated following the Chinese aggression in 1962 and the Pakistan aggression in 1971. Tension in the border areas prompted the initiation and strengthening of welfare services in these areas with a view to promoting their emotional and cultural integration with the rest of the country. At present there are 87 projects functioning in the remote border areas of the country for which an amount of Rs.269.65 lakhs has been released to 1 A State Boards uptil December 1998.

Innovative scheme

It was felt that there are certain areas and social sectors which have remained untouched and uncovered in the entire process of development and social welfare. The Central Social Welfare Board has identified priority areas where there is a need for policy intervention and programme inputs. The areas which are identified by the Board are:—

— Women, who are victims of atrocities and have been assaulted by antisocial elements, etc., widows, who need socioeconomic rehabilitation, counselling, etc.

— Children of prostitutes who need care and development.

— Help in education of mentally retarded.

Rehabilitation of prostitutes & their children

The following institutions are implementing the scheme of Child Development & Care Centres for the rehabilitation of prostitutes:

— Bhartiya Patita Uddhar Sabha, New Delhi.

— Centre for Development Studies & Action, New Delhi.

— Gram Niyojan Kendra, Ghaziabad.

— Indian Council for Child Welfare, New Delhi.

Assistance to needy children

The Central Social Welfare Board has assisted the Indian Council for Child Welfare to set up a Toy, Clothes and Book Bank for poor and needy children. A sum of Rs.1.55 lakh has been provided to the ICCW for this purpose.

Montering and Evaluation

There is a Research, Evaluation and Statistics wing in the CSWB which is responsible for functions related to monitoring and evaluation of various programmes and the maintenance of a data bank on various indicators. During the year 1998-99 the following monitoring and evaluation activities were undertaken by CSWB :

— Continuing monitoring of Scheduled Castes Components of Plan (SCP) & Tribal Sub -Plan (TSP) of the Annual Plan of the Department.

— Compilation of "Directory of Facilities & Services in Delhi" through Women's Feature Services, New Delhi.

— Coordination & facilitation of a study by NIC on "Institutional Strengthening, Study of Central Social Welfare Board" (a study by National Productivity Council).

— Compilation of a list of Voluntary Organisations funded by Central Social Welfare Board.

— Installation of Hindi software in the Computer Systems and training of the staff for using Hindi software.

— Regular updation of data bank.

— A Research Study "Identification of 24 most Backward Districts in terms of Status of Women" in India was brought out.

Publicity and Publications

During the year 1998-99 the programmes and functions of the Board received wide coverage in the print and electronic media. The Board continued to publish its monthly journals 'Social Welfare' in English and 'Samaj Kalyan' in Hindi.

'Social Welfare' which was founded in April, 195.4 soon after the inception of the Board brought out theme issues and special articles this year on subjects relating to economic reforms and Indian women, women workers, disabled women, empowerment, drug abuse, women's education, population control, ICDS and health.

'Samaj Kalyan' was introduced in August 1955 and has been focusing on topical issues. In the year 1998-99 Samaj Kalyan highlighted women's education, drug problem, child labour, environment, population increase,

Panchayati Rai, disabled, crime against women, AIDs, etc.

Hindi

During the year 1998-99 (upto 30 November 98) official language Hindi has been used progressively in Central Social Welfare Board as done in previous years. During the period under report the meeting of Official Language Implementation Committee was held.

An incentive scheme for original Hindi noting and drafting in official work was implemented for the propagation and spread of Hindi and cash awards were given to the winners of last year's scheme. With a view to develop proper mental environment for the successful implementation of Official Language Policy, 'Rajbasha Week' was celebrated during the month of September 1998. A Hindi Essay Competition and a Hindi Debate Competition were organised during the week.

9

Women's Rights and the Law

Education work for prevention of atrocities on women
Linked with social advocacy and legal literacy issues, this programme started in 1982, provides financial support to research and academic institutions and voluntary organisations to conduct legal literacy camps, para-legal workers training, produce publicity materials, seminars, workshops, campaigns and to promote studies on gender and violence. The focus is on educating people on legislation and its enforcement to prevent social crimes against women. Assistance has been given to the Central Social Welfare Board to conduct legal literacy camps through voluntary agencies under the Scheme. Assistance has also been given to Women's Development Centres set up in colleges to take up activities under the Scheme.

In the year 1997-98, 7 projects were sanctioned and an amount of Rs. 30 lakh was released. In 1998-99, 3 projects have been sanctioned and Rs. 3.00 lakh were released.

National commission for women
The National Commission for Women, a statutory body, set up under the National Commission for Women Act, 1990 has a mandate to safeguard the rights and interests of women. The Commission continued to pursue its mandated activities, namely review of law, interventions into specific individual complaints of atrocities and

remedial action to safeguard the interests of women, whatever appropriate and feasible. The Commission has accorded highest priority to securing speedy justice to women.

Smt. Vibha Parthasarathy has been appointed as Chairperson of the National Commission for Women, and assumed the charge on 18 January 1999. Smt. Vijay Daksh and Dr. Poornima Advani have been appointed as Members of the Commission w.e.f. 10 December 1998 and 28 December 1998 respectively.

Commissioner for Women's Rights

In the context of the rising trend of crimes against women, the need for establishment of an effective machinery to monitor the delivery of justice to women has long been felt, The National Perspective Plan for Women 1988-2000 AD has recommended the setting up of the Office of Commissioner for Women's Rights.

The Department has accordingly formulated a proposal for creation of a Cell in the National Commission for Women and similar Cells in the offices of State Secretaries in-charge of Women and Child Development/ Social Welfare in 5 States and in the office of District Magistrate in 50 selected districts.

The Department has requested the State Governments to set up District Committees for protection of Women's Rights to monitor and expedite disposal of cases of atrocities against women. The proposed Committees, would consist of the District and Session Judges, the District Magistrate, Superintendent of Police, Deputy Director of prosecution and others. The State Governments of Andhra Pradesh, Assam, Sikkim, Himachal Pradesh, Kerala, Madhya Pradesh and Maharashtra have set up such Committees.

National commission for women

The Department is examining a proposal to set up a National Resource Centre for Women (NRCW) and three State Level Resource Centres for Women (SRCW). The NRCW/SRCW will be an autonomous body to give technical backing to the draft National Policy for the Empowerment of Women by information dissemination, training, advocacy, policy support, research and documentation. This would be a nodal agency to mainstream gender issues in policies and programmes.

Laws affecting women

Under the Government's Action Plan for Effective and Responsive Government, the Women's Development Bureau of the Department initiated steps to review the following laws administered by the Bureau with the view to repealing and modifying procedures operating against the interests of women and to effect reforms:

i the Dowry Prohibition Act, 1961

ii) Indecent Representation of Women (Prohibition) Act, 1986.

iii) The Commission of Sati (Prevention) Act 1987 and

iv) The Immoral Traffic (Prevention) Act, 1956.

A Group of Experts was constituted in the Department to review the laws keeping in view the above objectives. The Group of Experts consists of representatives of the law enforcement machinery, consumers of the relevant laws and experts in laws affecting women. The Expert Group met on 5th February, 1998 and reviewed the Acts administered by this Department, including the four Acts mentioned above. The Expert Group took the view that none of the four Acts mentioned above need to be repealed. The Group also recommended codification of criminal laws concerning women mentioned in the Acts mentioned at (i) to (iv) above and inclusion of various substantive criminal offences against women in these Acts in the Indian Penal Code. The recommendations made by the Expert Group are being processed.

The Department of Women and Child Development is also reviewing the four Acts mentioned above with a view to make their provisions more stringent and to remove lacunae. The Department had entrusted the work of reviewing the Indecent Representation of Women (Prohibition) Act, 1986 and Immoral Traffic (Prevention) Act, 1956 to the National Law School of India University, Bangalore. The reports received from the National Law School in this regard have been sent to the NCW for comments. The comments of NCW with regard to the report of the National Law School of India relating to the Immoral Traffic Prevention Act have been received. The proposed amendments are being considered in consultation with the Ministry of Law & Justice. In respect of the other legislations namely, Dowry Prohibition Act and Commission of Sati (Prevention) Act, inter-ministerial consultations are being held with a view to carry out the amendments.

SAARC regional convention on preventing and combating trafficking in women and children for prositution

India hosted an Expert Group meeting to negotiate the SAARC Regional Convention on Prevention and Combating Trafficking in Women and Children for Prostitution prepared by it, in New Delhi on 18-19 June, 1998. The Draft as approved at the Expert Group meeting was further deliberated at the XIIIth Meeting of the SAARC Technical Committee on Women in Development at Kathmandu from 28-30 June, 1998. The Regional Draft Convention has been endorsed by the SAARC Council of Ministers meeting held at the Xth SAARC Summit at Colombo from 29-31 July, 1998 for adoption by the SAARC countries and is awaiting ratification by the

Government of India. The Convention is expected to be signed at the XIth SAARC summit.

The Convention would seek to take measures to prevent cross-border trafficking through proper international governmental coordination as well as harmonising of various laws and legal provisions relating to trafficking and rehabilitation of rescued victims.

In order to give greater teeth to the provisions relating to child prostitution in the Immoral Traffic (Prevention) Act, 1956, the Government is considering several amendments in the Act. These amendments were considered by the Central Advisory Committee on Child Prostitution on 16 October, 1998 and the recommendations are being consolidated for approval by the Government.

The Government has decided to involve Non -Governmental Organisations in the implementation of the Plan of Action prepared by the Government to combat trafficking and commercial sexual exploitation of women and children for prostitution. A meeting of NGOs active in this field was held on 2 December, 1998 to finalise the nature of help they expect from the Government to implement the Plan of Action. It has emerged that they would welcome financial support from the Government for rehabilitation of rescued victims as well as for awareness generation amongst the victims and their guardians.

10

Child and the Law

The United Nations Convention on the Rights of the Child (CRC), the recent major human rights instrument, is based on a commitment to a solidarity effort on behalf of the children of the world.

The CRC, as compared to any other human rights instrument, has been ratified and accepted as a binding multilateral treaty by the largest number of countries in the shortest period of time. Countries that have yet to ratify the international covenants which are part of the international bill of rights, have ratified the CRC. This indicates a core reality. In a world full of conflict and violent confrontation, we have found a single issue that can evoke a positive sense of agreement. If we widen this small window of reconciliation and realise even a few of the core values of humanism that the CRC articulates, we may well succeed in having an impact on the quality of life of all people.

The record of many countries in implementing international standards has not been one of which they can be proud. State Parties ratify Conventions and yet decades later continue to recognize laws, policies and practices at national levels which infringes on those standards. Most international instruments refer to "the people" on whose behalf these instruments have been ratified. Yet it is only recently that the people are becoming aware that international law has been transformed. It is no longer exclusively a matter for diplomatic relations between States but rather a set of norms that can be used to promote accountability in government within the state and at the national level. The European Convention of Human Rights has adopted a radical procedure in this regard and even gives individuals right of relief and redress for any infringement of the standards of the convention by their governments.

There are those who will argue that a rights strategy and realizing justice through the use of law are superfluous or irrelevant concepts, particularly in developing countries which suffer problems of poverty, social divisiveness and economic limitations. Yet the history of the past and the realities of today must surely convince us that the State has to be a presence in governance. It cannot "wither away" if we are to prevent anarchy. It is therefore vital to recognize that reality and develop structures and institutions that will humanise the interaction between the State and the people. Laws and a legal system fashioned according to norms of justice and international human rights standards which reflect the anguish and inspiration of human experience in struggling with authoritarianism are important for all peoples and their governments. They represent a universal and common heritage for ensuring that State power does not emerge as authoritarianism, but is exercised in a democratic environment.

The CRC is based on a strategy of rights and the implementation and enforcement of those rights. It envisages an important role for the legal system in realizing those rights. International agencies such as UNICEF, which are committed to the interests of children, have a critical role in helping to interpret those rights and in refining them within the context of international human rights law standards. It is the responsibility of both the State and the people to ensure that these rights will not remain aspirations or concepts of international law that we have no hope or expectation of realizing. We cannot afford to create an impression of international consensus, a common vision and a value system, where there is no real commitment to move our societies towards fulfilling their promises to children.

Accepting treaty commitments under international law often becomes only a gesture, because most of our countries do not recognize that international law and domestic law are one system. According to this dualist approach, international law can be enforced domestically, only if treaty standards are incorporated into the national legal system. National courts therefore perceive treaty standards as having moral rather than legal authority. This is why it becomes vital to ensure that the standards set by the CRC are incorporated into the national legal systems.

In setting about the task of incorporation, we must stand committed to certain basic values that are enshrined in the CRC. The CRC, like certain other human rights treaties, recognizes the concept of cultural pluralism and diversity. Nevertheless, Articles 2 and 3 of the CRC, which can be described as the "non-discrimination" and "best interests of the child" clauses, require that States Parties commit them selves to realizing the same framework of core rights for all children. Article 2 in particular clarifies that a child's right of survival and development, protection from exploitation and aggression, and the right to participate in matters that concern the child, consistent with evolving maturity , must be realized for all children within ratifying countries. Factors such as the child's or the parent's or guardian's birth, economic class, disability, ethnicity, religion or gender, cannot be a justification for denying these rights or diluting them.

The commonality of the core standards set by the CRC in Articles 24, 26, 27 and 28 must stimulate uniformly applicable policies on education, health and a safe environment. We can no longer justify different standards in the treatment of children on the basis of a different vision of the nutrition, health, safe environment or education needs of "our children" and " others' children." It is difficult if not impossible to adopt a culturally relativistic approach which would argue that the State had no right to intervene or impose common standards. The articles in the CRC on compulsory education and attaining the highest standards of health, mandate policy intervention by the State to prevent or undermine social practice that would be an obstacle to the realisation of those standards for all children.

We must also remind oursel not priorities one set of rights but treats them all as indivisible and interdependent. It is not possible to realise the child's right to survival without projecting towards and committing efforts to realise the rights of development, protection from exploitation and participation. This inevitably means that law making becomes not merely a task for the legislator and the law reformer. Laws have to be put in place with a holistic perception of their linkages, and a commitment of the resources necessary for implementation. It is not therefore possible to prohibit child marriage or child labour by setting minimum ages by law, without legislative and administrative decisions that provide for compulsory education, facilities for registration of marriage, and the general implementation of relevant socio-economic policies. Resource allocation for education, immunization, nutrition and sanitation, and legislative and regulatory mechanisms to ensure the proper delivery of these services becomes as much a part of law reform as legislating on minimum age for marriage, employment, and juvenile justice. These social and economic policies can no longer be considered issues of political choice outside the realm of law and enforceable rights.

Is this an impractical agenda or framework of international standards for implementation at the national level? In order to answer this question we must recognize the social costs of our past experience in law making without providing adequate socio-economic support or making enforcement a reality. Many developing countries in Asia and Africa face problems of infant mortality, child marriage, maternal mortality, and the phenomena of child widows, child trafficking even across national borders for prostitution, and child labour. We are used to consider these children as high risk, exceptional categories who as children placed in difficult social and economic circumstances need protection by law. Yet the reality is that these children are a product of our countries' inability to realise their rights and the right of their families to national resources.

When families are given minimal allowances to care for children, when maternity leave is grudgingly granted or perceived as a "benefit" to the working mother, we are perpetuating the myth of alleviating poverty and destitution while supporting a welfare payments and benefits ideology. Many of our countries have vagrancy laws that perceive poverty as a fault. Juvenile justice laws which deal with neglected street children speak of the need to rehabilitate them, and impose sanctions on parents for their poverty and neglect. Because we do not provide adequate resources for education or registration of marriage, we are reactant to impose sanctions on parents and the family for infringement of laws on child marriage and child labour. We recognize the validity of child marriage even as we set a standard of a minimum age of marriage by law. In a vicious cycle the inadequacy of the facilities is used as a justification for not imposing sanctions for violations. In the process we do not begin to touch the fringes of the problem of gender discrimination and denial of children's access, girls in particular, to minimum standards of health and education. We cannot ameliorate adult female illiteracy or the health of the working mother. Maternity leave laws make it more difficult for a woman to compete with men for employment. Law making is perceived as ambivalent, and fails to have an impact on these problems.

The CRC focuses on our past failures in recognizing that we should shift from the "poor law" and "welfare benefits" approach that has fertilised the jurisprudence of our countries for many centuries. Access to basic education, health care and a safe environment become the socio-economic rights of all children and their families who are entitled to resources allocation for these purposes. State parties are required to "take measures" to diminish infant and child mortality, combat malnutrition, ensure pre-and post-natal care for mothers as a social responsibility, and make at least primary education composure. It is only if these policies can be put in place, that it will be possible to realise the protection and participation rights of children. A reduction of the level of gender-based and other types of violence in our societies against children cannot be expected unless prohibitive sensations are combined with socio-economic policies that encourage responsible parenting and life chances for all children.

The concept of people's and children's core right to basic services in the area of health, education and environment is not as radical for national legal systems as it seems. Indigenous norms and even laws often recognised the concept of "community rights" in land. Even the legal systems derived from Roman law accepted that "the people" had certain rights in public rivers ad the sea shore. We already have on the statute books of countries, composure education laws, or laws on immunization, sanitation, community health and maternity leave that are often not monitored or enforced.

Countries with written constitutions also have powerful mechanisms for using their chapters on fundamental rights to promote social action in areas such as health and education. Many of these constitutions adopt the typical standpoint in the traditional human rights discourse and treat civil and political rights as enforceable rights and social and economic interventions as uneforceable guidelines to state policy. However, the Indian Supreme court with its extensive power of judicial review has developed the concept of using rights litigation to link the directive principles to justifiable fundamental rights. Social sanction litigation has expanded the scope of Constitutional redress for violation of child rights in areas such as child labour, adoption, children in prison, prostitution and trafficking. The right to life has been recently interpreted as broader than a negative duty of the State to refrain from infringement of personal liberty. It has been interpreted as a positive duty to provide the basic conditions for survival. These initiatives reflect the same perspective, that core needs in the area of health, education and the environment are part of the basic justiciable fundamental rights that accompany citizenship. Citizenship laws which discriminate on the basis of gender have been challenged in the courts of Pakistan and Bangladesh.

The new Constitutional Bill proposed for the Republic of South Africa is unique in the area of constitution making for its integration of international law standards on children's rights and for recognising socio-economic needs as justiciable rights. Children's rights to nurturing, basic nutrition and health, are recognised as their particular fundamental rights to basic education and a safe environment. This constitution is also unique in making the link between child labour and education, following **International Labour Organization** standards and the standards of the CRC. Unlike many other constitutions, the South Africa Constitution defines the right to protection from hazardous labour as a right to be protected from labour that is prejudicial to health and education.

The CRC Therefore provides an incentive to the people, legislators, courts and lawyers to expand the scope of fundamental rights by constitutional amendments and/or interpretations of the law that link national constitutional standards to obligations of their states under international law. If an ethos is created in which there is widespread awareness of the CRC, courts and lawyers can be motivated to interpret constitutional and legal standards so as to incorporate the concept of child rights into dispute settlement.

In countries that face problems of divisiveness it is important to remember that common legal values have already been forged by certain processes. Many countries continue to recognize the "choice concept" which permits persons to be governed by State law instead of personal laws based on ethnicity or religion. Certain laws and policies apply to all citizens, irrespective of choice. The cords in most countries have used the concept of the "child" best interests" in guardianship litigation to forge uniform standards that undermine gender discrimination, discrimination against nonmarital children and the separateness of personal law that can have a negative impact on children. Constitutional standards already recognize equality before the law and even provide for affirmative state action on behalf of women and children so as to achieve substantive rather than formal equality.

Gender discrimination and discrimination against non-marital children is a remarkable feature of the jurisprudence of many countries. With constitutional closes on equality and non-discrimination, the standards of the CRC can be used to bobby for those areas that have been ignored in law reforms, since they strengthen and relate to the constitutional standards of domestic legal systems.

Where Judicial discretion is exercised, an understanding of the framework of rights can stimulate dynamic interpretations of law that will give the child access to justice through the court system, and influence other methods of dispute settlement. The absence of a childcentred focus in legal proceedings in largely due to the tendency to treat the child as a miniature adult before the courts of law. A child-centred approach stimulated by the standards of the CRC can help to create spaces for providing the child access to justice even within the constraints of existing laws. It may be argued that this kind of judicial activism is in consistent with the traditional role of the judiciary as an agency concerned with interpreting rather than making law. Yet the judiciary has expanded and expounded the content of major areas of law precisely because the arrival at a decision in legal proceedings involves policy choices. To day, written constitutions are the basic law of the land, and courts must interpret them to realise fundamental right's. It is hardly possible to argue that they can not interpret the constitution to promote the realisation of rights.

The obligation of State to publicise the CRC and the regular country report, as well as the concept of national and international cooperation in realising child rights prevents arguments of State sovereignty being used to restrict the monitoring of state performance. Nationally and internationally, the CRC envisages a partnership between many actors and encourages dialogue and cooperation. Just as it requires and assumes a joint parental and family responsibility, it assumes a shared state and family responsibility for realising the rights of children. This concept of a shared commitment makes law making and law enforcement something more than the exclusive preserve of lawyers, judges and law enforcement agencies or their critics. There is indeed no places for professional exclusiveness in formulating strategies to realise these rights.

As we see the massive violations of rights in many of our countries it is easy to lose faith in a strategy of rights and their advancement through legal processes. Yet a rights strategy has been usually forged through the experience of human anguish in containing the abuse of power. Rather than allow social and economic injustice to continue and spawn the terror of violence and disillusionment which impacts all our lives, civil society and governments can work together to promote State, community and family accountability in the use of power and authority.

If we can ensure accountability and humanism in the process of governance on an agenda of child rights based on the value system of this new and important human rights convention, we will have found a path to improving our past record on rights and move from rhetoric to action. We can then truly say to children, "you are indeed the wonder tree plant, grown of ruins."

Ours is a deeply perplexing age in relation to rights. On the one hand there is a virtual explosion of human rights annotations; on the other hand, there is growing disregard of rights and cynicism about their future. The proliferation of human rights instruments seems to have caused critics of human rights to form a rights-weariness and a rights-wariness. They insist that only a lean and sparse articulation of rights provides hope for their enforcement. Thus we are in a situation where there is a notable increase in affirmation as well as violations of human rights, where all struggles articulate themselves in the language of human rights and invoke the "politics" of rights; making human rights into bargaining points for the enhancement of power.

Even so, the convention on the Rights of the Child, the World Summit Plan of Action, as well as the Jomtien World conference on Education for All, mark triumphant inaugural articulations of human rights. "Human rights," of course, in some way or other, have tacity included children's rights. But the range of inclusion was never so comprehensive and caring as is the case now. The Vienna Decoration on Human Rights accelerates, in so many ways, the dynamics of the international movement for the promotion of "respect for the rights of the child to the CRC by 1995 and urges State to withdraw "reservations to the Convention" which are "contrary to the objects and purpose of the Convention or otherwise contrary to international treaty law." In particular the Declaration insists that all States, with international cooperation, should:

— combat "exploitation and abuse of children by addressing their root causes:,

— devise "effective measures against female infanticide, harmful child labour, sale of children, child prostitution, child pornography, as well as other forms of sexual abuse",

— organise "means of improving the protection of children armed conflicts" and programmes of

> "aftercare and rehabilitation of children in war zones" as well as those in "especially difficult circumstances." The minimum age of recruitment to armed forces is also addressed.

It is difficult to imagine even the most conscientious critics of human rights enuncitations as having any cogent critique of the expansion of child rights. Critics of human rights enunciations must surely respect the achievements of these measures and realise that inaction would be costly. The neglect of the rights of children would mean the confiscation of our common future: the world's children.

Human rights articulations represent human hope in a brutal and brutalizing world. They provide arenas for he struggle for a just national and international legal order in relation to the child; hey mark an insurrectionary protest against the savage uses of power in the state and society. Even if we fail to achieve our collectively formulated human aspirations, not to try to achieve them is, starkly put, to belie our claim to be and to remain, human. For as state and society which is callous to the right of the child can never aspire to be a just society.

What then is our appointed historical task? And how do we achieve it? Happily, the agenda for action is now abundantly available. What is needed, first of all, is the elimination of adult illiteracy about children's rights. Adult illiteracy about children's rights is widespread among policy makers, intellectuals, ideogogues, opinion makers (e.g. the media), and even among human rights communities. This illiteracy also makes possible the comprehensive and continual ignorance about linkages between the rights of the child and human rights enunciations which are not child-centred and yet affect heir and our common future. Promotion of adult literacy about children's rights is a sine quo non for their realisation. It must be realized at the outset that the problem of adult illiteracy with respect to children's rights is as massive, complex and in need of urgent resolution as the problem of general illiteracy addressed at the Jomtien World Conference on *Education for All.*

Second, we must acknowledge and develop linkages between the rights of the child and other instruments of human rights. There is no danger in such an endeavor of losing the focus on children's rights. Rather, awareness and advocacy of such linkages will enable us to advance the plan of action on children's rights.

The World Health Organization had in 1993 activated the advisory jurisdiction of the International Court of Justice on the use of nuclear weapons by a state in war or other armed conflict as constituting a breach of international law. The World Court accepted the reference and asked all states to make submissions by June 10, 1994. No. effort is necessary, I hope, to underscore the critical relevance of this event to the future of all human rights including children's rights. Whether or not explicit so far, the right of all persons, especially children, to immunity from a world with nuclear arms, as a part of the right to peace, is the matrix of all other rights. But there is little awareness of enthusiasm in children's rights communities (indeed, human rights communities in South Asia) on this laudable intuitive. Similarly, we have little appreciation of the implications of the Dunkelt text on the life and world of children. It should not require any apologies to seek to review world economic development from the standpoint of children's rights.

Third, we need to promote awareness of what the Vienna Declaration describes as the "Undoubtedly, the quest for "root causes" is inordinately complex and it would not help to have any reductionist or simplistic understanding or answer. At the same time, we can not defer action on children's rights until the outcomes of scholarly and scientific engagement emerge. It may even be said that the lack of such involvement is among the "root causes" of the plight of the world's children! At any rate, reorientation of education and research traditions in "children's rights-friendly" directions is a task which ought to be high on our educational policy agenda.

Among these "root causes," clearly, is the state of the law (both normative and institutional). In India, legislative initiatives for the promotion and protection of children's rights are sparse and their enforcement impoverished; some recent movement does, however, point to an emergence of a more active involvement. But insofar as rights are to be enforced by courts, the whole nature (and history) of the adjudicatory system and lowering manifests itself as among the prime "root causes." For India at least, the need to rethink its adjudicatory system, to retool it, to recreate it, is a need which emerges most sharply in the context of child rights. If the rule of law (legality) is to have any meaning for tens of thousands of India's children as they grow into "adulthood," then legal education and research, the transaction of the legal profession and court-craft, and the reogranisation of the court system should engage the attention of children's right advocacy in India. In a profound sense, the career and future of a rule-of-law society and state in India remains closely linked to children's formative perceptions about "rights," law" and "democracy". This remains unexamined but even so it may be said that a nation determines the reproduction or repudiation of legality by the formative experiences of justice and injustice that it imposes on its children.

Fourth, human rights instruments on children's rights stress "participation" as a core value, along with "survival," "protection" and "development." What strategies should be devised to encourage "participation" by children in designing policies for "survival", "protection" and 'development" is, indeed, a most critical question. Policy and legal paternalism is the very basis of the movement towards the enunciations of children's rights. The ideology of "participation, "however, interrogates the institutionalized paternalism of policy, law, administration. Even to raise this kind of question may seem to be a kind of luxury given the misery and powerlessness of masses of children, especially in many parts of the Third World.

But it seems tome that giving children a voice, a forum, empowering their opinion, may accelerate the adult world's pace of progress towards realising their rights. To delink though and action on "participation" in my opinion, is to contribute, knowingly or otherwise, to a strategy or to a deferment of policies regarding the rights of "survival," "protection" and development."

It seems imperative to me that India should develop resources - intellectual, ideological, institutional and praxeological - for sustained children's rights advocacy. I know how institutions often become "traps" or generate a "deadweight" of their own over time. But given the nascency of the movement for children's rights, the persistence of historic formations that suppress and exploit children, and the need to accelerate history, some sort of institutional arraignment might enhance the capabilities of concerned citizens in their struggle to redeem our common future.

Protein-Energy Malnutrition (PEM), Iodine Deficiency Disorders (IDD), Vitamin A Deficiency (VAD) and Iron Deficiency Anemia (IDA) are the major problems of malnutrition in less developed countries, attacking more than half of the young child population. In society, malnutrition in any form is a problem with medical manifestations. The biochemical and medical complexities of malnutrition are dealt with by the science of human nutrition, while the problem of malnutrition in society calls for a much broader approach, requiring sciences, and others.

Like all other societal problems, malnutrition has a scientific and ethical aspect. Science deals with what "can" be done, while ethics deals with what "should" or ought to" be done. It is a scientific fact that iodisation of salt increases the intake of iodine and reduces the risk of IDD. It is, however, an ethical question whether or not salt should be iodised. It is a scientific fact that early initiation of exclusive breastfeeding reduces morbidity and mortality among very young children. The extent to which manufacturers should be allowed to distribute free breast milk substitutes in hospitals is an ethical question.

Science and ethics are dialectically related. Scientific discoveries influence ethics. For example the new discoveries in nuclear science pose some very difficult ethical challenges.

Ethics, on the other hand, may influence science, such as the way in which human beings may be used for medical experimentation.

Both science and ethics progress through the constant interaction between theory and practice. Theory has no meaning without practice, and practice is "blind" without a theory. In science statements like, "one finds what one looks for" (T. Kuhn) and "nothing is more practical than a good theory" (A. Einstein) reflect the way theory influences practice. Testing theories in practical situations, often means that the theory needs to be revised, i.e. practice influences theory.

Problems most often reflect current needs. The nutritional needs of young children have been known for a long, time, even if details continue to be debated. These needs are expressed in quantified daily requirements of energy, protein and micro-nutrients. The definition of these requirements is a scientific task.

Unfulfilled needs pose an ethical challenges, depending on how serious the deficiency is judged. When a need is recognised as being worthy of sympathy and serious consideration, this need becomes a claim. A need becomes a claim when people find it unethical not to do something about it.

Claims, however, are of different strengths. Some people may claim that young children should have their requirements of minimum intake of iodine fulfilled. This is no more than a descriptive statement. Nobody is identified as having the duty to fulfill this claim. Stating that children have a claim to adequate iodine intake is stronger, but still no duties are defined. Stating, however, that children have a claim against their parents, the community, or the government are expected to do something. Such claims are called justified claims, valid claims or duty-claims.

The World Summit for Children (WSC) and the International Conference on Nutrition (ICN) specified and agreed on a set of nutritional goals. These goals transformed well-known nutritional needs into recognised claims. Heads of Governments/States in the WSC and Governments in the ICN promised to achieve these quantified goals (objectives) before the year 2000.

Rights are more than claims. Rights are entitlements to something, even if they do not constitute valid claims against a particular individual or entity of society. Most often, however, rights imply obligation with the respondent clearly identified.

Human rights have been defined as rights which all persons equally have simply insofar as they are human. Gewirth (1984) defines human rights as "personally oriented, normatively necessary moral requirements." "Personally oriented," because they are morally mandatory and not a result of charity. "Moral requirements" refer to (a) necessary needs, (b) justified entitlements and (c) claims on others.

An example from nutrition may help clarify these distinctions. Every child needs a minimum intake of iodine ("personally oriented"). Every child should get an adequate intake of iodine, or his/her mental development will be negatively affected ("normatively necessary"). This moral requirement constitutes (a) the fact that iodine is necessary ("necessary needs"), (b) that children have a right to optimal mental development ("justified entitlement") and (c) that the governments have an obligation to ensure the availability of iodised salt ("claim on others"). Human rights are primarily claim-rights, because they imply correlative obligation to other persons or groups. Eide et al. (1991) define these different aspects in the implementation of human rights: (1) to respect, (2) to protect and (3) to fulfill. They also suggest that human rights need to be implemented at different levels of society, from individual/household to international levels. This approach is used by Jonsson (1993) to operationalise the implementation of nutrition as a human right.

Rights imply duties or obligations. Rights also imply goals. Goals, however, do not imply rights. A goal is a necessary, but not a sufficient condition for a right. This means that human development goals, including nutritional goals, can be achieved without any rights.

Feinberg describes this in a thought-experimen "Nowheresville," where most of the human goals were achieved but where there was no self-respect, no dignity no rights. The full implementation of the CRC requires or implies the achievement of all WSC goals. On the other hand, the achievement of the goals does not necessarily mean the full realisation of the CRC.

The challenge, therefore, is not only to achieve the WSC goals but to achieve them in such a way that the processes required for the realisation of the CRC are strengthened and accelerated. Such a rights-based approach combines elements from a goal-based strategy and a duty-based strategy. It constitutes a goal-driven, process-conditioning strategy.

Kant stated that "ought' implies 'can' - or it is otherwise Utopia." Rescher (1987) questions this statement and suggests a new interpretation of Kant. He argues that if "ought implies can" this logically means that "obligation implies capacity", which in turn is equivalent to "incapacity removes obligation." This, however seems unacceptable. He qualifies this problem by two arguments.

a) "To all appearances, an obligation can persist despite an incapacity. We have to be prepared for the prospect of undischargeable duties and unmeetable obligations."

b) "...incapacity does not actually defeat an obligation, it can, however, negate all blame for a failure to carry it out."

He suggests a distinction between the weaker mode of "should" and the stronger mode of "must." Based on Rescher's analysis, a choice needs to be made between:

a) "Absolutistic" rules with "realistic" expectations, and

b) "realistic" rules with "absolutistic" expectations.

In this sense "ought" does not imply "can", while "must" does. In the ideal world, "ought" implies "can," while in the real world only "must" implies "can." Seen in this perspective the WSC goals represent "realistic" goals with absolute expectations, i.e. the goals must be achieved, and they can be achieved.

The full implementation of the CRC, on the other hand, should be interpreted as "absolutistic" with "realistic" expectations. Rights are not divisible and cannot be graded; they are absolute. Many goals are "absolutistic" and not attainable. Rescher argues that it is completely rational to pursue unattainable goals. "Truth" has been the goal for scientific progress. As both Popper and Kuhn argued (and agreed for once!), this goal is not attainable. Science, however, can come closer and closer to the "truth" (of. Popper's definition of "verisimilitude"). The same is true for democracy in political development. The CRC as a whole represents an unattainable goal, although many parts of the CRC can be defined is "absolutistic" goals, e.g. the WSC goals.

It is very important to pursue morally important goals even if they are unattainable. By doing so, other attainable goals will be achieved faster. The promotion of the CRC contributes to the achievement of the WSC goals.

Further, aiming "too high" often gives a better end result than aiming lower. Finally, pursuing unattainable goals gives a clear direction and can often mobiles and create new resources.

Rights implies duties and obligations, but most often nobody can be punished if the obligation is not met. When a right becomes a law, the respondent is identified and if the law is violated the respondent can be punished through the judiciary system.

Practice, however, does not necessarily follow from law. There is therefore a need to enforce a law. Several countries have laws against distribution of non-iodised salt or against aggressive marketing of breast milk substitutes but their practices have not changed, because the laws have never been enforced.

The World Summit for Children Declaration and the Convention on the Rights of the Child can be seen as "social contracts" between the Heads of States and governments and the states themselves and the world's children. More than 300 years ago, Thomas Hobbes (1651) defined in his Leviathan the concept of a "contract" as, "the mutual transferring of rights" and that "...he that is trusted to perform in time to come, being trusted, his performance is called keeping the promise." The challenge is now for leaders of governments to keep the promise they gave at the WSC and for states to keep the promise they made when they ratified the CRC.

Countries are used to being compared on their economic development. Now the time has come when countries should be compared for the way they take care of their children. Signing the WSC Declaration or the ICN Declaration or ratifying the CRC means an obligation to give "a first call on resources for children." Only the future will tell who will keep the promise.

Hobbes, however, also stated "...covenants without the sword, are but words, and of no strength to secure a man at all." What "sword" do we have? An immediate action that can be taken is to establish national monitoring systems for the gradual achievement of the WSC goals, which are necessary for the implementation of the CRC.

The WSC goals represent moral minima (Goulet, 1988), supported by all major religions and political ideologies. A rights-based strategy aims at achieving such fundamental goals, but in such a way that their achievement becomes a right. This implies, for example, sustainability. Such a strategy will contribute to the development of a non-ethnocentric global development ethic.

Gradually the information from monitoring systems will contribute to an increasing "global embarrassment" for those countries that have the resources but avoid the necessary political choices to achieve the goals.

This will contribute to an environment where it becomes "good politics" to ensure the rights of children and "bad politics" to deny children their rights. In an increasingly democratic world more people will both know that the WSC goals can be achieved and think that the should be achieved. Ultimately this will not only influence what political leaders choose to do, but also why political leaders are chosen.

As a Lawyer who has Discharged duties in the executive as well as in the legislative organs of the state, I will try to evaluate the Turkish legal system and existing practices in terms of the rights envisaged in the Convention on the Rights of the Child. Before that, I would like to point out the duties imposed upon the State by the Convention and some principles cited in the same document

The Convention obliges States Parties:

a. to make the principles and provisions of the Convention widely known to adults and children (Article 42);

b. to submit to the Committee on the Rights of the Child, through the Secretary General of the United Nations, reports on the measures they have adopted which give effect to the rights recognised and on the progress made on the enjoyment of these rights within two years of the entry into force of the convention for the state party concerned and every five years thereafter (Article 44/1);

c. to make their reports widely available to the public in their own countries (Article 44/6);

d. to take all legislative, administrative, economic and social measures for the implementation of the rights recognised in the Convention (Article 4);

e. to ensure that the institutions, services and facilities responsible for the protection of children shall conform, in terms of safety, health, the number and suitability of staff, with the standards established by competent authorities (Article 3/3); and,

f. to ensure that the best interests of the child shall be a primary consideration in all actions concerning children (Article 3/1).

Of course, this is not an exhaustive list of the obligations that States Parties have undertaken with respect to the Convention. Some duties that States Parties have to fulfill, particularly those which relate to the duty of making booth the Conventional and the reports widely known by the public, have the potential of mobilising the public. This mobilization can make a significant contribution to the material realisation of the rights included in the Convention.

Besides emphasising the economic and social rights of children, the CRC lays down many principles relating to the rights of the child. The legislative, executive and judicial organs of States Parties have to take these principles into account in all activities relating to children.

Among these principles are:

a. regarding the best interests of the child as a primary consideration in all actions concerning children (Article 3/1);

b. assuring the child who is capable of forming his or her own views the right to express these views freely in all matters affecting the child and giving due weight to these views in accordance with the age and maturity of the child;

c. showing respect to his or her basic rights while taking decisions concerning the child;

d. recognising the principle that parents have the primary responsibility for the upbringing and development of the child, and that appropriate assistance will be rendered to parents by the State in the performance of this responsibility (Article 18);

e. ensuring that a child shall not be separated from his or her parents unless such a separation is necessary for the best interests of the child (Article 9);

f. respecting the rights of parents or those who are responsible for the child (Article 3/2 and Article 5);

g. ensuring review of any penal decision concerning the child by an independent and impartial authority or judicial body (Article 40).

All these principles and provisions clearly show that there has been a change in the overall approach to the child. At the beginning of the present century, the relationship between the State, the child and parents was dominated and governed by quite different principles. Within the frame of these principles, the child was regarded as an "object" rather than a "subject."

Throughout the first half of this century and even in the most advanced countries, the dominant view was that in all actions relating to the child, his or her needs could be best considered and met by "adults". If parents did not or could not fulfill their duties in relation to children, the State undertook to place the child in an institution under State surveillance or in another family. The child's view was not considered at all and there was little regard for the rights of parents.

Today there is a very different approach to the child, and due concern is also paid to the rights and duties of parents. It is accepted in principle that the child has the right to state his or her opinion freely and that this opinion should be properly considered in decisions concerning the child.

The CRC is one of the documents which fully reflects this overall change in approach relating to the child. States Parties have the obligation to respect the rights and personality of the child and to ask for his or her opinion while they are engaged in legislative arrangements relating to the child and preparing the environment in which the child will be able to grow to his or her full potential.

The CRC was signed by the former Turkish Government on September 14, 1990. In order to ratify the Convention, the former Government immediately prepared a bill and presented it to the Parliament. However, in November 1991 the country had a general election and the composition of the Parliament, as well as the government changed. As a result, he provisions of the Turkish Parliament Proceedings Regulation, the bill that would provide for the ratification of the Convention, became void. Therefore, the new Government had to draft and present another bill to the Parliament.

This New Bill is Currently on the agenda of the Turkish Grand National Assembly for ratification. Efforts are being made by a group of parliamentarians to ensure the speedy ratification of the Convention.

When the Turkish legal system and related practices are analysed in terms of the provisions of the Convention, we can reach the following broad conclusions:

a. As far as some provisions of the Convention are concerned, there is no contradiction at all with respect to legislative arrangements or to legal practices. For instance, the child's right to a name and citizenship are guaranteed under the Turkish Civil Code, the Surname Act and the Act on Citizenship, which are all in effect currently. With these acts, it is impossible for a child in Turkey to be deprived of his or her right to a name or citizenship.

b. For some rights stipulated by the Convention, there are problems relating to practical aspects though no problem exists as far as the legislative frame is concerned. The child's right to education can be cited as an example. In Turkey, the child's right to education can be cited as an example. In Turkey, the child's right to education is recognised firstly by the Constitution (Article 42) and further elaborated by the Basic Law on National education and the Code on Primary Education in a manner fully conforming to Article 28 of the Convention. Under these acts, primary education is compulsory and free for all children irrespective of their gender. Furthermore, the State has the obligation to provide appropriate support to children who are talented but lack the material means to reach the highest stages of education in line with their specific interests and capacities. While these provisions are clearly stated in laws, there are some difficulties in actual implementation. For example, despite the face that primary education is compulsory and free for both boys and girls according to our Constitution, many families, especially in he region of southeastern Anatolia are reluctant to send their girls to school because of traditional beliefs.

In order to enable our children to benefit from some of the other rights stated in the Convention it is necessary to introduce new legislative arrangements, as well as certain administrative, economic and social measures. Some efforts in this direction have been made.

Article 32 of the Convention recognises the right of the child to be protected from economic exploitation. According to this article, States parties shall effect all legislative measures in conformity with the relevant provisions of other international instruments to provide the following: minimum ages for admission to employment; appropriate regulation of the hours and conditions of employment; and prevention of the performance of any work that is likely to be hazardous or to interfere with the child's education, or to be harmful to the child's health or physical, mental, spiritual, oral or social development. The same article obliges States Parties to take all relevant administrative, economic and social measures to protect children from economic exploitation.

When the Turkish legal system is analysed in terms of the right to be protected from economic exploitation, it is seen that the relevant provisions are scattered among the various acts (viz. Labour Act, Apprenticeship and Vocational Training Act, Primary Education Act and the Act on the Duties and Authorities of the Police Force). In some cases provisions actually contradict each other. The Labour Act stipulates the minimum age for employment as 15 (Article 67) According to the standards of the International Labour Organization (ILO) agreements. Nonetheless there are some exceptions to this rule. The very same Act states that children above 13 years can be admitted to employment if the nature of the work is such that it does not impair their health, development and school attendance. On the other hand, according to the Apprenticeship and Vocational Training Act, elementary school graduates may be given training at enterprises for the purpose of preparation for an occupation before the minimum age limit. This means that children around 11 or 12 years may be legally employed in light work.

The working conditions of children are also taken into consideration by the Turkish legal system. According to the Labour Act, working hours of children must not exceed 7.5 hours and must not interfere with their school hours (Labour act, Article 67). Before employing children, employers must ensure, through a health check-up, that the child's health is appropriate for the job. The health examination has to be repeated every six months (Labour Act, Article 30). Employers who do not fulfill these obligations are liable to be fined (Labour Act, Article 104).

These legal provisions, which are designed to protect children from economic exploitation, cannot be enforced in most cases since relevant administrative, economic and social measures have not been taken. Moreover, since the Acts mentioned above do not cover children who work in the agricultural sector or in the streets, such children are vulnerable to conditions that are potentially harmful for their mental and physical health, education and development. Street children particularly are frequently subjected to physical, emotional and sexual abuse.

As examples of the Provisions of the Convention

which require new legislative arrangements and some economic, social and administrative measures, we can cite those which are related to delinquent children and others who are abused and neglected. The programme of the previous Coalition Government, in which, gave priority to human rights as well as children's and women's issues. Hence, that Government had, in addition to presenting the bill which provided the ratification of the Convention, prepared another bill which revised the current Juvenile Court Act. In preparing for the Juvenile Court Bill, the Ministry of Justice considered both the Convention on the Rights of the Child and the UNs Standard Minimum Rules for the Administration of Juvenile Justice.

The Cooperation Programme largely includes backward provinces, those which have been prioritised for development and big urban centres. The rationale behind this is the fact that these provinces are the ones in which children are affected much more adversely by such phenomena as poverty, unhealthy urbanization, intensive migration and distorted patterns of income distribution.

In addition to those which are valid for all children, the CRC includes special provisions, which cover children in especially difficult circumstances. This category includes children who are:

— in need of protection or special education;

— subjected to abuse and neglect;

— used in crime, drug trafficking, prostitution and pornography; and

– working.

A point which we would like to raise here in relation to children in need of protection is the change taking place in the overall policies of the Social Services and Child Protection Institution in conformity with the provisions of the CRC. This agency no considers keeping children with their own families as the priority solution and strives to create supportive institutions for the family and to extend assistance to needy families. Alternative care such as placing children with relatives, protective family, adoption, etc. is resorted to only in the most pressing cases. It is now accepted also by the Ministry in charge that institutional care should be the last resort. In spite of this, more than 90 per cent of children who have been taken under protection by the State are placed in protective institutions. We hope that this situation will change soon with the introduction of new policies.

In consider the absence of special legal arrangements for abused and neglected children and the lack of institutions specialising in providing assistance to the families of such children as important items of deficit in my country.

Given that the legislative, executive and judicial branches of the State recognise the best interest of the child as a priority issue, act in coordination on child related issues, and consider the child not as an "object" but a "subject," I believe that the realisation of the children's rights will be a relatively smooth process. Naturally, the State also has to cooperate with the Children's Rights committee of the UN; international organizations such as UNICEF, UNESCO, ILO, WHO and FAO; and international and national non-governmental organizations.

From Jesus to Gandhi, before and after, every sublime soul has beheld divinity in juvenility. Yet with the march of mankind this glorious gift has suffered culpable neglect and callous cruelty for so long and so lawlessly. The hallmark of culture and advancement of civilization consists in the fulfillment of our obligation to the young generation by opening up all opportunities for every child to unfold his or her personality and rise to his or her full stature-physically, morally, mentally and spiritually.

Ages of criminal neglect, despite protests by humanists, thinkers and sages in every country, have given place at long last to a gentler perception of juvenile justice and a chastened jurisprudence of the rights of the child. Human rights are inalienable and so are the rights of the child. So long as children suffer, are victimized or are not nourished, there is no true humanism in the world. Juvenile jurisprudence, during our heartless century, burgeoned after World War I and blossomed after World War II when the UN placed emphasis on the dignity and worth of the child.

The Convention on the rights of the Child, represents an instrument of infinite significance which binds peoples everywhere to cooperate "for improving the living conditions of children in every country, in particular, the developing countries and to evolve a viable jurisprudence of juvenile justice."

The Universal Declaration of Human Rights and the International Covenants on Human Rights, which together make the magna carta of making, confer rights without discriminating as to age, race, sex, religion, birth or other factors.

The Universal Declaration of Human Rights rightly stresses that childhood is entitled to special care and assistance. It further maintains that the family, as a fundamental unit of society, should focus on children as the new hope of tomorrow and provide all the necessary conditions for their growth, the lack of which would result in the stunting of the community. So it is that the Universal Declaration specifies in Article 24 that:

1. Every child shall have, without any discrimination as to race, colour, sex, language, religion, national or social origin, property or birth the right to such measures of protection as are required by his status as a minor, on the part of his family, society and the State.

2. Every child shall be registered immediately after birth and shall have a name.

3. Every child has the right to acquire a nationality.

The voiceless child has title to legal protection before or after birth, according to the canons of international justice. But the harsh truth is that the welfare of the child ranks tragically low in the agenda of State action. In our present day world, the trauma and torture, the illiteracy and deprivation, the hard labour and gross neglect which are the lot of the Third World's juvenile generation call for sensitive social action, united mass mobilisation and affirmative justice processes. Every child everywhere belongs to one global family and is entitled to a universal minimum of rights, fullness of expression and development of faculties. One hundred and thirteen nations, by consensus, promulgated the Vienna Declaration and Programme of Action where the rights of the child and of the girl child in particular, have justly received humane emphasis worldwide.

The Vienna Declaration and Programme of Action makes a humanitarian summons on nations in the articles relating to the rights of the child. Part D of the Vienna Declaration dealing with the rights of the child must become the locomotive of juvenile jurisprudence. The World Conference at Vienna emphasized the principle of "first call for children," and underlined "the importance of major national and international efforts especially those of the United Nations Children's Fund (UNICEF), for promoting respect for the rights of the child to survival, protection, development and participation."

The Vienna Conference Specifically refers to female infanticide, child prostitution, child pornography as well as other forms of sexual abuse and enjoins that measures be taken by specialized agencies "to ensure the effective protection and promotion of human rights of the girl-child" and "urges States to repeal existing laws and regulations and to remove customs and practices which disriminate against and cause harm to the girl child."

Childhood and youth are subject to many visible and invisible suffering and disabilities. Thus, several conventions and other instruments have included juveniles as part of International Jurisprudence by the United Nations. Each nation must have a special ombudsman for juvenile justice, with power, suo motu, to investigate, here cases, render verdicts and take action, including punishment.

Cultural cooperation among nation, acceptance of common values and the introduction of a world watchdog, which will not become an instrument of imperialism, but will operate in the juvenile field as a functional and effective Human Rights Commission is an urgent desideratum. If the Charter of the United Nations and the International Bill of Human Rights are to be taken seriously humanity worldwide, there is a need to transform the Declarations, Covenants, Conventions, Resolutions and Programmes of Action from pious wishes and paper projects into stern commands and operational obligations.

The ideals and goals projected in the UN instruments are a global gain. But shaping children's future by law, and harmonising their lives with the right to health and a happy environment has a long way to go.

Laws on the books and law in action often occupy different streets. If environmental degradation and betrayal of human health are not corrected by law and affirmative action by the executive, legislative and judicial wings of the State, tomorrow may castigate today as treacherous. So what we need is the development of a community conscience in the field of child justice, without which social justice and sustainable development will be a mockery of democracy.

The Constitution of India states specifically that affirmative discrimination in the form of special provisions for women and children is permissible. Article 39(e) of the India Constitution shows special concern for children and directs the State to secure conditions in favour of children so that in their tender age, they are not abused nor coerced by economic necessity to enter avocations unsuited to their age or strength.

Article 45 directs the State to provide free and compulsory education for all children until they complete the age of 14 years. There is no doubt whatever that these obligations have been violated. There has been a chronic dereliction of duty on the part of the State. Vast numbers of children have been kept illiterate, uneducated and without protection against exploitations of childhood such as forced labour and unwholesome activities, which condemn them to moral and material abandonment. If the State betrays its obligation, the Court and the people must rise to monitor and correct this delinquency.

The needs of children and our duties towards them have been expressed in the Constitution. The Resolution on a National Policy on Education has been adopted by Parliament. It gives direction to State policy on the Educational needs of children. India is also party to the UN Convention of the Rights of the Child. Goals set out in this document can reasonably be achieved by judicious and efficient use of the available national resources.

The vision projected covers a comprehensive health programme, nutrition service of a formal or informal nature, free and compulsory education, special attention to the children of weaker sections and those who are socially handicapped, delinquet or otherwise in need of rehabilitation. Even in litigation involving them, children's interests are to be given paramount consideration.

Although nominally a National Children's Board was constituted in 1974 and reconstituted in 1981, the majority of Indian children in India belong to the via lnerable sections and poverty' stricken families. The International Year of the Child (1979) was followed by a whole decade dedicated to the redemption of children from neglect, destitution and deprivation.

The International Year and the decade have come and gone, statistics have escalated and the dimension of the problem remains frighteningly colossal.

The Constitutional obligation has not been implemented and although the international instruments, such as the Universal Declaration and the two Covenants and the Convention and Declaration regarding the rights of the child, have persuasive power over the State, their fulfillment continues to be a low priority. Nevertheless there has been at least one step forward, the Government is committed to the National Policy for Children which emphasises the importance of education in Human Resource Development.

The vicious circle of child illiteracy, cheap child labour, and poverty cannot be used to deny the child his/her basic right to develop as a full human being. In fact, other countries with repent poverty have fared better. China is far ahead of us. African countries have advanced beyond us. Among the 21 largest developing countries, India ranks 15th in overall literacy and 12th in the percentage attending primary schools. The denial of education is the denial of the creative potential of the child and a culpable deprivation by the State since education of the young is a categorical imperative.

India's future, bearing mind that there are over 20 million children below 14 years of age, depends a great deal on juvenile justice in its development dimensions. The National Policy is a printed tribute; but if, alongside it, ill-health and illiteracy, child labour, squalor, shanties and infant mortality flourish, the future remains bleak and the country's failure to provide juvenile justice, an ominous shock. The challenge of the child continues.

In 1979, the International Year of the Child, the Government set up the Gurupadswami Committee to submit a report on child labour. That Committee notwithstanding, the Ministry of Labour accepted child labour as a "harsh reality," taking the view that abolition of child labour is not an economic feasibility.

The culpability of the establishment is aggravated by the fact that, far from withdrawing children from labour, provision for training of children to labour better, is being organized.

For example, in 1978, the Handloom and Handicrafts Exports Corporation (HHEC), a Delhi-based Government body, had set up a training centre to train children between ages seven and 14 to weave carpets. This job has been declared hazardous and forbidden by law since the woolen fibers are dangerous for the child's lungs, eyes and skin. These children, after undergoing training eight hours a day for one year, enter into the carpet industry for employment.

During February and May 1983 a series of reports appeared in the newspaper regarding rampant child labour in the fireworks and match factories of Sivakasi, a town in the Ramanathapuram district in the state of Tamil Nadu. The children in these factories are made to work nearly 15 hours a day, in spite of the fact that the occupation has been scheduled as hazardous for children. This issue of child labour is Sivakasi has ignited a national debate on the question of the legitimisation of child labour.

Social paediatrics, in the sense of eliminating the infrimities - social, economic and other - of children, has received statutory consideration at the hands of our legislatures. Public interest litigation in the area of bonded labour of children has made some change or at least awakened the people to their crime against the younger population. It is an equally well known fact that trafficking in children is becoming resistant to the law. Cheap labour through dalals is something blinked at by officials. girl children often end up in the flech trade. Indeed, the worst atrocities relate to the girl child. Middlemen buy and sell children while the law offers little resistance.

The legislature may reasonably claim that laws against employment of children have been made as partial implementation of the promise of justice to children. The minimum age of employment has been fixed by law and hazardous employment prohibited. The period beginning with 1950 has witnessed a spate of legislation based on the Labour Investigation Committee Report (1946). Today it can be claimed that in the eye of the law the right to life, which includes the right to education and development, interdicts child labour. this labour not only risks life and opportunity for growth but also denies those freedoms and facilities without which a child is condemned to dwarfism, moronism and penury of creativity. The ILO Convention has gone a long way in the amelioration of children's status.

The Plantation Labour Act, the Mines Act, the Factories Act, the Motor Transport Workers' Act, the Beedi and Cigar Workers (Condition of employment) Act, the Employment of Children Act (as amended in 1978) have provisions which are benignly disposed towards children.

The present priorities of the government ignore the child. The minimum one expected was the implementation of the National Labour Commission recommendations of 1969. Scattered pieces of legislation are not equal to a uniform code which liberates the child and gives him his entitlement for development.

A similar situation holds true regarding child labour, child education, child nutrition, and child development. Swami Agnivesh, Chairperson of the United Nations Trust Fund for Contemporary Forms of Slavery, alleged at the Vienna World Conference that child labour is still rampant:

> Mahatma Gandhi always said that the test of human rights and human dignity was when "the last among the least" were empowered to realise them first. Amongst these the most defenseless and the most voiceless are the children. The International Labour Organization has recently estimated the number of contemporary slaves at around 200 million in bonded about and/or servitude.

The working conditions of child laborers are extremely deplorable causing various physical and mental hazards, depriving children of the bliss of their childhood, education and flowering, all of which constitute their natural rights. Numerous cases of torture, beating, sexual harassment, and other forms of inhuman treatment are reported which are a reflection of the medieval slavery.

A child's welfare cannot be compromised; a holistic

approach to Project Juvenile Justice must deal with the negative and positive aspects, as in the English Children Act. We cannot claim that the Children Act of 1960 and the Juvenile Justice Act of 1986 passed in India are as effective as the English counterpart although the inspiration for both came from the English statues. When we deal with the child we have to deal with parents too, especially in societies where divorce is frequent and poverty is omnipresent. The guardianship of the child must depend upon the interests and well-being of the child, not only on the personal law.

Likewise, the question of criminal responsibility of a child when an offense is committed needs special attention. The question of neglect and delinquency vis-a-vis children is a delicate and sensitive branch of law, and depends very much on concern and commitment for the tender age of the juvenile. In India, more and more crimes are committed by adults using children as tools. Here we come upon the need for a Penal Code dealing with young persons which meets the manifold difficulties of the problems of juvenile culpability and curative methodology. Psychiatric inputs may be necessary to help the Court pass appropriate sentences, custodial or non-custodial. After care organizations also call for careful design, depending on the country and culture and social milieu. Certified schools, industrial schools, children's' homes and the like, along with foster care, adoption, sponsorship and other human techniques have to be compassionately created. In India there is not even an adoption law because religious differences have made it difficult for a facultative national legislation on adoption. Intercountry adoption has its own dangers although the India Court, at the highest level, has laid down guidelines.

Even so, the fact remains that intercountry adoption

deprives the child of its title to native culture and citizenship and promotes the likelihood of being a second-class citizen in later years in the foreign country. Cacism, cultural discrimination and the helplessness of the child in a foreign jurisdiction cannot be overcome by all that the Supreme Court has laid down.

The finest hour of Juvenile Justice Jurisprudence arrived in India when the Juvenile Justice Act, 1986 was passed. Prior to that, there were many imitative Children's Acts which when put into operation produced chaos.

The Children Act of 1960 was preceded by the United Nations Declaration of the Rights of the Child in 1959. Concepts became more refined and juvenile justice was adopted by the UN General Assembly in 1985 followed in India by the Juvenile Justice Act of 1986. These is more scientific and comprehensive treatment of the subject in the 1986 law which deals with neglected juveniles as well as delinquent juveniles. Prostitution, narcotic drugs and psychotropic substances, observation homes and places of safety are relevant topics in the juvenile context and are receiving legislative attention now.

The Indian Jurisprudence of Juvenile Justice is the wayward victim of legislative chaos and statutory slumber. And even when a fine piece has been put on the statute book, meaningful execution is distances away. If inaction is a form of action, the executive is culpable of non-enforcement of the law as any serious student of the subject will agree. The tragic irony is that the State Children's Acts continue de facto in many parts of the country, because the Juvenile Justice Act visualises various structures, functionaries and expenditures for which the States may not be ready.

Neglected juveniles and delinquent juveniles fall under different categories and punitive provisions regarding each must therefore be different. Many of miscellaneous matters regarding duties of parents, appointment of officers, people's participation through Advisory Boards, health care for juveniles and the like, find specific statutory expression in the Juvenile Justice Act. Had this justice legislation been brought into force throughout the country, the protection, development, correction and rehabilitation of younger delinquents would have received therapeutic jurisprudential attention sufficient to meet Constitution obligations.

There are many sins committed by the State which cannot be forgiven but those which relate to the welfare of children deserve condign public censure because the child has the first call on the State's resources. Because children are voiceless and voteless they are neglected with impunity by those in power who will be held guilty by the future.

The convention on the Rights of the Child is a landmark—a landmark for human rights, a landmark for children internationally and nationally, a landmark for human progress and the gradual establishment of universal standards for civilization.

The Convention has also become a landmark in several other more specific respects:

— in the speed with which the Convention first came into force, less than 11 months after it was adopted by the United nations General Assembly, and in less time than any other human rights convention;

— in the number of countries which have ratified it through national legislation- now 159. Indeed the goal has now been set fair ratification by all countries by the end of 1995, with the objective of making it the first truly universal international convention; and

— in the development of a set of international priority goals to meet the basic needs of women and children in health, nutrition, education, water and sanitation, ad family planning. These were adopted in September 1990 at the World Summit for Children, only a month after the Convention came into force. These have by now been translated into National Programmes of Action by 92 countries and are in draft or underway in 50 others. Thus over 90 per cent of children in all continents (except Africa) now live in countries which have ratified the Convention and prepared a national programme of action to implement its priority goals by the year 2000.

Nearly 50 years ago, Arnold Toynbee, the visionary historian wrote, "Ours is the first generation since the dawn of history in which mankind dared to believe it practical to make the benefits of civilization available to the whole human race."

These developments encompassing the creation, adoption, ratification and impending implementation of the Convention on the Rights of the Child are major milestones on the march towards the gradual realisation of this vision.

Index